Marketing Communications in Tourism and Hospitality

Marketing Communications in Tourism and Hospitality
Concepts, Strategies and Cases

Scott McCabe

AMSTERDAM • BOSTON • HEIDELBERG • LONDON • OXFORD • NEW YORK
PARIS • SAN DIEGO • SAN FRANCISCO • SINGAPORE • SYDNEY • TOKYO

Butterworth-Heinemann is an imprint of Elsevier

Butterworth-Heinemann is an imprint of Elsevier
Linacre House, Jordan Hill, Oxford OX2 8DP, UK
The Boulevard, Langford Lane, Kidlington, Oxford OX5 1GB, UK

First edition 2009

British Library Cataloguing in Publication Data
A catalogue record for this book is available from the British Library

Library of Congress Cataloging-in-Publication Data
A catalog record for this book is available from the Library of Congress

ISBN: 978-0-7506-8277-0

For information on all Butterworth-Heinemann publications
visit our web site at elsevierdirect.com

Printed and bound in Hungary
09 10   10 9 8 7 6 5 4 3 2 1

To Lisa, Kieran and Harry.

Contents

List of Figures

List of Tables

List of Plates

List of Case Studies

Acknowledgements

There are many people who have provided invaluable help, encouragement and support as well as practical assistance in the preparation of this book. I would first like to thank Professor Conrad Lashley and Sally North for commissioning this book as part of the Hospitality, Tourism and Leisure Series at Elsevier Butterworth-Heinemann and for all their help and encouragement throughout. I would also like to say a huge 'thank you' to Sarah Long, whose editorial support has been incredibly helpful during the process.

A great thanks also to Clare Foster, who provided invaluable research assistance on the case studies and illustrations as well as some really helpful comments and ideas on an early draft. I would like to thank all those colleagues at TTRI who have supported me during the time I have been writing: Chris, Adam, Anita, Rob, Karen, Peter, Isabel, Steve, Ann, Enrico and Debbie.

I owe an enormous debt of gratitude to my great friend Ralph Footring at www.footring.co.uk. Any creditable aspects of this book in terms of readability, sense and logic must be largely attributable to his unstinting critical comments and constructive guidance on the first draft of the book, given in his own time in the depths of winter. Throughout the whole process, Ralph has remained interested and incredibly supportive, and I cannot overstate how much I continue to appreciate his help.

I would also like to thank Claire Flint at www.whatifcoaching.com for occasional coaching and a sense of perspective and Dan, Ralph (again) and Neal for sympathy and sarcasm over weekly 'Pubminton' bouts. Of course, the greatest thanks go to Lisa, Kieran and Harry, without whose love, support and understanding would have made this project impossible.

I would like to acknowledge the assistance of the following people for help providing permission to reproduce copyright material: Rich Brown, Nicola Swankie and Annabel Evans at Rainey Kelly Campbell Roalfe (a division of Young and Rubicam Group Limited) for help in sourcing the still from the 'Return of the Train' advert; Suzy Young at the World Advertising Research Council (WARC) for the 'Virgin Trains, Winning Hearts and Minds' and 'Making Travelocity the Number 1 Choice for Online Bookings' case studies; Hannah James at Visit Wales for 'Visit Wales – UK Consumer Marketing Campaign' case study and images; Bill Wilson at the Outdoor Advertising Association (OAA); Lucy Huxley Editor of Travel Trade Gazette for 'Technological developments and the Impact of Marketing Tourism'; 'Thomas Cook's Campaign for an Extra Holiday puts "Clear Air" between Them and the Competition'; 'XL.com Sponsor West Ham United to Grow Awareness'; Sorcha Proctor at Internet Advertising Bureau (IAB) for 'Online Adspend – 2007'; Jane Kroese at Thomas Cook for still images of 'Campaign for a Free Day'; Natasha Woollcombe at First Choice Holidays for still image of First Choice Sale; Alistair and Eleanor Watters at www.travelblog.org for the Travel blog mock-up plate; Varsha Meswania at www.lastminute.com for the Lastminute image; Kerry Dean at Thomsonfly for the Thomson image; Alan Whicker (and Melissa Robertson at Miles Calcraft Briginshaw Duffy) for the Travelocity Alan Whicker plate; Margaret Ellis at Gleaneagles Hotel, Tamsin Andsell and Brian McGregor at Mightysmall.co.uk for the Gleneagles outdoor image; Anthony Crocker at CBS Outdoor; Louise Alexander at VisitLondon for the 'Totally London' image; Gillian Breen at Murray Consultants for the Ryanair plate; Matthew Wilson at the Advertising Standards Authority (ASA) for updated figures and for the rules governing standards in travel advertising; Stuart Smith at Centaur Publishing for the article 'Be Careful of What You Wish for…' from Marketing Week; Marzanna Misztela at Solo Syndication for the Mail on Sunday article 'How Far should We Trust Website Reviews'; Simon Tunstill at 'Thinkbox'; Bashni Muthaya at South African Tourism for 'Segmenting the UK Long Haul Market to South Africa: Profiling Positive Convertibles' case; Tessa Gooding at the Institute of Practitioners in Advertising (IPA); Laura Scott at www.google.com press office; Sarah Anderson at Thomas Cook and Sarah Longbottom at RBI (UK). Apologies to anyone whom I have overlooked in this process.

Positioning Marketing Communications for Tourism and Hospitality

At the end of this chapter, you will be able to

- Define tourism and hospitality marketing communications.

- Understand the importance of communications in tourism and hospitality services.

- Describe the changing role of marketing communications in the tourism and hospitality system.

Introduction – Defining Marketing Communications for Tourism and Hospitality

Marketing communications forms a key aspect of the delivery of tourism and hospitality services. This sector is heavily dependent on marketing because of the industries special characteristics as services. However, marketing communications is a great deal more than simply about advertising. Getting the right messages to the right people is perhaps one of the most important factors in determining the success of this sector. Indeed marketing communications forms its own sub-field of study within the discipline of marketing. And yet there are few textbooks that focus specifically on marketing communications for services, and none of them that look in detail into the communications issues, theories and strategies facing the contemporary tourism and hospitality sector. This is despite the fact that this sector is an experiential services sector which relies so heavily on 'representations'. Representations can be described as impressions, images and depictions about the experiences or about what might be expected from service providers. Although there has been a great deal of academic attention given to the various dimensions of marketing in tourism and hospitality services within the business and management literature, and within sociology on the semiotics of representations of tourist brochures, there has been remarkably little attention given to the broad dimensions of marketing communications, the concepts, strategies, issues and challenges underpinning this important function in a dynamic service sector environment. This book aims to at least partially address this omission. It is important, therefore, that the book begins by attempting to define and limit its scope given the broad nature of the topic and the wide variety of concepts that fall within the remit of marketing communications.

Defining Tourism

Tourism has been defined as the sum of the relationships arising out of the activities of persons travelling to and staying in places outside their usual environment for not more than one consecutive year for leisure, business and other purposes (Wall and Mathieson, 2005). This physical movement from the familiar to the unfamiliar puts a great emphasis on the need for practical and relevant information on the characteristics of the destination and the means of travel by which consumers can access it. The tourism industry is broad, focusing on the idea of a tourism system (Leiper, 1990) comprising 'generating regions', 'destinations' and encompassing the discrete elements of the tourism service sector, also known as 'principals': transport services, accommodation providers and visitor attractions; as well as tour operators who package these elements. together to provide an organised itinerary; and travel agents who are the intermediaries forming the link between tour operators and consumers (Cooper *et al.*, 2005). A range of supplementary and ancillary services are also partially included within definitions of the tourism industry. This is important for gathering statistical data in order to record and attribute spending to this particular form of activity. These ancillary services include more as well as less obvious sectors of the economy, such as car-hire firms, taxis, insurance services, building and construction and public sector services. The nature of tourism partially as a 'lifestyle' activity lends itself to entrepreneurial activity and self-starter or sole trader businesses predominate and so the industry tends to be characterised in terms of structure by a very large number of small and micro-operations (whose primary concerns may not even be profit motivated; see for example Getz and Carlson, 2005) alongside a small number of extremely large and powerful multinational organisations. This means that there is a great deal of variation in the types, resources and practices of marketing activity in the tourism industry. This activity is often in the form of marketing communications, and because its structure, the industry creates a great volume of marketing activity by a wide range of organisations.

In addition, central to the tourism industry is the concept of a tourism 'destination'. All places can potentially become tourism destinations, and many local, regional as well as national governments now realise the potential contribution that tourism can make as a tool for economic development or regeneration by providing resources to coordinate and facilitate the development of the tourism industry in their region. This is usually undertaken through a national tourism organisation (NTO) which is responsible for devolving resources to regional tourism organisations whose role is to coordinate activities through destination marketing partnerships (DMPs). These non-governmental organisations (NGOs) consist of partnerships between the public and the private sectors, and a large part of the activities of these organisations are directed towards marketing the destination, be that at national, regional or local level. It is recognised that tourism destinations are some of the most difficult entities to market because of the complex nature of the relationships between stakeholders (Buhalis, 2000).

A further crucial point to make about tourism when trying to identify its defining characteristics is that it is essentially a consumer activity. Tourism, and particularly leisure travel, vacations or holidays, can be considered as a discretionary consumer activity. This means that it is often portrayed as a non-essential item of household's disposable income. Although many commentators have pointed out that holidays are often perceived by the highly developed service-driven economies of Western Europe as essential, there is little doubt that tourism is especially vulnerable to fluctuations in the economy where consumers' disposable household income changes. A key issue in terms of marketing communications is that tourism is the 'experiential' consumer product par excellence, and this experience service creates the need to emphasise messages which appeal to consumers' emotions in marketing. In addition, tourism is highly vulnerable to external forces or changes to the economies of destination countries, such as political crises or sudden and severe changes to exchange rates. News media coverage of places and events both exposes consumers to information about destinations, which can be negative or positive, and provides people with an image of the place and culture. Consumers of tourism can be highly fickle. Tourists are sometimes driven by a desire to 'see the world' and explore new places, so they are, perhaps, less likely to be loyal to a destination or country, although this conception of tourist motivation can be challenged. Trends in tourist consumer behaviour change very rapidly, and analysis of these trends can be useful in identifying wider social mores and patterns of behaviour or attitudes. One highly important aspect of tourists' behaviour is that they like to talk about their experiences to other people – this is called 'word of mouth' communication, and it has always been cited as the most used, trusted, and reliable source of information influencing tourist choices and consumer behaviour.

Defining Hospitality

Lashley (2000) argues that hospitality in the historical sense concerns a duty of charitableness, offering protection (shelter) and succour (food and drink) to 'strangers' (2000: p. 6). This is in recognition of the fact that hospitality studies have in the past emphasised the commercial orientation, hospitality management, over the more intuitive and humanistic nature of hospitality in the social domain. Conventional definitions of hospitality focus on the provision of domestic labour and services for commercial gain. These services include food, drink and lodging which are offered for sale. Obviously, hospitality services are much more than simply about selling food and drink or providing people with a roof over their head for a night. It is clear that commercial hospitality organisations draw on images and a rhetoric of hospitality which connects more deeply with those historical and socio-anthropological meanings of hospitableness which holds importance for marketing communications.

There is an enormous variation in the range of prices for which these services can be charged and so the features of the products and services, and the quality of the service must be very carefully defined and communicated to the selected audiences. It is evident that hospitality services are intrinsic to the tourism industry, and although the hospitality industry serves a much wider range of clients' needs than passing strangers and some would even argue that hospitality services form a vital and vibrant part of any community, there are sufficient synergies that link tourism and hospitality together in terms of the issues, challenges and contexts that conjoin them in relation to marketing communications.

The hospitality industry can be divided into components which deal in purely the provision of accommodation such as guest houses, hostels and backpackers, youth hostels and camping and caravan sites. Those that offer the full range of services, such as hotels, provide bar, restaurant, conference and meeting rooms, leisure, health, beauty and spa treatments as well as accommodation. A further distinction arises taking into account only those that offer food and beverage, such as restaurants, pubs, and bars and inns. A distinct but complementary sector arises out of the meetings, incentives, conference and events (MICE) markets which provide hospitality services and are often attached to hotels but are regarded as somewhat separate to conventional notions of hospitality. The sector can also be differentiated by an orientation to particular markets or consumers. Some sections of the trade focus solely on local markets, whereas others cater solely to tourists – in the case of the latter, this is mainly in the context of tourist resorts where there is little indigenous population and development is linked explicitly to the tourist trade. Thus again there is a huge variety in the size, scope, ownership structure and orientation to marketing in the hospitality industry making the challenge of understanding the usefulness and application of marketing communications complex and worthy of a specific focus of attention.

The hospitality industry is also characterised as a lifestyle consumer activity. Although its services are essential needs, the basics of life – food, drink and shelter – they are delivered as a consumer experience, and in recent years, there have been trends which reveal the 'lifestylisation' of hospitality, particularly used as a reward for hard work in advanced consumer economies. Therefore, in a similar way to tourism, hospitality has become an experiential consumer good, which explicitly aims to appeal to consumers' emotions.

Marketing Communications in Tourism and Hospitality

Marketing communications has been considered as saying the right things to the right people in the right ways (Delozier, 1976). In defining marketing communications, it is useful to consider the two distinct elements: 'marketing' and 'communications'. According to the

> ### Illustration
>
> At the heart of every tourism and hospitality activity, experience is an act of communication. Think of the greeting received when entering into a restaurant or hotel, or at the check-in desk at the airport, the friendly chat with strangers met at the bar, or the first encounter with a person from another culture in the tourism destination. The inter-action-rich context of these service encounters means that the role of communication in the production and consumption of tourism and hospitality services cannot be underestimated. It is this interpersonal communication which sets the tone for the entire experience of the service or the destination and underlines the importance of communi-cations to the successful functioning of the wider contemporary busi-ness sector.

Chartered Institute of Marketing (CIM), marketing is the managerial process by which goods, services and ideas are exchanged for profit. Communication can be conceived as a process of 'meaningful informa-tion exchange'. Marketing communications, then, can be understood to be tied to a commercial intent, which means that whilst communica-tions might include a broader range and remit of information provision, when considered in the context of marketing there is an assumption that the purpose of communications activity will result in benefits to the organisation and thus, either directly or indirectly, to profits. There must be a meaningful exchange of information, because the organisa-tion needs to know that its messages are being received and interpreted in the ways in which they were intended. In this way, communication is not simply about sending messages out to audiences but requires a two-way process, a meaningful dialogue. Fill (2005) states that

> Marketing communications provides the means by which brands and organisations are presented to their audiences. The goal is to stimu-late a dialogue that will, ideally, lead to a succession of purchases. Complete engagement. This interaction represents an exchange between each organisation and each customer, and, according to the quality and satisfaction of the exchange process, will or will not be repeated. (Fill, 2005: p. 9)

Marketing communications in a contemporary sense, however, is more than simply 'presenting the brand' through advertising. It can relate to other forms of information and can be widened to bring in consideration of the broader strategic position of marketing in organisations. Marketing communications can be thought of as bringing a 'strategic approach' to *all* information originating from and coming into an organisation – potential and actual customers, suppliers, shareholders, wider publics, the media or anyone. By adopting a strategic approach towards information, organisations take care of and pay attention to the processes of information exchange and ultimately recognise its strategic function in helping the organisation achieve its strategic aims. Communications, therefore, form a vital part of the marketing strategy of the organisation. This book takes a broad approach to include a range of activities and contexts and defines marketing communications as follows:

> The strategies, methods and processes through which meaningful information is exchanged between people about an organisation's activities.

Strategies, methods and processes refer to the marketing communications' goals and tactical methods used to develop dialogue and exchange of meaningful information between senders of messages and audiences. These conventionally consist of a set of marketing disciplines or tools: advertising, personal selling, sales promotion, direct marketing and public relations. They can include a range of informal and formal communications, which can be delivered through a variety of means and channels. These means and channels consist of a range of media such as television, radio and newspapers and magazines, in which space and time can be bought or used to provide messages to selected audiences. It is important to understand that in order to achieve success in the contemporary tourism and hospitality business environments, organisations need to adopt a marketing-led or marketing-oriented approach to their business decision-making, with the consumer as the ultimate focus of operations and strategy.

Therefore, marketing communications' planning and strategy needs to understand how, where and when consumers access information, how they respond and the means by which this process can be effectively managed. The term 'information' is used in preference to 'advertising' or 'promotions' in recognition of the wide variety of types of businesses and organisations within the sector including public and voluntary organisations as well as the private sector. Not all communications within the sector are concerned with the promotion and selling of 'products' and 'services'; in fact, much information is created and delivered to provide awareness and knowledge of a whole range of activities, such as changes in timetables or schedules, weather problems, opening and closing times, and in reaction to media coverage or places or organisations or health messages for example (Peattie *et al.*, 2005).

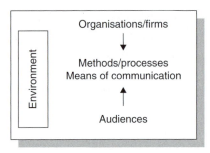

Figure 1.1 Basic elements of marketing communications.

The fact that information is exchanged assumes that there is a two-way process and that this process needs to be managed by the organisation. Within the context of tourism, information about a destination and/or activities which might affect tourism within a region or country can be generated by events or the media which are outside the control of the destination marketing organisation, and in many other contexts an organisation might be affected by media exposure, wanted or unwanted, negative or positive. A crucial function of marketing communications is the ability to react, counteract or capitalise on information which is propagated outside the direct control of the organisation. This is becoming an increasingly important function in an 'information age' characterised by a proliferation and fragmentation of media forms and channels and currently dominated by the rise of Internet social networking and peer-to-peer interactions through review and recommendations.

The marketing communications process involves both proactive and reactive elements, and thus a concerted and strategic approach in which timing is crucial. Marketing communications must be targeted to defined audiences largely because of the information-rich nature of contemporary society: consumers are both inundated with media and marketing communications and extremely aware of their own conscious ability to screen out unwanted or irrelevant information. Thus consumers are likely to react strongly against service providers that do not understand their needs or interests, and in any case the cost of delivering broad-scale information to non-target audiences is likely to be prohibitive to most organisations. Figure 1.1 illustrates the key elements of marketing communications.

Integrated Marketing Communications

Another important development in marketing in recent years has been the move towards an integrated approach to marketing communications (De Pelsmacker *et al.*, 2004). Integrated marketing communications (IMC) requires a coordinated approach to marketing across individual campaigns and across different forms and channels of information. This has been driven by issues of costs reduction and maximisation of marketing effectiveness outlined earlier. It is also due to the dominance of brands and branding for consumers as well as organisations. The need to ensure that all marketing and non-marketing information reflects the brand personality and values to maximise the potential of organisations and to create a strong 'message' across all its communications has become a critical success factor in the highly competitive marketplace of tourism and hospitality services. In the international hotel market for example, there is often little differentiation between the core offers of competing chains. In this sector, firms aim to discriminate between their offers finding or creating essential points of differentiation and conveying these unique features through a strong brand identity. In order for this to be successful, all stakeholders must be aware of the aims and vision of the brand and so all information must reflect these brand or organisational values. Therefore an integrated approach to marketing communications ensures that internal audiences are aware of the strategic aims of the organisation and its vision in terms of brand values. Internal audiences consist of employees, but also suppliers, shareholders and other stakeholders including wider society. These developments are indicative of the changing nature of the marketing communications environment, and this book aims to discuss the applications of these approaches in the context of tourism and hospitality marketing services, which are characterised by special features with specific issues. The following section outlines why these services can be considered unique raising interesting issues for marketing communications.

Marketing Communications Characteristics in Tourism and Hospitality

In the context of the marketing literature, tourism and hospitality fall into the field of services marketing. However, there are many differences between marketing a hotel and marketing banking products such as a personal loan. Tourism and hospitality share many important services marketing characteristics which have an impact on the ways in which they are marketed to potential consumers. This is important because marketing communications for this sector is affected by these particular features. They are, to a lesser or greater degree, depending on the types of service:

- intangible
- perishable

- inseparable
- heterogenous

Tourism and hospitality are said to be *intangible* services because it is not possible to experience the service prior to purchase. A great many textbooks focus on these characteristics, but there are few which consider the ways in which they impact on the communications issues and strategies of these services. Mittal and Baker (2002) focus on the difficulties posed by intangibility in terms of knowing how to communicate the attributes and benefits of these services. They argue that intangibility poses four key challenges:

1. *Abstractness*, difficulties in communication of abstract concepts of the services – such as 'a good night's rest'
2. *Generality*, difficulties in conveying distinctions between one organisation's service offer, such as 'cabin service', from another
3. *Non-searchability*, the fact that customers cannot search the credentials of the organisation or test the service prior to purchase, meaning they have to be taken on trust
4. *Impalpability*, refers to the problem of being able to imagine the physical experience and thus a need to convey an understanding and interpretation of the service in communications

They also argue that organisations have three key aims from communications strategies: creating brand identity, positioning of the brand and creating demand. Further, they argue that within these general goals, hospitality firms must work to communicate the intangible benefits of the service, be specific about the distinct features and characteristics of the services, providing concrete details, provide key information about the evidence about which claims for 'trust' can be made and, finally, take consumers through the exact steps of the experience to make them more palpable. They provide useful examples that illustrate how tourism and hospitality services can overcome the difficulties of intangibility and yet each of the other three main characteristics also present challenges to marketers.

Services are said to be *perishable* since they cannot be stored or stockpiled to be sold at a later date (a six-night Mediterranean cruise leaving Athens on 14 August cannot be sold after that date). This factor puts a strategic emphasis on the role of price-setting in the marketing mix. Marketing which aims to communications aspects of pricing strategies, including sales promotions and discounting, is a key feature of tourism and hospitality marketing communications for example. The concept of *inseparability* refers to the fact that it is not possible to separate the point of production of the service from the point at which they are consumed. It means there is a great emphasis on the role of people in the service encounter. Again, the importance of people and quality of service linked to expertise of individuals or within the organisation collectively is a key force in marketing communications strategies in the sector. *Heterogeneity* refers to the fact that it is very difficult to replicate the same experience for different people within the same service environment and to replicate the same experience at different times. These factors mean that marketing strategy for tourism and hospitality is often tied to organisational and operational concerns, and in summary, marketing messages often highlight the following features and issues in delivery of the service:

- the highlighted role of people
- experiential and emotional nature of messages
- timing and process issues
- quality of service delivery and products
- tangible features and benefits
- pricing strategies, promotions and discounting
- standards and guarantees

However, Mittal and Baker also point out the need to communicate how the services will benefit consumers. Earlier in the chapter, some special characteristics of the consumption of tourism and hospitality services were outlined. These are also influential factors affecting the marketing approach and the content of communications. These can be expanded to include

- the importance of word-of-mouth communication in consumers' decision-making processes
- the links between consumption and status/identity
- the impact of consumers' personality traits and motivations on brand loyalty
- macro-social factors which influence consumption
- the extent to which tourism and hospitality consumption is an established norm of social life.

Tourism and Hospitality Marketing Communications: Concepts, Strategies and Cases

The previous sections have outlined the ways in which tourism and hospitality make an interesting and unique focus for an exploration of marketing communications. It was noted that these two sectors

Illustration

The tourism and hospitality industry is rapidly changing. Even though the industry is traditionally a people-intensive service industry, the role of interpersonal communications between service providers and consumers is becoming less prominent. Automated services, online booking and self-service are becoming more commonplace as companies try to reduce costs to consumers and increase consumer choice. As a result, it is increasingly difficult to know how consumers feel about places, experiences and services before, during or after purchase. Traditionally, service personnel understood how their customers felt about their experiences by their immediate reactions during the service encounter. These expressive forms of communication enabled the service delivery workers to respond accordingly. In many contexts, personal service has been reduced to key 'moments', which both makes them more important and increases the need for more systematic forms of consumer feedback. Communication is not simply something which is 'done' to consumers. Communication is a dialogue between people requiring an exchange of information. Communication is taking place all the time.

are diverse and dynamic and that they are undergoing a period of unprecedented change. Change in the focus and orientation of marketing theory and the impact of this on marketing communications were highlighted as a factor worthy of discussion. Therefore, the book is structured into three parts in order to understand and assess these changes and to identify and discuss marketing communications strategies which can be used to illustrate current practice in the industry. Part 1 deals with the concepts which underpin analysis of the changing marketing environment for tourism and hospitality marketing communications. It first sets out key concepts in communications theory (Chapter 2). Communications theory has many facets, and communications has been theorised from differing perspectives. Chapter 2 outlines these main perspectives and discusses how current thinking affects the marketing communications of the two service sectors under discussion. Chapter 3 aims to introduce the global context in which communications is produced. Recent trends and developments in the structure and organisation of the marketing communications industry are discussed in relation to the function of the marketing department for tourism and hospitality organisations. Marketing communications is discussed in the context of the constraints and challenges of the external business and regulatory environment. Consumers' attitudes towards advertising and their consumption behaviour of different media channels has an important impact on organisation's approaches to packaging, delivering and marketing of tourism and hospitality services. Chapter 4 outlines consumer behaviour theory and assesses how consumers' reactions to marketing communications impact on the strategies employed.

Part 2 of the book deals with the strategic context for marketing communications and explores marketing strategy in relation to how strategic choices connect to communications strategies. Chapter 5 begins by examining the strategic marketing context. Here the focus is on the role of marketing within the organisational context and how the IMC approach to marketing communications strategies is related to wider marketing and organisational strategy. Chapter 6 begins to analyse communications strategies and tactics in relation to meeting the needs of specific consumers through a discussion of how markets are segmented into subgroups, which are then targeted through discrete marketing messages. Chapter 6 also outlines how services are 'positioned' through effective marketing communications in the minds of target audiences. Chapter 7, the last chapter in Part 2, outlines the role of marketing planning in the integrated marketing communications strategic process. It explores the relationships between organisations and brand development strategies and management. The importance of branding was highlighted earlier, and Chapter 7 outlines how brands are communicated to audiences.

In the final section of the book (Part 3), marketing communications applications are described and evaluated. Chapter 8 discusses the role of advertising in marketing communications, whilst Chapter 9 defines and describes how sales promotions, public relations, direct marketing, personal selling as well as events, sponsorship and other forms of marketing are integrated into marketing communications campaigns. Chapter 10 outlines the importance of the Internet as an information medium and describes the various types of advertising and communications strategies which can be used to establish dialogue with consumers and wider audiences. The book concludes with a discussion of the future direction and challenges of marketing communications for the industry.

Each chapter of the book contains a case study related to the themes of the chapter as well as shorter illustrations and examples of current practice. Hence, the third focus of the book is to provide relevant and current case studies together with discussion questions, learning activities and resources which relate to contemporary issues in the tourism and hospitality sector.

Summary

This chapter has outlined the defining qualities of tourism and hospitality as 'experiential' services, ones that have special characteristics. It is these characteristics which make the marketing communications issues particularly interesting as a focus of study. Tourism and hospitality was defined as lifestyle consumer goods, making them vulnerable to changes in the external market environment. This challenging contemporary business situation has an impact on marketing practice, which has resulted in many firms and organisations adopting a marketing orientation with a focus on the consumer, and an integrated approach to marketing communications. Chapter 2 extends this discussion of the external environment and its impact on the current trends in marketing communications. However, prior to this, the first case study begins by looking at future trends in technology for the travel industry particularly the ways in which technology will affect how organisations converse/connect with their audiences.

Discussion Questions

1. Outline the special characteristics of tourism and hospitality services and explain why and how these impact on marketing communications for these services.
2. What are the main elements included in a definition of marketing communications? Why is each element important to successful marketing of tourism and hospitality organisations?
3. Outline the range of types of organisations in the tourism and hospitality sector. What are the current issues facing the sector? What is the impact of these trends on marketing?

Case Study 1: Technological Developments and the Impact on Marketing Tourism

This first case study focuses on the role of technology for marketing tourism. Technological developments have been a key driver of change in the tourism and hospitality sector over the last 15–20 years and has radically affected the marketing communications environment and practices in the industry in the last 10 years. These changes will be discussed in greater detail later on in the book, but this case study outlines some of the predicted future trends and asks you to think about how these factors might impact on how the services in this sector are promoted to consumers.

Popular travel trade magazine *Travel Weekly* ran an article in October 2006 asking key industry experts "What does the future hold for travel technology?" (www.travel-weekly.co.uk).

In the 25 years since IBM launched its PC, a machine widely regarded as the first real personal computer, technology has all but taken over the workplace. Virtually all office workers now sit at computers, stay in touch via e-mail and receive information via a broadband connection. The travel industry is no exception. Advances in technology have moved travel in completely new directions, driving strong trends towards online purchasing, dynamic packaging and e-ticketing. But fast forward another 25 years and how will the travel industry be using technology then?

Of course, some things are impossible to predict. The rate of technological development is such that a quarter of a century from now, computers will allow us to do things that today we can't even conceive. But there are also some of today's trends that can be projected into the future. One that cannot be disputed is the growth of online purchasing. Today, 30% of all global travel products are bought online, but Amadeus director of travel distribution strategy Andy Owen-Jones predicts this figure will be nearer 80% in 15 years' time. He also foresees a future in which travel booking engines will be integrated into car satellite navigation systems, so travellers will be alerted to hotels and amusement parks situated along the route they have planned out. Wearable computers will also be commonplace in 20 years' time, said Owen-Jones. Pre-programmed with our preferences and built into a headset or jacket cuff, they will let us know if we are in the vicinity of our favourite kind of restaurant or bar. "In general, there will be far more data available, giving more power of choice to the consumer, while providing more ways for retailers to predict what the consumer wants," he said. Owen also thinks online kiosks, allowing consumers to research and book holidays in supermarkets or pubs, will be widespread in the future – a scenario that Thomas Cook chief information officer Carl Dawson is less certain of. "Kiosks seem to have been much-lauded over the last 10 years, but in most trials the public don't seem to like using them. It's likely that people will feel more comfortable using their own devices," he said.

Kamran Ikram, a partner in the travel and transport service practice at business consultancy Accenture, believes increased use of mobile technology by travel companies will be the key development in coming years. He said reduced roaming costs across Europe will enable the transmission of travel content, such as destination information or details of excursions, to clients on holiday – a trend that will take off as today's mobile-using youth starts buying travel products in around 10 years' time. Airline companies will also become bandwidth providers, according to futurologist Ray Hammond, who said more operators will follow Ryanair's lead, charging less for the air ticket and more for the in-flight services they offer. "By the time Internet services are available to air passengers, it won't just be business travellers wanting to use e-mail. Everyone will be demanding Internet access to update their MySpace profile and load their holiday videos onto YouTube," he said.

With the airline industry being asked to reduce emissions, we may see many aircraft powered partly by solar power by 2030. Other modes of transport will also be revolutionised. Proposals are already afoot to develop cruise ships powered by giant kites, while a group of engineers at the Massachusetts Institute of Technology have been advocating a transatlantic rail line, with trains running in a tube under the ocean at speeds of up to 5,000 miles per hour."

Some of the developments envisaged over the next 15 years:

Mobile technology

Five years: cheaper roaming and data access across Europe will open up the market for travel applications.
Ten years: IT-literate youth now have disposable income. This will accelerate the development of travel applications for mobile devices.
Fifteen years and beyond: mobile phones with foldout screens or a virtual projection of keyboard by laser to make use of mobile device easier.

Online purchasing of travel

Five years: 50% of all travel bought booked online
Ten years: 60% of all travel bought booked online
Fifteen years and beyond: 80% of all travel bought booked online

Holidays

Five years: significant growth of travel kiosks in supermarkets and high streets.
Ten years: web cams in every resort, so clients can view before they buy.
Fifteen years and beyond: new generation virtual reality jumpsuits and helmets mean clients can "go" on holiday from their front room, complete with sea breeze and the smell of suntan oil.

Use of data

Five years: airlines and agencies introduce personally targeted ticket prices based on analysis of customer value and ability to purchase.
Ten years: personal tour building systems – where consumer becomes self-bonding – gain market share over operators.
Fifteen years and beyond: personalised intelligent search engines replace agents, with staff moving to higher value-added roles.

Source: Ross Bentley (www.travelweekly.co.uk)

Learning Activity

- Discuss the extent you believe these changes will happen in the next 10–15 years.
- What other trends in technology development/applications can you identify?
- What impact will these technological developments have on the marketing and promotion of tourism and hospitality services?
- What other issues need to be considered alongside technological changes?

References and Further Reading

Buhalis, D. (2000). Marketing the competitive destination of the future. *Tourism Management*. 21: 97–116.

Cooper, C., Fletcher, J., Fyall, A., Gilbert, D. and Wanhill, S. (2005). *Tourism Principles and Practice*. 3rd edn. Harlow: Pearson Education.

DeLozier, M.W. (1976). *The Marketing Communications Process*. New York: McGraw-Hill.

De Pelsmacker, P.M., Geuens, J. and Van den, Bergh. (2004). *Marketing Communications: A European Perspective*. 2nd edn. Harlow: FT Prentice Hall.

Fill, C. (2005). *Marketing Communications: Engagement, Strategies and Practice*. 4th edn. Harrow, England: Prentice Hall.

Getz, D. and Carlsen, J. (2005). Family business in tourism: State of the art. *Annals of Tourism Research*. 32(1): 237–258.

Lashley, C. (2000). Towards a theoretical understanding. In Lashley, C. and Morrison, A. (eds) *In Search of Hospitality: Theoretical Perspectives and Debates*. Oxford: Butterworth-Heinemann, pp. 1–17.

Leiper, N. (1990). *Tourism systems*. Massey University Department of Management Systems Occasional Paper No 2. Auckland.

Mittal, B. and Baker, J. (2002). Advertising strategies for hospitality services. *Cornell Hotel and Restaurant Administration Quarterly*: 51–63.

Peattie, S., Clarke, P. and Peattie, K. (2005). Risk and responsibility in tourism: Promoting sun-safety. *Tourism Management*. 26: 399–408.

Smith, P.R. and Taylor, J. (2002). *Marketing Communications: An Integrated Approach*. 4th edn. London: Kogan Page.

Wall, G. and Mathieson, A. (2005). *Tourism: Change, Impacts and Opportunities*. Harlow: Pearson Education.

Key Resource and Link

www.travelweekly.co.uk

Part 1 introduces the major concepts, theories and challenges which frame the context of marketing communications in tourism and hospitality. Marketing messages are created and distributed to audiences in a purposeful way to meet organisational objectives, but it is important to understand the underlying concepts at work in working out why some messages are successful and others less so. It is also important to note that the environment in which messages are created and distributed is a dynamic one, and so there are a range of impacts and influences on consumers' behaviour which affect the ways in which messages are reacted upon. Chapter 2 begins by outlining the main concepts in communications theory including academic perspectives to assess how current thinking affects marketing communications for tourism and hospitality organisations. Chapter 3 assesses the global context in which communications are produced including the function of marketing and the changing structure of the marketing communications industry. Marketing communications are discussed in the context of the constraints and challenges of the external business and regulatory environment. Chapter 4 outlines consumer behaviour theory and assesses how consumers' reactions to marketing communications impacts on the development of marketing communications strategies.

Communications Theory and Applications

At the end of this chapter, you will be able to

- Understand different perspectives on communication theory.

- Identify and relate the development of models of communication within their historical context.

- Discuss contemporary debates in communication theory in relation to tourism and hospitality products and services.

- Identify the relationships between mass media, marketing communications in tourism and hospitality and semiotics.

Introduction

This chapter describes a range of theory approaches to understanding communications and discusses how knowledge about communications is applied to tourism and hospitality marketing communications strategies. The approach taken is to outline how theories of communication have developed over time from simple, linear models of communication to complex, relational and network perspectives. The discussion then moves on to a consideration of the role of semiotics in the representations of tourism and hospitality services. In Chapter 1, it was noted that these two services relied heavily on representations because of the experiential nature of the consumption of these services. Organisations need to inform consumers about what to expect from the company or destination marketing organisation (DMO) in terms of the more tangible features of the service or destination, but they also often try to communicate something about the ways in which consumers will feel about their consumption of the service or place. The role of visual imagery is very important to tourism marketing, and communications often rely on visual communications (Baloglu and Brinberg, 1997; MacKay and Fesenmaier, 1997; Yuksel and Akgul, 2007). The emphasis on the role of emotions to advertising in tourism and hospitality marketing communications requires a detailed understanding of how communications work to influence people's behaviour. However, this business-to-consumer approach belies the much wider range of communications contexts, purposes and stakeholders involved, and it is important to understand how different models of communication can be applied in different contexts. Furthermore, the importance of communication between consumers themselves necessitates a consideration of flows of communication and the role of networks to the marketing of tourism and hospitality services. The importance of relational and network communication approaches leads to a discussion on the vital function played by word-of-mouth communications to the industry.

The links between the types of information and modes of exchange of information is critical to understanding how communications work in different ways on audiences. Organisations, including tourism and hospitality organisations, government and the wider media, make considered choices to produce information and communicate with particular groups of individuals in society. Some of this information aims to persuade people to take action, to buy a package holiday, book a trip to a resort destination or call a telephone number to take advantage of an offer for a hotel, for example. This type of information would be classified as sales promotion and would be communicated through advertising. Other types of information are produced to inform or remind people about the existence of brands or places or to inform them of events, regulations or changes in circumstances which might impact on people's ability to access them. An example might be information about changes in visa regulations which would be created by the government and communicated to potential visitors, tour operators and transport providers.

News media stories which focus on events, people or organisations add to people's knowledge and their impressions of them. People communicate within their social networks to achieve social and/or personal goals. Marketing does not exist in a social vacuum. Consumers of tourism and hospitality receive information about places, products and services from a range of different sources. People trust information from some sources more than others. In order to understand how marketing communications 'work' on the target audience to get the desired reaction and to understand in what circumstances the messages fail to provoke the right reaction, it is important to understand how people decipher messages, react, understand, and create meaning from marketing communications.

There are a variety of ways in which an organisation can communicate to its audiences. The main ways are to

- inform
- remind
- persuade.

It is generally assumed that in product marketing, the most useful and pervasive form of communication is to persuade; however, in relation to tourism and hospitality it can be argued that a more complex blend of information is required because of the composite and multi-service nature of sector, and the nature of the 'total visitor experience'. This composite nature of the service outlined in Chapter 1 – the destination and its features, the character of the hotel bedrooms and facilities, the range of restaurants, bars, entertainments venues, visitor attractions etc. – often requires that marketing communications is collaborative and serves a complicated function of both informing *and* placing the company or the destination within the forefront of the mind of the consumer simultaneously.

However, to begin this chapter, early mass communications models are outlined to provide an understanding of the basic concepts, before the chapter proceeds into more contemporary and complex models and their applications to the tourism and hospitality sector.

Models and Concepts of Communications Theories

Although any attempt to reduce the wealth of theorising on communications over the last 75 years to a single chapter will inevitably result in an oversimplistic gloss, space does not permit a detailed elaboration on the various perspectives and historical antecedents of communications theory. However, this chapter aims to briefly outline these pro-cesses and relate to the current thinking on tourism and hospitality marketing communications environment.

There are four basic perspectives to communications theory:

1. *Mechanistic*: This view argues that communication is transmitted from sender to the receiver.
2. *Psychological*: This view considers the subjective processes involved (thoughts, emotions, etc.) in the way meaning is interpreted by recipients of messages.
3. *Sociological*: This perspective focuses on the social context in which communications are sent and received and how meaning is established and shared, and views communication as a socially constructed process.
4. *Systems and networks*: This perspective views communication to be a complex system of circulating messages which are being adapted and modified in a continual and complex process.

Early communications theories were developed in relation to understanding how information was transmitted from organisations to individuals from the perspective of mass communications through the media and the effects of propaganda on people. Simple linear models were developed and expanded as theorists recognised the internal, mental processes which were involved in giving meaning to messages. These theories were adopted by marketing and consumer psychologists and specifically related to the processes of communications through advertising. These theories were later developed to encompass relational and network models of communication exchange. Marketing communications is an attempt by organisations to develop a meaningful dialogue with its stakeholders, and so the communication itself can be understood as the process through which this meaning is established and shared. Evaluation and research needs to be undertaken to ensure that the right meanings have been shared. Sociological concepts can be applied to the processes of interpretation and meaning construction through the application of semiotics which will be discussed in the last section of the chapter.

Early Mass Communications Theories

Schramm (1954) developed the first basic model of mass communication, which he envisaged as a linear process, as in Figure 2.1. In this model a source is responsible for the production of some information – a message – which is then distributed to a receiver. A simple example might be given of a letter. A letter is written by someone, and the content of the letter can be conceived as the message. The letter is sent

Figure 2.1 Schramm model of mass communication.

via the postal service to a recipient, a target of the communication. This is a one-directional process and one that assumes no relationship exists between the originator of the message and the receiver. Finally, the model assumes the existence of a message as an independent entity, seemingly without any recognition of the way in which the message is directed purposefully or controlled in any way by the source. This linearity of communication process and lack of linkages has been strongly criticised, but it must be remembered that the theory was developed at a particular time in the post-war consumption boom, when marketing and consumer theorists argued that individuals were easily persuadable by marketing stimuli and that they could be conditioned to 'need' products through advertising.

Schramm conceived the communication process in the context of the study of mass media and human communications. These basic components were developed and adapted in the early 1960s by Shannon and Weaver. Shannon and Weaver were concerned with the technology of communication, and this is evident by the centrality of the technological concepts connecting the information source, message and receiver. However, their model of the flows and processes of communication has become applied in the context of marketing communications as well as in the study of person-to-person interaction. It has become one of the principal models of communication process.

The Shannon–Weaver model is shown in Figure 2.2. This model builds on the basic concepts of the Schramm model but expands the basic components to include consideration of the factors which could affect the ways in which messages are sent and received. An *information source* such as a tour operator or hotel, for example, identifies a need to create and send some information, a *message*, to a specific individual or group. The *transmitter* can be considered as the translation of the message into an appropriate format of words, symbols and images into a *signal* which can be equated to the 'channel' or the medium by which the message is distributed to the audience. The concept of *noise* refers to distortion or barriers which prevent the message reaching the target recipient in the ways it was intended. This can be broken down into 'physical noise' which might impact on the receiver, meaning the sensory perception of the message is blocked, such as a distraction during the television advertisements, or an airplane flying overhead drowning out the sound of the communication on a radio. Or it can refer to 'semantic noise' which could include the cultural, attitudinal or other external sociocultural factors which might mean that the original intention of the message is not received in the way it was intended – or simply that the message is not understood. The *receiver* refers to the equipment required to understand or interpret the message, and the *destination* is the person for whom the message is intended. In fact, the receiver and the destination is the same in terms of the individual, but the model breaks down the process of receiving the information via the senses (sights, sounds, touch, taste and smell) and its interpretation, or decoding into a meaningful message.

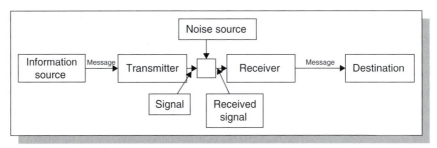

Figure 2.2 The Shannon–Weaver (1962) model of communication.

The Shannon–Weaver model is generally referred to as a 'transmission model of communication', because it assumes that messages can be conceived as simple 'objects' which are sent out – transmitted and received in a very uncomplicated way. The model recognises that a process of adaptation is required to modify the message into a form that can be transmitted as a signal. It also shows how communications can fail to reach its intended audiences because the signal can become 'lost' or distorted. A process of interpretation and assessment is then required to transform the signal back into a message which is understood and given meaning by the receiver.

The Shannon–Weaver model was adapted and developed by Osgood and Schramm, who argued for the need to recognise in more detail the processes of transmission and to explicitly recognise the interpretive work that is required by the receiver in interpreting the meanings of a message. Also for the first time, Osgood and Schramm made reference to the fact that receiver's role does not end when the message has been received and given meaning appropriately and that, indeed, communication is less linear and more circular in form. Their circular model emphasises the fact that information, messages, do not simply 'end' but are reacted to and acted upon through more communications of different types. In effect, individuals play an active role in communications and are endlessly circulating information, receiving it, interpreting it and then passing it on to others.

In the Osgood–Schramm model, the person or organisation responsible for the creation of a message is called the *encoder* and sends out

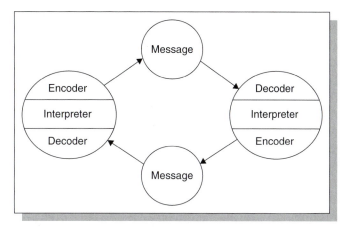

Figure 2.3 The Osgood–Schramm model of communication.

a message via a process of interpretation. The *interpreter* can also be equated to the marketing channel. The *decoder* is the recipient of the message, who then interprets the message and becomes the encoder to communicate the message onwards (Figure 2.3).

The Osgood–Schramm model reminds us that the communication of information is never a simple one-dimensional process whereby the message is encoded, transmitted and decoded as intended. The circular nature of the model shows that individuals change roles as they decode the message and by the process of interpretation then recode the message to pass on to another individual.

Illustration

Information is never neutral. It is 'produced' for specific purposes. This does not just relate to marketing communication which is often directed at persuading us to buy a product. All information reflects an ideological (political) and often subjective (opinion) position, or purpose. Even everyday conversation can be thought of as being purposeful in this way. We are always engaged in presenting ourselves to others through the things we say and do, reflecting the types of people we like to think we are, our own ideology or subjective opinions. Individuals are constantly engaged in a process of working out how to respond to the situations in which they find themselves, an endless interpretive process of ordering, and organising information and responding to that information in specific ways. Some of the information is filtered out, or deemed as not relevant to the individual in some way, and other information is acted upon and transmitted onwards. It is very often re-interpreted; however, and it is very difficult to track how messages are changed in this process or to know whether people truly respond to information as it is difficult to measure people's feelings.

Marketing Communications Transmission Models

The final type of transmission model discussed here is that presented by Fill (2005) in Figure 2.4. Fill blends together elements of the previous models in a composite which has been adapted to take account of the differences between persons in their interpretation of and orientation to different types of information in different contexts. Fill relates the model specifically to the context of marketing communications and organisational goals. Feedback comes directly back to the source in this model – the organisation which produced the message – since the content of many marketing messages contains some form of 'call to action', a specific instruction to 'call this number now for a free brochure' or 'visit the website to discover how easy it is to book' or 'send off the coupon the claim your gift'.

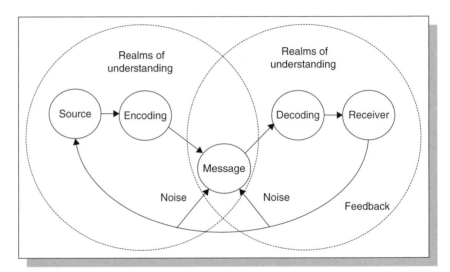

Figure 2.4 Fill's adaptation of the Schramm and Shannon and Weaver model.

In addition to the processes and concepts discussed previously, Fill stresses the importance of 'noise' in the marketing communications process. As mentioned previously, noise occurs when a receiver is prevented from receiving the message or the message is distorted on its way to the receiver or by the receiver. Although noise is always present in communications, the task of the marketing communications is to minimise the potential for noise to disrupt or corrupt the content of the message. Noise can occur through either cognitive or physical factors. Fill argues that cognitive factors could include instances when the organisation makes an error in encoding the message, in these cases, the organisation has misunderstood the way in which the target audience interprets the information, or the audience has difficulty in decoding the message. In these cases, there is deemed to be a mismatch between the *realms of understanding* of the source and the receiver (2005: p. 42). The realms of understanding refer to cultural inter-subjective meanings shared between the source and receiver.

Successful marketing communications is likely to occur when the person producing (or encoding and transmitting) the message shares understanding with the person receiving the message about what is being communicated and how the message communicates these symbolic or practical meanings. These shared meanings – or in the case of failure, a lack of shared meanings – are formed by an individual's attitudes, perceptions, behaviour and experience. The ways in which marketing communications aims to influence consumers' behaviour is discussed in the Chapter 4; however, it is important to note here that there are individual and personally held beliefs and attitudes and that there are also culturally shared values. Organisations which purport to a market-led orientation to their activities put a great deal effort into market research developing detailed knowledge and understanding of their target markets at a deep level in order to minimise the risk of a mismatch in understanding and to ensure the successful transmission and appropriate interpretation about the meaning of the message.

Criticisms of the Transmission Models of Communication

Transmission models have been criticised largely because they fail to capture the enormous complexity of communication, and the fact that communications theories attempt to cover a great many social and psychological processes, and an immense variety of possible communications contexts within fairly broad and encompassing models. These models have then been applied to marketing situations which perhaps cannot reflect the differences in nature between marketing promotions and other forms of communication such as political campaigning.

In the transmission model scenario, a source, usually an organisation or an individual, identifies a need to communicate something and creates a message using appropriate words, images, symbols and/or music which best represents the type of message to be transmitted. Once the message has been encoded into the chosen format, which could include written or verbal forms, or heavily laden with symbolism or very practical and simplistic, the format needs to be capable of transmission through designated channel(s). The channel can be either personal, that is using personal selling or word-of-mouth forms of communication or non-personal, which are characterised by mass media advertising for example. Of course, the type of channel selected will influence people differently and many tourism and hospitality organisations rely on a mix of different channels particularly in relation to tour operators' packaged trips. Personal selling techniques are highly influential but are only capable of communicating to small numbers of people at any one time, whereas mass media advertising is, or can be, less persuasive yet can reach a very large audience.

Through the concept of 'realms of understanding' the importance of shared meaning between the source and the receiver overcomes many of the criticisms of the transmission models of communication. However, many other influencing factors also affect the transmission of messages. These criticisms focus on the one-dimensional framework in which communication is conceived, the context in which the communication is received, the medium used as the channel, and the relationship between the sender and the receiver. The linear models assume that information is simply objectified in a 'container' which is then received and feedback, if at all provided, is slow to arrive and one directional. Context is important since the place and time and feeling state of the receiver at the time the message is received may influence the way in which the message is decoded. The medium used to transmit the message will impact upon the way that the message influences the receiver. And the relationship between the source and the receiver is crucial in determining the extent of trust in the truthfulness of the message and belief in the credibility of the source. However, there is great variance in terms of the tourism and hospitality sector. Travel advisory notices such as those provided by national government offices, such as the Foreign and Commonwealth Offices in the UK are impersonal forms of information, with little relationship expected or required and yet they are trusted forms of communication.

Multi-modal Communications Models

In order to overcome some of the problems identified hitherto with regard to transmission models of communication, multi-step and network models have been developed. This is to recognise the social processes involved in the production and interpretation of messages. In multi-modal models of communication, messages are conceived as being constructed by an organisation and transmitted via the mass media but then come under the influence of other people in society. Fill presents this scenario as a two-step model of communication (Figure 2.5) where the messages being transmitted through the mass media reach some target members but not all, but crucially, the message flows to 'opinion leaders', who may be able to reach members of the target audience who were not exposed to the message. Fill's model does not explicitly show this link between the mass media and the opinion leader, who must also be exposed to the original message.

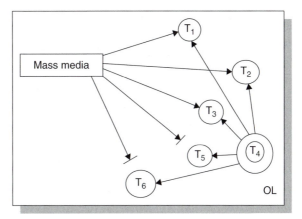

Figure 2.5 Two-step model of communication.
Source: Fill, 2005: p. 46.

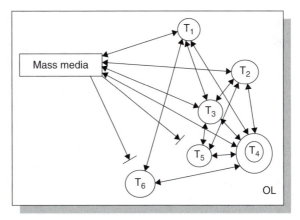

Figure 2.6 Multi-step process of communication.
Source: Fill, 2005: p. 47.

What is most important about multi-modal models of communication is that they recognise the important supporting role that peer groups can play in translating, reinforcing, mediating and influencing behaviour, which will be discussed in greater detail in the following sections.

In most common communication processes, however, networks of people interact in a more fluid and multi-staged process, and Fill extends the flows of information in a multi-step model as seen in Figure 2.6.

In Figure 2.6, people can be seen to interact in a networked way, communicating to each other about the product or service, reinforcing the messages received through the official media channels and also that the communication lines travel backwards to the mass media. In many ways, this reflects a more contemporary analysis of communications exchanges. The importance of peer interactions – those communications between people who share certain characteristics such as age, gender, ethnic background or special interests – are increasingly influential and are relied upon more often by the 'official' producers of communications messages. Networks help spread information to members of a specific target group or market. Referrals, testimonials and peer reviews are all new forms of communications which have been appropriated and incorporated into authorised marketing communications and these strategies will be discussed in Part 3 of the book. Not all people are the same, and some members of a peer group have powerful personal, social networks – sometimes referred to as social capital – and these people can have an important impact on the ways in which messages are perceived. However, as we will discuss later, the role of 'word-of-mouth' communications and ordinary peer interactions are fundamental to tourism and hospitality marketing.

Relational and Network Models of Communications

The previous discussion has highlighted that information and communication about places as tourist destinations, and other tourism and hospitality services and products, is likely to be influenced by prior learning, as a direct result of circular and diverse types of information from different parties in differing contexts, through a wide range of channels of communication which are accorded different levels of trustworthiness. Although the linear transmission models are intuitively easy to understand and serve many useful purposes in understanding basic processes of communication transmission, they lack the sophistication to account for the nuances which arise considering that humans communicate with each other all the time and to account for the variety of contextual factors which might impact upon the process. Multi-step models of communication allow for human interactions and a range of different information source inputs to the communication but still fail to account for the many different ways in which people evaluate and decide to act, or not, upon any given marketing message. A term which has been applied to understand the more complex matters of how communications flow around in organised systems which are linked to varying modes of interpretations and actions is called the 'relational approach' to communication.

This approach argues that the importance of 'context' needs to be factored into an analysis of how communication works. All communication occurs in a context. The multi-step models of communication recognised the importance of social background, but social context is equally important in determining how communication will be received and acted upon. These approaches also recognise the importance of the relationship between the sender of the communication and the receiver.

If a relationship is surface level, the communication may be interpreted in a different way than if there is a strong and trusting relationship between the parties. This is particularly relevant in the case of personal selling or business-to-business communications. Relationships develop over time and need not be a simple dyad but can consist of a whole network of participants with complex and different levels of engagement or affiliation occurring within a specific context.

However, the issue of context is crucial to understanding the level of relationship between the participants and the subsequent effects of the communication. In the hotel sector in particular, and some other sections of the tourism industry, a great deal of emphasis is placed on the importance of customer relationship management (CRM) as a technique to develop and maintain loyalty based on the formation of personal and deep relationships between the organisation and the individual (Hollensen, 2003). The principle behind this approach is that it is more cost-effective to communicate with existing customers who know and recognise the organisation and its services than it is to try and gain new customers. Through a 'connective' relationship the organisation can also make adjustments to its service offerings to exceed the customer's expectations and win long-term loyalty. This is made possible by large databases of customers' preferences and past consumer behaviour profile. However, communications between the organisation and these target customers not only consists of advertising and impersonal mass circulation direct mailing, but is also deeper and consists of detailed evidence gathered over multiple points of feedback and connections. These new forms of 'relational' approaches to marketing communications rely much more heavily on the idea of 'exchange', reciprocity and mutual gains whereby communication is more interactive and based on producing deeper levels of trust and commitment.

Communications in the network approach are not restricted to organisational boundaries, but by the social networks of people who communicate with each other independently of the organisational environment. Individuals participate in the network and exchange communications depending on how 'connected' they are to the network and how 'integrated' (how well they are linked to each other) into the network they become. Flows of information pass through and around the network by reciprocating individuals. These networks can be either prescribed, in that they are formed by the organisation in order to achieve an organisational agenda, or they are emergent, in that they are informal and emerge through the social and interpersonal actions of the participants. These types of network and relational approaches to communications theorising are important in helping understand how communications spread, particularly in the context of electronic communication systems, and therefore can help us to locate and develop viral or other types of e-marketing communications strategies which will be discussed later on in Chapter 10.

Illustration

Think about geographic knowledge. We become aware of the world at school through our learning of geography, culture, religion, politics and history, and yet the character of our knowledge of the world changes as we grow older and through our own experiences as travellers. We become more aware of some places through their exposure in the news media or through a wide variety of different means and contexts. We may grow deep connections with certain places, and we may visit some places many times as tourists. Often it is difficult to think back to how our knowledge of particular places was formed or how our image of a place became fixed. It may be down to the exposure of the place as a tourist destination in the media or through interpersonal communications through everyday conversations with peer groups, associates, employers or even in chance social encounters with strangers. Our experiences of the world make for very easy topics of conversation. Knowledge of places might also be derived from television programmes or movies which are located in particular places. There is a whole variety of ways in which information about places is communicated and circulated, much of which is independent of official marketing communications in the form of tourist brochures or guide books. The range of information together with the variety of modes of communication means that information about places evolves and develops through a learning process and communication circulates, weblike. The information is valued differently depending on the type of information channel and context used. For example, we can become inspired by individuals' stories about their own adventures in places and are more likely to trust some information sources more than others. Our attitudes, stage of life and upbringing are likely to affect how we feel about a place and its culture, as much as our ability to purchase a holiday to it. These issues make communications in tourism and hospitality much more complex than for other consumer goods.

Communications Effects

In discussing the importance of different gatekeepers in the community such as opinion leaders in terms of their roles in influencing other consumers about tourism and hospitality services and products, it is easy to assume that this information and communication process will inevitably lead to the adoption and consumption of such services or destinations by the majority of the population who can be conceived as 'opinion followers'. This is not the case, of course. People react differently on information, and it is conceivable that many people would not automatically become consumers based on the advice or advocacy of certain opinion formers or leaders. Also a great many variables will impact upon people's preferences for and decisions to act on messages about new products and services, such as other elements of the marketing mix, including, importantly, the pricing strategy.

New products such as a new restaurant opening in town or a new niche holiday product or new destinations in themselves generally can be conceived to follow a process of adoption. This process begins with people becoming aware of the product or service. Knowledge is built up over time until the potential consumer is persuaded by the messages that the service could potentially meet their needs. A decision is then taken whether to adopt or reject the offer. This decision is followed by action, the experience of the service which will lead to either a confirmation or disconfirmation that the service did or did not meet the needs.

Over time, this process of adoption is 'diffused' throughout the marketplace. Here, structural processes of adoption can show how new products or destinations, are diffused across the society. This process is conceived as beginning with a small number of 'innovators' who are followed by larger numbers of 'early adopters', in turn followed by the 'majority' and lastly 'laggards'. In relation to tourism development theory, there is a correlation here between the tourist area life cycle (TALC) model devised by Butler (1980). Butler developed the idea of the TALC in relation to physical development of tourism resorts, but it was based on the normative distribution curve for product life cycles and relates very clearly to this process of diffusion (Figure 2.7).

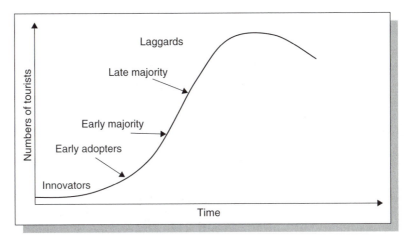

Figure 2.7 Adapted TALC model.

This is a fairly simplistic representation of the process of adoption of new destinations, however, and in reality a host of contextual factors influence the adoption of new destinations and hospitality services. These can be summarised as follows:

- Socio-economic characteristics (stage in the family life cycle, age, education, gender, employment, household disposable income, household composition, social networks and peer groups)
- Personal characteristics (attitudes, beliefs, values, personality traits, attitude to other cultures, motivation)
- Communication behaviour (responses to communications)

Another critical issue in understanding why tourism and hospitality marketing communications and related flows of information do not lead to automatic consumption is the concept of buyer readiness states. Consumers are considered to be more receptive to different kinds of communication depending on their readiness to consume. This process is linked to concepts of need recognition and motivation which are dealt with in Chapter 4. However, it is important to note that at certain times in consumers' activity cycles, they may be more responsive. In the context of holidays in Northern Europe, families and individuals traditionally think about their summer holidays in the time immediately after the winter festivals of Christmas. Although the model of buyer readiness states shown in Figure 2.8 relates more to the realm of physical products as opposed to service sectors, it is clearly applicable to some contexts such as a new tourism destination.

The models and theories discussed so far have described and evaluated flows of communications of messages from organisations to individuals, from organisations through individuals to reach other individuals and between networks of individuals. Furthermore, processes of consumers have been briefly mentioned, as has the processes on interpretation and meaning making. Communication has been described as the meaningful exchange of information. In Chapter 1, it was argued that tourism and hospitality relied heavily on representations because of

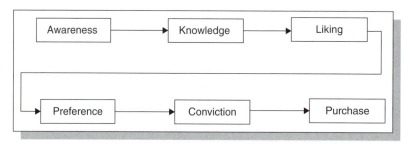

Figure 2.8 Buyer readiness states.

their characteristics as intangible lifestyle services and the use of emotional and experiential messages. In the final section of this chapter, we discuss how meanings are constructed and presented through semiotic analysis of communication messages.

Semiotics and the Communication of Meanings

Thus far, the models of communication theory outlined can be classified as process models. This is they try because to relate *how* messages are passed from one individual to another. We now need to look at the processes of *interpretation*, to understand how meaning is created and shared through symbolic uses of words and images. Although we discussed the importance of understanding how meaning is shared through a process of encoding and decoding – which was equated to the process of interpretation – a further discussion is needed on how *meaning* is created through *representations*.

This section outlines the basics of semiotic theory, which will be useful to develop understanding of how marketing communications uses symbolic objects and ideas in a creative process. Semiotics as a branch of social science has been developed and applied in many different contexts; it is, in fact, a complex set of theorisations and limitations of space necessitate a brief discussion. This, though, will help underpin knowledge on how marketing communications encodes meaning and enable an understanding of how marketing messages relate to specific need states which will be discussed more detail in Chapter 4.

Semiotics is the study of signs and symbols, in particular how meaning is constructed and shared between people and/or organisations. Semiologists or semioticians are concerned with the study of how signs are transmitted through the use of codes. In this way, there are some similarities between communication theories and semiology. Both recognise the fact that the message must not only be received but must be acted upon through a process of interpretation. In the earlier section on transmission models, this process was defined as 'decoding' but in semiology, however, the emphasis is different in that the focus is on the processes of meaning construction and how meanings are dependent on the variety of ways in which objects can be interpreted according to what the objects signify for people.

Semiotics was first developed by the American pragmatist Peirce and the French linguist Ferdinand Saussure. Peirce argued that an object or a thing involves the cooperation of three elements for it to be meaningful: the sign, its object and an interpretant. Saussure, coming from a linguistic approach, is recognised as the father of semiotics, and he elaborated the dualistic nature of signs. He argued that for a sign to have meaning, it must contain a *signifier*, the image, or form of words, and a *signified*, which is the mental construction. The 'sign' is thus a combination of a 'signifier' and a 'signified'. The thing that is being signified takes on meaning only when it is accompanied by its relevant 'context', the 'signified'. In contemporary semiotics, the signifier can be any type of sensory object – something seen, touched, smelt, etc. – but Saussure initially conceived it within the context of written language.

In Figure 2.9, Saussure explains the relationship between the signified and the signifier. The arrows show the relationship between them, which is called the 'process of signification'. This relationship exists because it is not possible to have a sign without the relationship between the signifier and the signified. When an object (signified) comes into our gaze, it is assigned (signification) a mental concept (signifier), as in the example of Figure 2.10. Of course, in any given

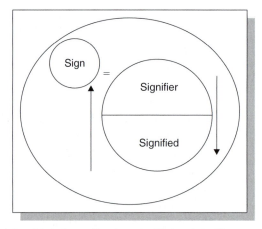

Figure 2.9 The relationship between the sign, signified and signifier.
Source: Saussure and Harris, 1983.

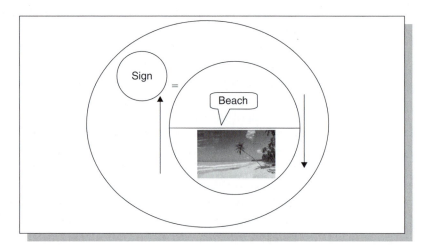

Figure 2.10 Example 1 of the signifier/signified relationship.

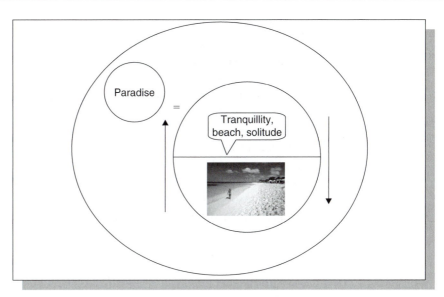

Figure 2.11 Example 2 of the signifier/signified relationship.

situation an object (signified) may be attached with a different signifier, depending on the context in which the object is received and how the individual decodes the signifier.

In Figure 2.11, the positioning of a beach with a solitary figure walking away out of view allows us to make connections between an imagined escape from hassle filled, everyday lives and pressures to a place which is free from mobile phones, work and drudgery, a tranquil world where peace and freedom can be experienced. One interpretation of this signification process could be 'paradise' which is a well-worn trope in tourism imagery. The idea of a 'paradise beach' is so infused into tourism mythology that a Google image search using this as a search term yielded 2,100,000 related images.

In this way, objects can mean a great deal more than their surface (face, or use) value. Objects take on a symbolic value, and this is the great contribution that semiotics can make to social science thinking: in its ability to explore beyond the immediate use value of things, to reveal deeper levels of meaning and the ways in which people, organisations and whole cultures interpret different things out of material objects. As a species, human beings are always trying to find ways of interpreting the meaning of things. Indeed, Peirce argued that we think only in signs. And so the study of signs is very important to understanding cultural activities. In later chapters, the processes of interpretation and meaning construction are picked up in relation to specific case studies and also in the context of developing marketing communications strategies.

This is extremely relevant to marketing communications in tourism and hospitality services, since as we will discover in relation to consumer behaviour processes in Chapter 4, consumption of these services and products is very often discretionary and linked to a person's identity as well as to wider individual concerns of class, status and what Bourdieu (1977) refers to as 'habitus' – our individual social backgrounds which ultimately define who we become as people through our cultural capital, our ability and desire for social distinction (see also Holden, 2005). Since consumption of these services is often to achieve identity goals through the symbolic association conferred through the consumption process, many tourism and hospitality services must construct and communicate messages based on the 'sign value' of consumption as opposed to the 'use value'.

In terms of tourism, the consumption of certain types of tourist experience or places (extreme climates or extremely difficult physical, social and cultural environments, for example) can confer a status of explorer or adventurer upon the individual. In other contexts, tourist places can be conferred with identities, particularly when they are related to particular forms of consumption practices (McCabe and Stokoe, 2004), and a rich tradition in social science thinking in tourism has concerned with the issue of 'myth making' through travel. Tourism is often linked to a desire to experience a mythical heritage, the meaningfulness of life in pre-industrial society (MacCannell, 1975; Selwyn, 1996), and so the tourism industry creates mythological representations that suggest such an experience is actually possible. Tresidder (1999), for example, conducted semiotic analyses of 18 Irish tourism brochures to show how Ireland was constructed as a mythical landscape of pre-industrial society based on representations of heritage, wildness and rurality (see also Holden, 2005: pp. 139–140). This is only one example of a whole plethora of studies which have analysed the semiotic content of tourism brochures, indicating the richness and depth of interpretation that is possible out of the content of tourism and hospitality marketing communications which will be explored in further in later chapters.

Recent years have witnessed changes in the importance conferred to different types of consumption experiences. There has been a postmodern turn in touristic consumption and an increase in emphasis placed on the visual aesthetic, modernist design and urban culture in consumer societies. These developments have taken place alongside the growth in DIY holiday making and low-cost airline routes between cities. In the context of hospitality, particularly the hotel sector, the precepts and ideals of postmodernism are used in marketing communications, both in the increasing attention given to the visual aesthetic in the design and décor of the physical environment of the hotel, here high art and high architectural design are incorporated into the core product in so many ways and the design and architectural features are used to communicate and convey meaning about the nature of the hospitality service provided.

Summary

This chapter has outlined the various different communication theories which can be applied to tourism and hospitality marketing communications strategies. The key concepts underpinning these strategies are that an organisation or an individual identifies that there is a need to communicate something to a group of people – most often a target market, but this can also include all other stakeholders such as suppliers, internal marketing communications to employees and so on. The various types of communication models were discussed, including linear transmission models which assume that information is transmitted in an uncomplicated and one-dimensional way. Even though transmission models can be criticised, there are circumstances in which mass communications must adopt a linear approach, such as in adverse weather warnings or other travel advisory notices. However, most communications models now assume a more reciprocal, communication exchange approach, whereby the dialogue between sender and receiver potentially involves other individuals and organisations who can potentially influence the impact of the message. The chapter went on to outline the importance of relational and network communication approaches and discussed the vital function played by word-of-mouth communications. In concluding this chapter, the discussion turned to the role of interpretation and meaning in the construction and deconstruction of marketing communications messages. Subsequent chapters will investigate the deconstruction process further, and Chapter $ examines how marketing communications target various drives, motivations and needs of consumers of tourism and hospitality products and services.

Discussion questions

1. Explain the differences in linear transmission models and multi-step, relational and network approaches.
2. Discuss the factors which might affect how communication is received by target individuals.
3. Explain three key differences between psychological theories of communication and sociological theories.
4. Discuss the process by which signs are created and meanings are understood.

Case Study 2: The Stuff of which Dreams Are Made – Representations of the South Sea in German-language Tourist Brochures

Schellhorn, M. and Perkins, H.C. (2004). *Current Issues in Tourism.* 7(2): 95–133.

This article investigates how places become 'representative' of mythical paradisal utopias through marketing materials – in this case tourism brochures of the South Sea Islands which are created for a German language audience (Germany, Austria and Switzerland). The article argues that the study of tourism brochures is important because of their historical function in promoting destinations to tourists and for the wide array of promotional objectives, broad distribution and marketing effectiveness of the material in a single promotional tool. Through their comprehensive literature review on the analysis of these promotional tools, Schellhorn and Perkins article shows us that tourism brochures have been subjected to a great deal of academic scrutiny largely outside the discipline of marketing where they are an accepted form of advertising. Sociologists (Dann, 1996), geographers (Shields, 1991), and anthropologists (Bruner, 1991; Selwyn, 1996) have all developed theorising about the construction, representation and consumption of places through analyses of tourism brochures. Broadly speaking, the main concerns of these researches have been on trying to work out whether what is being promoted about the place actually matches the reality of sociocultural life in the destination and what are the implications for local cultures, tourists and their effects on the nature of interactions between them. The answer is invariably that they do not match and that such representations act both to subjugate locals and present culture as something which can be consumed (see Echtner and Prasad, 2003, for a good discussion on the image of the third world). And yet, this lack of match between images portrayed, and what is actually experienced does not seem to matter. In fact, the role of the brochure might be much more complex in that it might specifically act to represent 'dreams' about places at the deliberate expense of 'reality' of existence. In the context of the South Sea Islands Schellhorn and Perkins argue that

> Organic images of island destinations are supplemented with deliberate tourism marketing which creates impressions of adventure and self-discovery. While some potential tourists might have menacing connotations of island experiences lurking in their subconscious minds derived from European fiction such as *Lord of the Flies* and *Robinson Crusoe*, marketers have systematically built up positive images of the islands. King (1997: 145) also argues that tourism promoters exploit the early literary work based on a Eurocentric island mythology noting that the fictional dream of paradise can become a reality for European consumers. As a result, consumer perceptions of South Pacific islands owe more to the mythology of the palm-fringed coral atoll than to the realities of life in the tropics. This is despite the fact that island environments and experiences are not always hospitable and include such things as coral cuts, sunburn, spiders, sharks, stonefish, sea wasps, and the cyclone season. (Schellhorn and Perkins, 2004: pp. 97–98)

Schellhorn and Perkins link a search for a fictional dream of paradise to socio-anthropological theorising on the motives for tourism being deeply connected for a search for meaning and authentic experiences (MacCannell, 1975) and akin to a sacred journey of self-discovery (Graburn, 1989). The move towards more postmodern theorising in recent years has only served to legitimise the symbolic, superficial and heterogenic associations between

representations of place and the nature of contemporary tourist experiences (Urry, 1995). In discussing the ways in the idea of 'paradise' has been transformed from its original context in religious iconography and mythology as the ultimate utopia alongside the process of secularisation, Cohen (1982) argues that paradise has become a consumer product through these representations. Ultimately, according to Schellhorn and Perkins analysis, place-marketing which draws on these types of images and representations, specifically where local, indigenous cultures are portrayed in destination imagery in stereotypical, mythological or sexualised ways can lead to transformations of place including perceptions, attitudes and behaviours. However, the reflexive agency of tourists must not be underestimated, and it cannot be assumed that representations of place cultures in tourism brochures have a negative effect or that commodification in this way necessarily diminishes tourist's experience.

In their study, Schellhorn and Perkins analysed the images and texts in 18 German language brochures containing tours to the South Sea Islands. Their data consisted of 986 photographs and text contained on 365 pages within the brochures. Their method of analysis was informed by content analysis, discourse analysis and deconstruction. Deconstruction was thought to be especially useful because it asks questions about the meanings of representations. Particularly, deconstruction is useful as a method to look at the politics of image, to acknowledge that representations are 'authored' and so are purposeful and contain references to ideological positions of the authors, and to uncover the implications of these representation processes (Feisenmeier and MacKay, 1996).

Schellhorn and Perkins analysis revealed that the South Sea Islands were represented through the concept of 'romantic discovery' drawing on early discourses of colonial discoverers. Not only do the texts of the tourism brochures construct the Islands as 'gentle' and tranquil, they also emphasise the feminine in their descriptions of the culture and conflate historical colonial imagery with current life in the Islands (Schellhorn and Perkins, 2004: p. 107). This portrayal is totally at odds with historical reality and contemporary life. But it is the portrayal of the Islands as 'paradise' which forms most of the analysis of their article. Notions of paradise are constructed and represented through the imagery and text of the brochures, and the authors contrast these notions with the political, environmental and social reality of contemporary life on the South Sea Pacific Islands. The specific examples they raise include political unrest, poverty, deforestation and environmental degradation. Schellhorn and Perkins go on to assess the presence and role of people in the imagery of the brochures. They found that people featured in only 36% of the photographs, demonstrating the emphasis on the South Sea Islands as a natural paradise. However, within this figure, 41% focused on images of local people only. Schellhorn and Perkins (2004: pp. 116–118) assess the gender relationships and stereotypes within these representations:

Solitary women are the largest of various gender-based groups, nearly twice the size of the solitary men category. There is, however, not just a quantitative difference in the portrayal of unaccompanied local women and men. The local male is usually depicted within an active context, often engaged in professional or ceremonial activities that are integral to everyday domestic life. Thus a 'brochure man' might be fishing, working the gardens, climbing a coconut tree, mixing a kava bowl or patrolling in a police uniform. The stereotypical solitary 'brochure woman', on the other hand, is almost exclusively depicted as inactively 'just being there', often portrayed in close-up form posing for, or smiling at, the camera (and, ultimately, the brochure reader). She might be lying on the beach or standing in the ankle deep waters of a turquoise lagoon. Occasionally, she sits in front of a hotel room or on a guest bed. In the few exceptions when a solitary woman is portrayed as working, she holds the role of servant, usually smiling over a tray of exotically decorated drinks.

Not only are these roles in stark contrast to the normative roles of men and women in South Sea Island society, but also Schellhorn and Perkins point out that the images of women portray them largely in a sexualised, way often with flowers in their hair, or in partially dressed attire again at odds with social norms. These brochures create a mythical fantasy, a dream-like version of the South Sea Islands, making the places available for consumption in a particular and stylised way. The representations and constructions of these Islands in this way tells us more about our own (Western Eurocentric) culture and values than those it purportedly reveals.

The ubiquitous dream metaphor is the most persistent common denominator of the brochures' advertising narratives and connects the South Sea's core image to an ancient myth. The promise of a distant paradise, Utopian in character, builds upon a romanticised organic image which continues to be popularised by artists, writers and popular culture. Through tourism advertising, however, the Utopian myth is being converted into a marketable consumer product. For this purpose, dreams have to be traceable, paradise has to become discoverable, Utopia must be realised. (2004: pp. 127–128)

Learning activity

What can we learn from this article? Read the full article by Schellhorn and Perkins. Hold a class debate on the role of tourism brochures in marketing tourism destinations. Consider the following debating issues in your discussion:

- Tourism brochures need to reflect the reality of life in tourism destinations.
- Tourism is about 'selling dreams' and therefore tourism advertising should focus on myths and fantasies.
- Local, indigenous cultures should not appear in tourism brochures at all.
- Tourism and hospitality marketing has a moral responsibility to represent people accurately and ethically in tourism brochures.
- Should we aim to control how places and people are represented in tourism brochures? Who should be involved?

Find examples of tourism brochures for a range of destinations. Work in small groups, ensuring a good spread of different destinations in each group, try using content, thematic and deconstruction techniques to analyse the images and textual representations.

Think about classifying 'what' is represented, 'how' it is represented, and 'what implications' arise from the representation.

References and Further Reading

Baloglu, S. and Brinberg, D. (1997). Affective images of tourism destinations. *Journal of Travel Research*. 35(4): 11–15.

Bourdieu, P. (1977). *Outline of a Theory of Practice*. Cambridge: Cambridge University Press.

Britton, R.A. (1979). The image of the Third World in tourism in marketing. *Annals of Tourism Research*. 6: 318–329.

Bruner, E. (1991). Transformation of self in tourism. *Annals of Tourism Research*. 18: 238–250.

Butler, R. (1980). The concept of a tourist area life cycle of evolution: Implications for management of resources. *Canadian Geographer*. 24: 1–24.

Cloke, P. and Perkins, H.C. (1998). 'Cracking the canyon with the awesome foursome': Representations of adventure tourism in New Zealand. *Environment and Planning D: Society & Space*.

Cohen, E. (1982). The Pacific Islands from utopian myth to consumer product: The disenchantment of paradise. *Cahiers du Tourisme* (série B) 27.

Cohen, C.B. (1995). Marketing paradise, making nation. *Annals of Tourism Research*. 22: 404–421.

Crick, M. (1989). Representations of international tourists in social sciences: Sun, sex, sights, savings and servility. *Annual Review of Anthropology*. 18: 307–344.

Dann, G.M.S. (1996). *The language of tourism: A sociolinguistic analysis*. Oxon, England: CAB International.

Echtner, C.M. and Prasad, P. (2003). The context of Third World tourism marketing. *Annals of Tourism Research*. 30(3): 660–682.

Fesenmeier, D. and Mackay, K. (1996). Deconstructing destination image construction. *Review de Tourisme*. 2: 37–43.

Fill, C. (2005). *Marketing Communications: Engagement, Strategies and Practice*. 4th edn. Harrow, England: Prentice Hall.

Graburn, N. (1989). Tourism, the sacred journey. In Smith, V. (ed.) *Hosts and Guests. The Anthropology of Tourism*. 2nd edn. Philadelphia: University of Pennsylvania Press, pp. 21–36.

Holden, A. (2005). *Tourism Studies and the Social Sciences*. London: Routledge.

Hollensen, S. (2003). *Relationship Marketing*. Harrow, England: Prentice Hall.

MacCannell, D. (1975). *The tourist: A new theory of the leisure class*. New York: Schocken books.

MacKay, H. (ed.) (1997). *Consumption and everyday life: Culture, media and identities*. London: Sage in association with the Open University Press.

MacKay, K.J. and Fesenmaier, D.R. (1997). Pictorial element of destination in image formation. *Annals of Tourism Research*. 24(3): 537–565.

McCabe, S. and Stokoe, E.H. (2004). Place and identity in tourist accounts. *Annals of Tourism Research*. 31(3): 601–622.

Miller, D., Jackson, P., Thrift, N., Holbrook, B. and Rowlands, M. (1998). *Shopping, place and identity*. London: Routledge.

Morgan, N. and Pritchard, A. (1998). *Tourism promotion and power: Creating images, creating identities*. Chichester: Wiley.

Saussure, F. de. and Harris, R. (1983). *Course in General Linguistics*. Trans. Charles Bally and Albert Sechehaye. Illinois: Open Court.

Schellhorn, M. and Perkins, H.C. (2004). The stuff of which dreams are made: Representations of the South Sea in German-language tourist brochures. *Current Issues in Tourism*. 7(2): 95–133.

Schramm, W. (1954). How communication works. In Schramm, W. (ed.) *The Process and Effects of Mass Communication*. Urbana: University of Illinois Press, pp. 1–15.

Schramm, W. and Porter, W.E. (1982). *Men, Women, Messages and Media*. 2nd edn. New York: Harper and Row.

Selby, M. and Morgan, N.J. (1996). Reconstruing place image: A case study of its role in destination market research. *Tourism Management*. 17(4): 287–294.

Selwyn, T. (1996). *The tourism image: Myths and structures*. New York: John Wiley.

Shannon, C. and Weaver, W. (1962). *The mathematical theory of communication*. Urbana, IL: University of Illinois Press.

Shields, R. (1991). *Places on the Margin. Alternative Geographies of Modernity*. London: Routledge.

Thurot, J.M. and Thurot, G. (1983). The ideology of class and tourism: Confronting the discourse of advertising. *Annals of Tourism Research*. 10: 173–189.

Tresidder, R. (1999). Tourism and sacred landscapes. In Crouch, D. (ed.) *Leisure/Tourism Geographies: Practices and Geographical Knowledge*. London: Routledge, pp. 137–148.

Urry, J. (1995). *Consuming Places*. London: Routledge.

Yuksel, A. and Akgul, O. (2007). Postcards as affective image makers: An idle agent in destination marketing. *Tourism Management*. 28: 714–725.

Key Resources and Links

http://www.cultsock.ndirect.co.uk/MUHome/cshtml/index.html
http://www.aber.ac.uk/media/Documents/S4B/sem02.html

The Marketing Communications Environment

At the end of this chapter, you will be able to

- Define the marketing function and the structure of the marketing communications industry.

- Understand the external environmental factors that impact on marketing communications for tourism and hospitality.

- Recognise changes in the industry and how these affect marketing functions.

- Understand the regulatory environment governing marketing communications and evaluate the need for regulation of marketing communications.

- Understand the role of ethics in tourism and hospitality marketing communications.

Introduction

Marketing management is concerned with managing the interface between the organisation and its environment (Jobber, 1995). The adoption of a marketing orientation puts satisfaction of customers' needs and values at the heart of all organisational decision-making, including strategy development. In the previous chapters it was noted that the tourism and hospitality industry is dynamic as it responds to changes in consumer needs and values, and that these developments affect the marketing environment of these services. Competition in the marketplace for the services offered by this industry places an important emphasis on marketing communications. Communication involves the exchange of meaningful information and represents the 'sharp edge' of the interface between the organisation and its environment since it is through marketing communications that strategic aims, marketing planning goals and tactical actions of the organisation are brought to the attention of its customers and stakeholders. This chapter focuses on the organisational and market environment interface and how that is managed through marketing communications. There are both external and internal constraints to marketing and the purpose of this chapter is to describe the main relationships and factors and explain how current developments and trends inform the direction and content of marketing communications in this service industry.

Marketing communications are shaped by and must respond to the external context, including the political, legal and regulatory context, socio-economic trends, the media and industry trends (see Figure 3.1). This chapter also outlines the internal organisational forces and defines the function of the marketing department in relation to developing a market orientation and an integrated approach to marketing communications. This leads to a consideration of the links between the organisation and the marketing communications industry, the structure of which is described. Chapter 4, then, goes into detail on how marketing communications relate to consumers' behaviour processes and explores the interplay between consumers' actions and reactions to marketing messages.

The marketing function is concerned not only with promoting the brand, organisation or service to maximise sales but also with understanding what consumers need and value from the services offered and make changes to the marketing mix accordingly. A further factor to consider is the competitive context. Organisations must meet and exceed consumers' needs better than the competition. How these competition factors impact on marketing communications for tourism and hospitality services is detailed in Chapter 5 whereas the marketing mix will be discussed in the context of communications strategies in

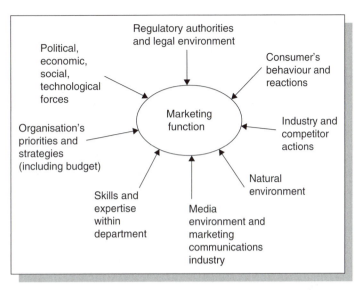

Figure 3.1 Factors impinging on the marketing function.

Chapter 7. However, the point to make in this chapter is that the marketing function is constrained by changes in demand and supply of the products and services and the relative importance of the services in the marketplace and the dynamic marketing industry environment itself. One of the most important functions of the marketing department is to respond to these dynamic conditions which in contemporary contexts demand a market orientation, good marketing planning and also flexibility to respond to developments beyond the organisation's control that might impact on sales or other targets. This is particularly important as, as noted in Chapter 1, the tourism and hospitality sector is susceptible to change in the socio-economic and political environment, the natural environment conditions and competitors actions in a largely international marketplace.

Figure 3.1 identifies the main factors impinging on the marketing function. Some of the factors relate to external forces beyond the direct control of the organisation. The marketing function is to understand the range of possible external factors which might impact directly on the organisation and to put in place controls, strategies and activities which might mitigate against their influence. Some factors are internal factors which the marketing department must try to exert influence to change. Before these main issues are considered in more detail, the following section briefly outlines the global issues currently influencing the context for tourism and hospitality marketing.

The Global Context of Tourism and Hospitality Services

Towards the end of the last millennium, Kotler (1997) outlined four key challenges for market-led organisations in the twenty-first century: new customers, new competition, new types of organisations and technological advances. These issues can be related to challenges for the tourism and hospitality sector.

1. *New customers*: Customers are becoming more experienced and have higher expectations of quality in relation to tourism and hospitality services; they are less likely to accept lower standards of product and service quality. Modern consumers are more sophisticated and knowledgeable. Because of high levels of exposure to marketing communications, they are more aware of organisation's strategies for sales and marketing promotion, are more able to choose between brands based on how much the purchase meets their needs as opposed to loyalty to the organisation and are more likely to be cynical in their attitude to marketing communications. They are also more aware of their power and their consumer rights. But also there has been an increasing globalisation of consumer tastes, especially in relation to the spheres of entertainment and sport. Global cultural icons in the worlds of acting, music, art, architecture and design, modelling and fashion, and sports have created an international celebrity culture. At the same time there are huge variations globally.

2. *New competition*: With globalisation, the competitive environment is changing rapidly. Consumers have access to information about places, destinations, brands and services which are not exclusive to their home nation. This has had the effect of forcing companies to re-orient their businesses towards globalised markets. Another impact of globalisation has been deregulation in terms of access and entry into new markets. It is this ease of market entry and a lack of barriers to competition which has led to a growth in internationalisation of brands in the tourism and hospitality sector in the part decade. For example, Doole and Lowe identify that growth in international trade in the overall service sector (which includes banking and financial and other services) reached US$1.5 trillion in 2000, and the service sector is one of the most rapidly growing sectors of the international trade of the advanced economies (Doole and Lowe, 2001).

3. *New type of organisation*: Businesses are changing their business models to focus on core aspects of their activity. New organisations are flexible and responsive to market conditions and are able to focus on delivery of customer value. These developments have led to a rise in outsourcing, collaboration and alliances in marketing tourism destinations

(Wang and Fesenmaier, 2007) and, importantly for the hospitality industry, franchising. Although franchising has been a long-established model in hotels and fast food restaurants there has been an increasing emphasis on the importance of the value chain. The value chain consists of orienting all the primary and support activities of the organisation to creating value for customers. The focus on value and quality is a key concern for all tourism and hospitality organisations.

4. *Technological advances*: Technology has already been mentioned in relation to future developments in tourism marketing communications in Chapter 1. However, technological advances have affected every sphere of business activity which is also affecting the ability of organisations to exceed consumers' expectations. Technology allows organisations to improve systems and processes, develop new products, promote and distribute services to consumers and contribute to internal systems including data warehousing for customer relationship management. The widespread adoption of information communication technologies (ICTs) in the marketplace has influenced a generation of consumers to become much more independent in their choices and consumption of these services.

These structural changes to the business environment are often associated with globalisation. There are three key features of globalisation that are particularly important for the present context:

1. The flows of capital across and between national economies
2. The flows of ICTs across national economies
3. The flows of cultural exchange between and across nations

These aspects of global trade are intrinsically related to the tourism and hospitality sector since it is reliant on exchanges of capital, culture and information as the very basis for its operations (*cf.* Wahab and Cooper, 2001).

Illustration

The spread of personal computing and broadband Internet connections has meant that consumers worldwide are able to access a wide variety of information from a range of different sources about travel and hospitality services, holidays, destinations or resorts. They can download personal testimonies of other travellers, read guide books and also access information provided by tour operators and the destination marketing organisations (DMOs). Consumers can access this information 24 hours a day, 7 days a week and can book their arrangements in real time. This, together with increased disposable incomes and a highly competitive holiday travel market where quality has improved and yet prices have remained relatively stable, has driven up demand for holidays and short breaks abroad particularly in Western Europe and the UK and changed the landscape of tourism marketing communications. There has been a large increase in UK residents' visits abroad, and in the 20 years between 1985 and 2006 these more than tripled, to a record 69 million visits in 2006 (International Passenger Survey, 2008).

A great deal of this demand has been driven by a fragmentation in the holiday travel market and a move to independent booking (so-called DIY holidaymaking). A key component of this fragmented marketplace is the low-cost airline (LCA) market. The business model of the LCAs relies on technology to reduce labour costs, drive productivity and enable direct distribution systems to deliver customer value. Doganis (2005) argues that within the space of 10 years (1994–2004) the demand for low cost air travel grew from less than 3 million to over 100 million passengers within Europe. The vast majority of these passengers either begin or end their journey at a UK airport. Not only does this growth demonstrate a willingness on the part of UK and European tourists to accept lower standards of service in some aspects of their overall trip in order to make cost savings, including perhaps to trade up to higher quality accommodation or to allow them to take more short break holiday experiences for example. It also demonstrates an experienced market which is able to search, arrange and book their holidays without the advice of travel agents. The decision-making process is less highly involved as is conventionally described in the tourism consumer behaviour theory. It is accepted that the majority of LCA flights are for short breaks as opposed to main holidays; however, research has shown that all types of travellers value the low cost air travel experience. Although abroad consumers can keep in touch using their mobile telephones, they can use their regular bank account debit cards to withdraw cash in local currency using automated teller machines (ATMs), and language barriers are less a problem for many tourists. This means that consumers face less risk during their experiences.

Thus, there are new types of organisations not only in the LCA sector, but also in terms of accommodation rental agencies and directories, price comparison services (new e-mediaries), which create new types of competition and new types of consumers.

The Function of the Marketing Department

As outlined at the beginning of this chapter, the function of the marketing department is to manage the interface between the organisation and the environment. In the context of the tourism and hospitality sector this has traditionally been concerned with managing the sales function. This has meant that marketing within the sector has been oriented to

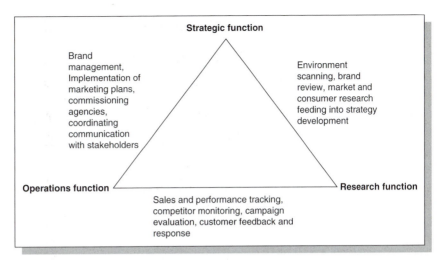

Figure 3.2 The triangular function of the marketing department.

generating sales through sales promotions. However, this is also chang-ing as organisations move to a marketing orientation and integrate marketing communications. Figure 3.2 shows the three main areas of functional activity for the marketing department.

Strategic Function

The marketing department has input into the strategic direction of the organisation. The marketing department provides research on the external environment which feeds into the identification of new mar-ket opportunities, product development or service innovation. The marketing function also directs the strategic decision-making at organ-isational level in terms of branding review and research on wider con-sumer trends and developments.

Operations Function

The marketing department takes direct control over the management of sales, planning and forecasting demand for the services, feeding in turn into the operations and human resources management functions. The marketing function is also responsible for the delivery of brand management strategies, and the implementation of marketing plans. At the tactical level, the marketing department commissions creative teams and marketing communications agencies to deliver the market-ing and promotions materials. The department controls budget and scheduling of marketing activity during the cycle of activity and coor-dinates communication with all stakeholders of the organisation.

Research Function

A great deal of the work of the marketing department is dependent on or driven by marketing research. Research feeds into the strategic and tactical functions. Some research is commissioned from market research agencies with specialist knowledge of markets or access to consumer databases. Similarly, brand reviews are often undertaken by external research and consultancy organisations. The marketing department collects and analyses sales data and customer satisfaction research. The department may also seek to find out about customers decision-making processes. This type of research often leads to service innovation and/or modification.

Processes of the Marketing Department

In terms of the practical activities of the marketing function, these can be categorised as planning and forecasting, organising and coordinating, directing and implementing strategies, and monitoring and controlling marketing activities.

- *Planning and forecasting*, utilising wider aspects of the marketing mix, product, price, distribution, promotion, physical evidence, people and processes, to create specific mixes for niche market segments and managing customer relationships. This not only shows how organisations have had to respond to changes in the market environment but also to changes in the marketing environment for the tourism and hospitality sector.
- The marketing department is responsible for *organising and coordinating* the development of products and services to ensure that quality standards are implemented in line with the financial planning and operations departments. The marketing department works with all stakeholders of the organisation.
- The marketing department takes a direct role in *directing and implementing communication* with stakeholders – suppliers, shareholders, employees as well as customers – and takes a direct lead role in determining the type and nature of the communications required, which could include messages about leadership, motivating or empowering employees, for example, as well as brand identity, strategies for sales promotions and public relations (PR).
- The key role of the marketing function is *controlling, monitoring and evaluating* the performance of the marketing and communications initiatives as articulated with the overall business strategies and goals. The marketing function makes certain that plans are implemented; championing the customer and ensuring that all aspects of

the company's promise to the consumer in terms of service quality are maintained and anticipating and responding to change.

The Marketing Planning Process

One of the most important functions of the marketing department is to understand the position of the organisation in relation to the market, the competition and the external environment and to develop and implement a range of strategies and plans which will help the organisation to realise its goals and mission. This is a constant process in which the marketing team evaluate changes in sales, performance and market share and provide accounts for any changes to the senior management, draw up marketing plans to manage future demand and implement strategies to stimulate demand or respond to competitor's activities. It is also a strategic function in that strategic marketing plans are developed to meet long-range objectives.

In many micro and small tourism and hospitality organisations, the focus remains on day-to-day sales activities, aiming to achieve sales targets and putting in place strategies, including sales promotions or marketing campaigns designed to realise these targets. This is often referred to as a tactical or short-range marketing planning approach and represents the core marketing function on a short-term activity cycle. Cycles in this context can refer to daily, weekly, or seasonal flows of peak demand or off-season periods. At periodic points in the annual cycle the marketing function must also provide an analysis of the future market opportunities and/or account for any changes in demand, and it is at these points in the cycle that an analysis or a marketing audit is undertaken. Similarly, this type of strategic planning function can sometimes be undertaken in relation to research and development of new products or in preparing for a new marketing communications and promotional strategy. This type of marketing auditing or market environment analysis is also referred to as market scanning.

Figure 3.3 highlights the linkages between marketing strategy development and the organisational strategy. Separate departments within the organisation including operations, finance and human resources coordinate activities and are aligned with the marketing planning function to implement organisational strategy. The marketing department is constrained by the financial planning function and an integral part of the work of the marketing division is to vie for resources to achieve planning objectives and goals. Once the marketing budget has been agreed in the context of research and analysis on the external environment, customer and market analysis, including competitor intelligence, the department begins to develop marketing mix strategies

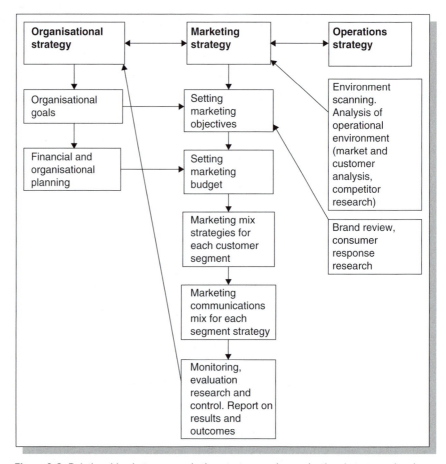

Figure 3.3 Relationships between marketing strategy and organisational strategy showing the marketing planning process.

for each identified segment. Chapters 5 and 6 provide more detail in the marketing planning and competitive strategy development whereas Chapter 7, then, outlines segmentation, targeting and positioning approaches in tourism and hospitality. In this chapter, the focus is on the importance of environment scanning and how this impacts on the marketing planning and marketing communications.

Environment Scanning

The process of environment scanning is sometimes called macro-environment analysis because these are the forces and factors which have (if the analysis serves to provide an explanation of sales performance) or are likely to (if the analysis seeks to inform and determine future strategy selection) impact upon the demand for tourism and hospitality ability of the organisation to attract customers. This type of scanning procedure is often referred to as a PESTLe analysis.

These analyses together provide the basis for strategic marketing planning in the following:

- PESTLe
- SWOT analysis
- marketing objective setting
- identification of target segments
- product positioning strategy
- marketing mix strategy selection
- marketing communications planning
- implementation
- evaluation and control

The key frameworks for understanding the external pressures which might impact upon sales and/or performance of the organisation is a PESTLe analysis (Cateora and Ghauri, 2000):

P – political forces
E – economic forces
S – sociocultural forces
T – technological forces
L – legal
e – ecological

According to Sandhu (2006: p. 210), the main functions of PESTLe analysis is in the context of 'environmental scanning', an analytic process described as necessary in terms of

- understanding about events and trends in the external environment
- establishing relationships between these events and trends
- making sense of them in relation to consumers' choices and behaviour
- extracting the main implications for decision-making and strategy formation.

It is often difficult to understand how PESTLe analyses feed into the marketing planning process of tourism and hospitality sector and hence how such external environmental factors impact upon marketing communications and so the next section provides a brief overview and a set of examples to indicate how this framework is relevant to marketing communications planning and actions.

The issue for many students and practitioners of this sector is a lack of clarity in terms of what is required by a PESTLe analysis in relation to external factors at the national and/or international level [i.e. should the focus of the analysis be on the external forces affecting the market (the generating economy) or the destination (the receiving economy)]. The simple answer is that both must form part of the analysis in some cases, especially if the following principle is applied.

Political and Legal Factors

These factors are driven by government and quasi- or non-governmental organisations. Increasingly, organisations are subject to the influence of international politics and intra(or supra)-national agencies such as the United Nations, and in particular the World Tourism Organisation, the EU and industry-wide organisations such as European Tour Operators Association (ETOA) and the International Air Transport Association (IATA) and so on. Government policies influence people's ability to travel such as the control of movement of people into and out of the country through the use of visa restrictions, the provision of statutory holiday time, and sometimes through the control and regulation of currency transactions or through direct control of the national central bank (although in many countries the central bank is an independent organisation from government).

In the UK context in particular, recent government initiatives have the potential to impact upon the tourism and hospitality business sector as follows.

Climate change legislation (such as that being introduced in the UK under the Climate change Bill) which will change the taxation structure on aviation and encourage some forms of transport and discourage highly polluting forms. The UK air passenger duty (APD) will be replaced in 2009 with a new tax system for aviation linked to flight distance which will encourage air transport firms to increase load factors.

Other legislation and policy areas which impact on the tourism and hospitality sector include licensing and regulation for the sale of alcohol and gambling, food standards and health and safety, crime and public disorder, anti-competition laws and minimum wage and wider employment law legislation. Another major area of political intervention is in terms of *anti-terrorist measures*, particularly in relation to flights between the UK and the US through the Department of Homeland Securities Transport Security Administration (www.tsa.gov) and the UK Department of Transport (www.dft.gov.uk), which were increased from November 2006 onwards in the light of terrorist threats have the potential to impact upon check-in times, travel times and perceived infringement on people's rights. This may lead in the longer term to 'fatigue' on the part of travellers for some routes or forms of transport. However, a positive outcome of these measures might be that travellers feel more safe and therefore are willing to accept the measures and perceive America and Britain as relatively 'safe' destinations. There are many areas of government policy which have the potential to intersect with the travel industry as the example of *education policy shows*. The UK government for example is concerned about the educational achievement of children and aims to place restrictions on absence from school to take holidays. The government aims to work with the travel industry to try to ensure fair pricing for family holidays during the main vacation times. However, pricing policies within the tourism industry will always reflect the peaks and troughs in demand which are associated with normal working and holiday times. One potential is that with an increase in flexible working practices, the demand for some forms of short breaks and other holiday trips will be an opportunity for some tourism organisations.

The potential for political issues to affect the marketing communications of tourism and hospitality organisations is demonstrated in Plate 3.1 which shows a full page advertisement taken out by Ryanair in late 2006 in response to Gordon Brown, the then UK Chancellor of the Exchequer, whose budget announced the doubling of APD, from £5 to £10 on short-haul flights (those served by Ryanair and hence only this is referred to in the advertisement) and to £80 for long-haul flights.

Ryanair, which through its low cost leadership strategy, aims to provide customers with the lowest cost short-haul air fares, sends a message to its customers that price rises were not the fault of the company but the 'greedy' government tax regime. Ryanair can claim success in that the UK government has agreed to move to a tax based on distance and flight loads for 2009 as identified earlier.

Economic Factors

The economic performance of the generating region is important, together with some aspects of the economic situation in the destination or resort to understand how customers' and markets' relative buying (consumption) power is affected by current economic conditions. These external forces affect the ability of consumers to purchase the tourism and hospitality products and services. The economic forces include: economic growth figures (including an analysis of whether the country is currently in recession) (Okumus and Karamustafa, 2005); income growth and relative distribution of income (i.e. relative size and growth of middle/working classes, and how these are changing); unemployment levels; gross domestic product and average annual wages/salaries; the levels of people claiming other types of state benefits including incapacity benefits, the availability of credit, exchange rates and interest rates.

Plate 3.1 Ryanair protest against doubling of APD.

High interest rates can either be a positive opportunity or a negative threat in relation to tourism industry. For instance, a combination of high levels of personal debt and high interest rates is likely to dampen demand for higher end discretionary goods such as tourism and hospitality, whereas with easily available credit and low interest rates demand may be very buoyant, as may be the case with high interest rates, low levels of debt but high levels of savings.

Exchange rates need to be assessed in relation to both the strength of the currency in the generating market and also the destination region. Times of turmoil in the financial markets such as that experienced in the recent credit crunch in the financial markets of the US which impacted on the global economy and may extend into a full brown economic recession has the potential to impact on demand for tourism and hospitality. A recent *Travel Weekly* article assessed how an economic downturn would affect the travel industry and concluded that

- The world's airlines only returned to profitability in 2007 (since 2000 in the aftermath of the 9/11 attack on the World Trade Centre) and so economic downturn would severely impact the aviation sector.
- Holidays remain a key part of family budgets so people would probably trade down in their holidays and take fewer breaks. But inflationary pressures including large increases in the costs of essential items such as housing, fuel, food and transport would mean that many consumers will take shorter breaks or book less costly destinations.

Sociocultural Factors

Social, demographic and cultural forces are crucial to the analysis of the external marketing environment because these factors are about people and people make up markets for products and services. The main social, demographic and cultural forces which have the potential to impact on tourism and hospitality markets are forces which can be characterised as being influential at the structural level (i.e. those that are slow to change and over longer periods of time) and at the surface level (i.e. those that can change more rapidly over shorter periods of time and are more responsive to other aspects in the external environment including the media).

Structural level factors include population size and structure, density, location, age, gender, race, occupation (characteristics thereof) and changes within different categories.

In the UK, there are profound structural changes within the social, demographic and cultural make up of the population. More women in full time occupations, a great tendency for women to settle down and have children later in life, a large proportion of marriages ending in divorce, a rise in single occupancy households and an ageing population continue to be the dominant structural changes in the UK social demographic structure (Wilson and Smallwood, 2007).

These trends are having a dramatic impact on the market for tourism. One-parent families now account for around a quarter of the UK family market and this figure is expected to increase in the future. In families where both parents are employed, pressures of work are often forcing families to holiday separately, where one parent remains working whilst the other takes the children on holiday.

Recent figures show that around one-third of holidays taken by a single adult were taken by people who were in a relationship but were not taking the holiday with their partner (ONS, Travel Trends, 2007).

These changes in socio-economic status and demographic patterns create both opportunities and threats to tourism and hospitality organisations. Understanding the social and demographic structural environment will enable companies to respond to new markets as they emerge and to create new segments. They will be able to identify new business opportunities and recognise threats to existing product markets. These companies will also be able to creatively use marketing communications to depict people and situations in ways which will garner sympathy and understanding from targeted segments.

> *Surface level* factors include, attitudes, values, beliefs, opinions and lifestyles. Examples of surface level forces are a growing interest in green issues, organic and healthy foods, 'slow food'; a related interest in general health and fitness; a growing interest in independent (DIY) travel and holiday making; and sports- and activity-related travel.

These forces can represent both threats and opportunities for organisations in the tourism and hospitality sector, depending on to what extent they have resources and competencies to provide services and products related to these types of interests. There is a need to recognise that some organisations cater to different types of interests, lifestyles, values and opinions which may not correspond to these broad generic types of interests. New destination products are likely to emerge as more people become interested in different cultures and their practices (such as religion and style of life). Communications can be created which respond to changing values and lifestyles of the target groups.

Technological Factors

Earlier on in this chapter, the importance of technological advances to the development of tourism was outlined. However, in all areas of the tourism and hospitality service industries, technological advances have made it possible for companies to create a better understanding of customers' needs and wants, their preferences and their values. Technology in hotel booking systems has enabled hoteliers to capture important information on customers' preferences and therefore has fuelled a dramatic increase in direct channels of marketing communication (Sheldon *et al.*, 2000).

The technology used to manage yield has led to more dynamic and responsive pricing strategies, opportunities to increase profit and to respond to customers' requirements for good value products and services and hence has the potential to contribute to customer loyalty. The mechanisation of systems and processes such as e-ticketing, electronic order pads and housekeeping systems and automatic check-in procedures at airlines all facilitate different aspects of the customer value chain, speeding up processes, ensuring quality, lowering prices and putting in place the capacity to develop customer relationship marketing and therefore customer loyalty (Buhalis and Laws, 2001). This most important aspect of all this technology is the marketing (or management) information systems (MIS).

Environment (Natural/Physical)

The protection of the physical amenities or resources in the natural/physical sense is essential in maintaining an attractive environment for modern tourists. However, in relation to hospitality companies, the ecological part of environmental scanning can also refer to the environmental policies in place in combating the effects of climate change. And in terms of both tourism and hospitality consumption debates have increasingly centred on the 'carbon footprint' of travel to and stay within destinations. Carbon offset schemes and the ability to communicate to stakeholders and customers about the company's policies towards climate change or the carbon imprint of the organisation will become an increasingly important aspect of future marketing communications strategies. This aspect of the external environment represents a significant threat to many organisations as many modern consumers are becoming more concerned about the impact of climate change, and, in the future, politicians and organisations will find this concern increasingly difficult to resist.

Henderson (2003) argues that tourism and hospitality are susceptible to a diverse range of exogenous events including extremes of weather as well as political unrest and terrorism and flight disasters in her paper. Henderson provides an analysis of the communications response to the crash of Singapore Airlines flight SQ006. In this case, severe weather had contributed to an even bigger crisis which resulted in 89 fatalities. She cites Ray (1999), who classifies five different communication strategies open to organisations in times of crises: denying responsibility, hedging responsibility, ingratiation, making amends and eliciting sympathy. Henderson argued that exogenous crises created special circumstances for communications responses. Audiences may differ; communications need to take account of who is responsible for the crisis and messages must be sensitive and timely.

Illustration

Stuart Smith (Editor). *Marketing Week,* 10 May 2007.

Be careful what you wish for, because it may come back to haunt you.

Transport companies, and in particular airlines, have recently been flirting with the green issue, in the belief that it can be used as a cheap, tactical means of knocking spots off the competition. Thus Virgin Trains, in an effort to cudgel the no-frills flights mob, has been running an advertising campaign which claims that a train journey results in 75% less carbon emissions than any comparable trip by air.

Rising to the bait, easyJet reported, with much glee, Virgin to the Advertising Standards Authority (ASA) on the grounds that Virgin has pumped up passenger numbers to illustrate its point. It has also lobbed a damaging grenade into the debating chamber by demanding that Virgin disclose whether its trains use electricity generated by nuclear power stations (deemed a social good, in this context if few others). Of which more later.

EasyJet, it will be remembered, has itself had a recent bruising encounter with the ASA. Late last year, it sought to use the claim that 'our planes emit 30% fewer emissions per passenger mile than traditional airlines' in an ad contrasting its own high ethical standing with the money-grabbing tactics of the Chancellor of the Exchequer, who was just about to double APD (allegedly for our environmental benefit).

Sadly for easyJet, the ASA didn't swallow the airline's argument. It accepted that easyJet's newer fleet was more carbon emission-friendly than any other European fleet. But, oh dear, the ASA then ruled that the only way easyJet could justify that 30% figure was because it crammed so many passengers into a plane, thus reducing the per passenger burn-rate. Not the most edifying of marketing platforms. Ad dismissed.

It is easy to see where this argument is leading. People standing outside greenhouses and lobbing stones can easily get cut by flying glass. Overall, the airline business has a fairly rotten green record. As it happens, Sir Stelios Haji-Ioannou – the public face of easyJet – is refreshingly candid on this subject: 'The fact is, we're part of the problem and should act,' he said recently at Davos. Others, like British airways (BA), have been mealy-mouthed about emissions schemes; or, like Ryanair's Michael O'Leary, too downright cynical about building their business to care.

But that is not to let easyJet's tactics off lightly. It may be that, in attacking Virgin Trains, the complainants thought they could get two for one. Take an artful sideswipe at one of their airline rivals, Sir Richard Branson (whose own record on carbon cleanliness is far from class leading), while reserving the broadside for the generic enemy: trains.

But all a wider discussion about planes and trains is likely to do is draw further invidious attention to the planes element. Airlines tirelessly point out that, currently, they account for far fewer carbon dioxide emissions than, for example, road transport or energy companies. Understandably, they are less evangelical about the fact that, if present growth projections are any guide, airlines will soon become some of the worst offenders.

Trains, regardless of the source of their electricity (a matter as it happens for Network Rail, not Virgin), must be a better bet, ecologically speaking, than road transport. And, inasmuch as they have an irreducible function as public transport, they are also a lot more indispensable than planes. The airlines should never forget that one blindingly simple way to radically reduce carbon emissions would be for people to take fewer discretionary flights.

www.marketingweek.co.uk

What makes this illustration from a recent edition of *Marketing Week* really interesting is that it demonstrates the lengths that many tourism organisations will go to communicate something about how much they are thinking about – if not so much directly caring for – the current concerns from educated travellers about global warming and the impact of their discretionary travel purchases on the global environment. Secondly, the illustration amply illustrates that transport providers recognise how consumers' choices relate to individual elements of the tourism package and just how competitive these individual component elements really are. And thirdly the illustration demonstrates well how tourism (in this case transport) promotion/advertising strategies are not simply about the generation of sales but are used to achieve a range of communications objectives (in this case the ecological credentials of the respective organisations involved). Finally the illustration demonstrates the importance of making sure that the research which underpins the content of the advertising or promotional message is correct, factually based and can be verified.

In this case the overall tone of the piece seems to suggest that the organisations are not trying to state their environmental objectives, or their commitment to environmental protection, or recognition of their respective role in the contribution to the global warming issue. The article suggests that the messages are more in the vein of 'propaganda' based on research which is at best open to interpretation and at worst easily disputable. Although it is perhaps easy to understand that organisations in a fiercely competitive business environment need to make sure that their advertising messages reflect customers' concerns about the impacts of their activities, it is also easy to gloss this case as industry in-fighting rather than being concerned with a focus on customers, and as such, could easily loose both organisations the respect of their respective customer bases.

In Figure 3.1 another area of impact on the marketing function was the impact of the media and marketing communications industry environment. The remainder of this chapter focuses on these influences and also on the regulatory environment for marketing. Connected to issues of regulation is the ethical environment, including social attitudes which are also briefly outlined.

Media Environment

An important area for consideration is the impact that the media can have on a business. Media attention can occur for a variety of reasons which are beyond the control of the organisation or tourism destination or resort and may seriously impact upon the image or perception of the company/destination in the minds of customers and markets. The direction of the impact is not easy to predict. A news story about a place for example could generate positive and wide ranging media coverage, which could create awareness and a desire to visit. However, equally the media coverage could cause a long lasting negative image of the destination which could seriously damage the ability of the destination to attract visitors for many years. Natural environmental disasters can adversely affect tourist demand such as the effect of Hurricane Katrina (August 2005) on tourism to New Orleans in the US (see Case study 3). A further role of the marketing department is to monitor and track media coverage and to engage in appropriate marketing communications through PR (which will be discussed in more detail in Chapter 9) to counteract or capitalise on media exposure. This leads on to a need to consider the structure of the marketing communications industry since changes in the industry also impact on the marketing communications environment.

Marketing Communications Industry

Once marketing departments have decided on a strategy in respect of meeting the needs of selected groups of consumers in the market through the provision of tourism or hospitality services, they can begin the process of commissioning the creative teams and media planning/advertising agencies to develop the communications strategies. The marketing communications industry is structured around to following key players:

- marketing communications agencies
- media providers

- creative and design sector
- clients and marketing departments

Again, size and scope of the organisation has an impact on the level and extent to which it can engage with the marketing communications industry. For a small guest house in a seaside resort with a very small marketing budget, possibly the only direct contact with the marketing communications industry would be with media providers. Marketing at this level is likely to be restricted to listings in accommodation directories, small adverts in newspapers and magazines and links to the local resort marketing partnership (the local authority tourist information bureau). A further contact may be through the development of a dedicated website which may be commissioned by a new media agency. Whereas large tourism and hospitality organisations such as national tourism authorities, multinational hotel chains and tour operators are more likely to engage the services of large marketing communications firms which will be able to offer a totally seamless in-house offer which includes all marketing requirements of the organisation. In the middle is a huge sector of specialist agencies and contractors which perform discrete functions.

Therefore the market is made up of agencies which specialise in the following:

- *industry sector* (i.e. agencies specialising in tourism and hospitality marketing communications);
- *type of client* (such as business to business, or business to consumer, third sector or public organisations);
- *type of communications* (agencies with specialist knowledge of PR, press, television, radio and cinema, direct mail, outdoor and transit, Internet).

In addition to these types of firms, the marketing communications industry is also connected to a wide range of support and specialist sub-functions as well as consultancy firms which can link marketing communications to product development and operations functions for examples. Therefore there are many firms which specialise in branding review and development. These companies help organisations to understand how their brands are perceived in the marketplace and combine creative development, research and marketing communications in the context of branding review, management and implementation.

Marketing Communications Industry Operations

The marketing industry has changed in organisation and structure in the past 20 or so years in line with structural changes in the global economy outlined earlier in this chapter, whereas the overall size of the marketing communications industry has increased in line with increasing fragmentation of media channels and the growth in marketing activities particularly in some areas such as new media (Internet advertising growth is outlined in Chapter 10). However, the basic functions of the marketing communications industry remain. Similarly, in the context of the tourism and hospitality sector, the trend is for marketing departments to outsource as many functions as possible. And so, the decision process for organisations outlined in Figure 3.3 means that when the research has been undertaken, marketing budget has been set and marketing strategies, objectives and segments identified, the marketing department (the client) then begins the process of contracting marketing communications agencies to implement the strategies.

Figure 3.4 shows the main functions and processes of the marketing communications industry. The tourism of hospitality organisation client, depending on the strategic issue or objectives, can either select a full service agency or consultant to work with it on determining which types of communication are needed to reach the target audience most effectively. Alternatively, the tourism or hospitality organisation may already know that it requires say, a direct marketing or an advertising campaign and thus selects an agency according to this need. The agency then works with the client through an account planner or manager, who will develop a close working relationship with the client to determine the communication needs and to work out the fine detail of the project/account brief.

The account planner will then engage the services of the creative team. This team consists of the artistic design and the copywriter. The

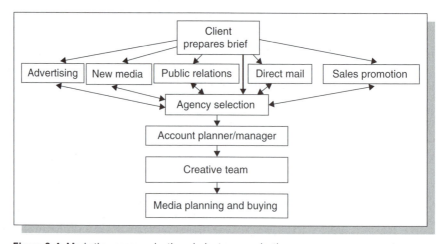

Figure 3.4 Marketing communications industry organisation.

job of the creative team is to interpret the project brief into an advertisement. In the context of PR, this is slightly different in that the PR agency works with the firm to translate the project proposal into a 'story' and to generate news media interest. This copywriting function may be undertaken in-house within the PR agency.

The work then passes to the media planning department – also increasingly now-specialist planning agencies. This changing structure is largely due to the fragmentation of media in recent years leading to the growth of advertising in alternative media forms, such as through events and event sponsorships, new forms of outdoor advertising in transit areas such as public toilets and roadsides, and so on (discussed in more detail in Chapter 8). This has meant that there is now a very wide range of choices for advertising products and services. Although the changing structure of the marketing communications industry does not directly impact on the tourism and hospitality sector per se, the influence is felt in terms of the competitiveness within the marketing industry opening up choices for organisations and leading to a dynamic and creative marketing environment affording greater opportunities for innovation in corresponding marketing communications strategies.

The Regulatory Framework of Marketing Communications

In the global environment of marketing communications, an important influencing factor to consider is the regulatory environment for marketing and considerations of ethics in marketing. In this book the emphasis is placed on the effectiveness of marketing communications messages to reach target audiences. Often these messages are used in an effort to inform, remind and persuade consumers about the attractiveness of the products and services on offer, compared to the offers of rival organisations. However, important ethical issues arise in terms of both the ethical orientation of the organisation and in the specific context of standards in marketing communications including personal selling, advertising and PR.

Organisational Ethics

The first relates to the nature of the organisation. Predominantly in the tourism and hospitality sector, organisations are in the private sector, although the important role of public sector organisations in the context of DMOs must not be overlooked. Ethical issues relate mostly to the strategic orientation of the organisation towards short-term profits or a long-term approach to business. The competitive nature of the industry and the intangible nature of services often require that the organisations focus on profit maximisation, and therefore in marketing messages, present their offers in the most positive light to target audiences. However, all organisations have duties to their stakeholders (customers, employees, shareholders, etc.) to conduct its activities honestly and responsibly. These responsibilities are mainly regulated by government. Forward thinking organisations also try to consider issues of justice, particularly the impacts of their activities on the wider community in which it operates. These are implemented through policies for corporate social responsibility (CSR) for hospitality firms or through an orientation to responsible tourism (RT) by tour operators and travel agencies (Hudson and Miller, 2003). This gloss on CSR and RT oversimplifies the complexities of issues relating to social justice, especially in the context of tourism destinations where local culture becomes the object of tourist curiosity or scarce resources (including land, water and food) are diverted away from local people for tourist consumption. The intention here is to distinguish between corporate ethics and issues of ethics in marketing communications. Of course, an organisation's approach to corporate ethics and social justice can become the focus of their marketing communications strategy.

Social responsibility has been used as a positive marketing strategy to engage consumers' confidence and sense of trust. It has become clear in recent years that ethical and moral considerations are having an impact on some consumer segments choices about products and services, and so competitive advantage can be gained for companies with a commitment to social and/or environmental issues. However, this creates both communications opportunities and potential challenges for organisations, whose messages must be informative but also honest. Travel Trade Gazette gives the example of tour operator 'Discover Egypt' which teamed up with a charity caring for horses working at tourist sites along the Nile. Discover Egypt promises to provide a local charity, the Brooke charity, with a donation for each client as well as sponsorship for the charity which provides free veterinary care and training for the owners of more than 100,000 horses and donkeys in Egypt. Discover Egypt will highlight the charity's work in its brochures (www.ttglive.com).

Advertising Standards and Miscommunication

This leads on to the second set of issues concerning of truth, misrepresentation, and taste and decency in marketing communications. Marketing can be an extremely powerful means of persuasion and

Illustration

There is sometimes an uneasy relationship between the marketing department and the wider media and regulatory authorities. The purpose of marketing communications is to reach the potential audience, as many people within those targets groups as possible. And given that we know some people encounter barriers to receiving marketing messages through noise, marketers often try to generate additional interest in their messages by creating distinctive campaign messages which get people talking, either in word-of-mouth communications or through wider media exposure. Most often this is achieved by means of contentious messages which aim to provoke a reaction from customers and/or the press. This type of action can have consequences in terms of sanction from the regulatory authorities or in an adverse consumer reaction. However, the main aim of these types of campaign is to generate media interest. Making a promotional message a news story in itself has the potential to add significant value to the overall reach of the campaign.

there are many examples where tourism and hospitality organisations representations do not match up to what customers actually experience. Some people think that marketing is inherently bad, and yet the reality is that we live in a world which is both heavily mediated and dominated by marketing messages. Although this is indicative of the pervasiveness of advertising and marketing messages, it is more and more difficult to reach consumers and convince them of the benefits of products and services. A classic example is that of tourist brochures which show images of resorts in a highly selective way to screen out urban development or crowds of people for example as discussed in Chapter 2. This aspect has two dimensions: the ethical orientation of organisations to be truthful and honest in its representations of tourist destinations or the intangible benefits of the organisation; and the consequences of mis-selling which can lead to compensation claims and further regulation.

It is important that marketing communications give fair and honest treatment of the benefits and value that the purchase will provide to the consumer and so it is important that advertising is not misleading. The aggressive selling techniques of representatives in resorts for timeshare apartments caused an enquiry in the 1980s, and the use of familiarisation trips and corporate hospitality are also key examples of potentially ethical issues within marketing communications in the sector. A cause of current concern in tourism and hospitality marketing communications concerns realistic pricing, particularly in the context of air travel tickets, as we can see in the following example from the ASA in the UK below.

A further issue relates to matters of taste and decency in advertising. The use of shocking, indecent or tasteless images in advertising can cause significant distress to many people to whom the marketing communication was not targeted. The use of provocative and sexually explicit words and images have landed UK tour operator Club 18–30 in trouble on numerous occasions over the past 10–15 years. Their advertising slogan of 1996 aimed at young people exhorted them to *discover your erogenous zone.* The ASA received 314 complaints which were upheld and Club 18–30 were forced to remove the posters. Similar complaints were received about subsequent campaigns, which featured slogans such as *Beaver Espagna*; and an image of a man wearing only boxer shorts under the caption, *girls. Can we interest you in a package holiday?* The campaigns were deemed to be offensive and could encourage young people to take risks with their sexual health. The company still uses suggestive advertising and themes, images and words oriented to a youth audience, but have been forced to tone down the provocative imagery. It is debatable if these advertisements caused any serious damage to the reputation of Club 18–30, since they are not likely to be deemed offensive by the core target audience and, given the amount of media coverage of the public outcry these campaigns produced, it is very possible that the campaigns improved the image and reputation of the company in terms of its target market group. The campaigns for Club 18–30 were led by Saatchi and Saatchi and were clearly designed to provoke a reaction from the wider media. They were designed for a 30 day exposure period in the knowledge that the ASA takes 30 days to investigate complaints, so that by the time the ASA had reached their judgement the campaign had ended and had achieved its aims of maximising impact.

Regulation in Advertising

In the UK the organisation which monitors the marketing and advertising practices of businesses (which is financed by a levy on advertising) is called the Advertising Standards Authority (www.asa.org.uk) and is a non-governmental organisation. In the USA, the sister organisation is called the Federal Trade Commission (www.ftc.gov).

The ASA provides a code for the industry to adhere to, and handles complaints from the public, and importantly the ASA adjudicates on whether the adverts breech their code in the case of such complaints. The ASA understands the importance placed by many people in their annual holiday for example and it aims to ensure consumer trust through its actions to ensure honest representation of destinations in brochures.

Illustration

The ASA and its practices for holidays and travel.

THE RULES

The British Code of Advertising, Sales Promotion and Direct Marketing [the Committee of Advertising Practice (CAP) Code] contains a number of requirements for holiday and travel advertisements. As a general rule, no advertisement should mislead consumers about anything likely to influence their decision about buying a holiday whether by inaccuracy, ambiguity, exaggeration or omission.

CAP code also recommends/requires that

All prices should be inclusive of all taxes or charges paid for at the point of purchase of the ticket. Any extras such as insurance, booking fee or surcharges should be stated.

Any limitations must be clear. If, for example, a price is dependent on two people travelling together and sharing a room this should be specified. The date of travel must also be clear.

Itineraries must be accurate both in terms of places visited and the amount of time spent there.

All amenities that are advertised (such as golf courses, shops, child care) should be available – if they cannot be used during the off-peak season this should be made clear.

If illustrations and photographs are used they must be up-to-date and accurate. The brochure should also make every effort not to omit any significant drawbacks regarding the location of accommodation, for example nearby building works, busy roads or airports.

Source: Committee of Advertising Practice (CAP) and the Advertising Standards Authority (ASA)

Other areas for complaints included

- Hidden extras

Since January 1998, travel operators have been obliged to state all pre-payable taxes in their headline advertised prices, and so this should increase consumer confidence. However, many quoted prices are subject to limited availability and consumers sometimes find the actual price much higher than advertised. However, the ASA states that consumers should be able to clearly understand what specific price-based offers consist of, the limits of availability and any restrictions.

- Sales promotions

The ASA also reports that recent complaints have been received concerning sales promotions for 'free' holidays. Prize winners soon discovered that in order for them to qualify, they faced numerous hidden costs including insurance, airport taxes and fees. Other regulatory bodies such as ABTA and IATA also have codes of practice dealing with holidays, which advertisers are also bound by. In addition, a key issue for the hospitality industry involves the use or targeting of children, as in the case of fast food restaurant chains.

Summary

This chapter has outlined the main contextual factors affecting marketing communications in the tourism and hospitality sector. Global forces in technology development, competition, consumer trends and regulation influence the industry sector and the marketing communications industry. The structure of the marketing communications industry is changing and this leads to a dynamic relationship between marketing departments in the tourism industry, the functions of marketing and the ways in which marketing communications are undertaken. One management tool available to marketing departments is the concept of environmental scanning. This allows marketers to track changes in the macro-environment which feeds into marketing planning and strategy formation. Chapters 5 and 6 follow up on the strategic role of marketing communications in relation to organisational strategy development. In the case of tourism destinations the media can play an important role in exposing the organisation/resort to unwanted or uncontrollable media attention, which needs to be monitored to ensure that media exposure can be either capitalised upon or mitigated against through the use of marketing communications. The ethical environment for tourism and hospitality communications is also a regulated environment. Each company has a responsibility to act in accordance with the code of practice which governs marketing communications and is bound by other industry codes of practice and EU and national government legislation. However, the use of an ethically driven approach to business could be a positive marketing communications tool, one which could be used to create a distinct competitive advantage.

Discussion Questions

1. Outline the main forces which influence the external environment for tourism and hospitality organisations. What tools do marketing departments have at their disposal to respond to changes in the external environment?
2. Explain the functions of the marketing department. How are these functions changing in response to structural changing in the marketing industry?

3. Outline the main ethical dimensions facing the tourism and hospitality industry. Discuss which consumer segments are likely to prefer tour operators who act responsibly, explaining the reasons which justify your answer.

Case Study 3: Uncontrollable Events and Negative Images: Tourism Marketing Recovery Strategies in New Orleans

Prior to 29 August 2005 when Hurricane Katrina struck the New Orleans coast resulting in a breach of the city's flood defences which ultimately caused the worst civil disaster in American history, New Orleans was a thriving city in which to live and a top American tourism destination. Renowned within the US and to a large international audience for its associations with jazz music, its world famous Mardi Gras and unique culture and history and well recognised for the warmth and friendliness of its citizens, tourism was in fact the primary industry in New Orleans generating more than 10 million tourists and $5 billion in direct visitor spending, supporting 85,000 jobs, in 6000 businesses out of a total pre-Katrina population of 500,000 (current population is only around 60% of 2004 levels).

Leisure tourism was by far the greatest type of tourism to the city, with three quarters of the total visitors followed by an important convention visitor market. Within the leisure market, families were an important segment. According to the Louisiana Department of Culture, Recreation and Tourism's 2006–2007 marketing plan (http://www.crt.state.la.us/), the numbers of jobs in tourism in post-Katrina New Orleans had fallen to 25,000, with reduced bed stocks and leisure and restaurant businesses open and 71% of New Orleans cultural institutions remaining closed because tourism had not been restarted.

However, it is negative media coverage which has caused the most damage in terms of exacerbating the problems and slowing down the possibility of swift recovery. This type of media coverage can be seen as equivalent to advertising worth billions of dollars.

Media reports containing images of a flooded and broken city infrastructure in the aftermath of Katrina as well as Hurricane Rita which followed less than a month after were prolonged by a perceived slow reaction to the crisis at the Federal level and images of violence and neglect, unhealthy and unsafe conditions effectively wiped out a return to business during 2006. These reports and images gave the impression to the general public that all of New Orleans was affected when it is clear that not all districts were in fact devastated by the flood damage. They send out a general impression that New Orleans was not a safe place to visit and that there is nothing to see or do there.

The 2006–2007 marketing plan presented research undertaken in January 2006 about current perceptions of New Orleans which found the following:

- Half of all respondents thought there was a lack of police presence in the city.
- About half believed that the important historic neighbourhoods including the French Quarter were severely damaged or destroyed.
- Almost 40% thought that some neighbourhoods were still flooded.
- Around a quarter believed the air to be contaminated and posed a health risk.

Source: Louisiana Department of Culture, Recreation and Tourism, New Orleans Marketing Corporation, New Orleans Metropolitan Convention and Visitors Bureau: Marketing Plan 2006–2007.

The plan identified the following strategic actions which had to be taken in order to take more effective control of the media messages and present the city's recovery and rebirth as a tourism destination of choice for American and international tourists.

- Change perceptions about New Orleans to show what is available to do and that it is open for business.
- Reach out to Americans everywhere and tap into a goodwill and a desire to be involved in the rebirth of one of America's greatest cities.
- Aim to rebuild market share to pre-Katrina levels.
- Control the channels of information distribution to ensure a consistent story, not to rely on the news media but to complement PR activities with an aggressive and impactful paid media campaign.

The marketing plan for 2006–2007 identified the following tactical steps:

1. A consumer awareness campaign to change perceptions about what is available, develop tactical offers, create a cooperative advertising programme allowing hotels and businesses to link together to improve effectiveness, produce 'advertorials' in regional and national consumer magazines to drive website visitation and build awareness; develop an online programme to provide tactical offers and incentives; produce an official city guide as a key communication tool to persuade potential visitors to make a booking.
2. Rely heavily on PR and publicity to capitalise on media attention on New Orleans and maximise positive images of current activities and events in New Orleans such as the Mardi Gras and Jazz Fest; hosting familiarisation trips for media.
3. Develop a new website with a focus on immediacy and fun.
4. Develop an online marketing programme.
5. Target niche markets with specialised programmes such as cultural, family and gay and lesbian markets, as well as sub-cultural markets including African American and Hispanic American segments.
6. Market New Orleans festivals.
7. Target repeat visitors. By focusing attention on those people who had already made a visit to the city who are more likely to return.
8. Launch an autumn campaign to promote seasonal visits at Christmas time.
9. Partner major travel promotion agencies and businesses.

Recent advertising campaigns have used humour to combat negative impressions and have developed a campaign drawing on Louisianan celebrities to promote visits to the state. The latest press releases (March 2008) indicate that flights into Louis Armstrong International Airport are forecast to return to pre-Katrina levels by 2009 and that visitor levels to key events such as Mardi Gras reached three quarters of levels achieved prior to the disaster.

This case study shows that some external events are beyond the control of a tourism destination and that negative media coverage can produce false impressions and negative perceptions which can cost a destination a lot in lost revenue and which requires a great deal of counteractive marketing communications.

Learning Activity

- Collect examples of current marketing communications for New Orleans. This can be in the form of website printouts or tourism brochures or other promotional material (www.neworleansonline.com/; www.crt.state.la.us/tourism/).
- Review archive media coverage of the aftermath of Hurricane Katrina.
- Discuss the main issues that you think have impacted on the public's perception of New Orleans as a tourist destination, and the extent to which you think the city has overcome the negative press coverage it received.
- Additionally, collect recent news items, market intelligence and other literature to compile a PESTLe analysis of the forces which might impact upon the inbound tourism market for New Orleans.
- In small groups in your class, identify and discuss which marketing communication tools would be best suited to overcome negative perceptions of New Orleans generated by adverse media coverage in the aftermath of Hurricane Katrina.

References and Further Reading

Beirman, D. (2003). *Restoring Tourism Destinations in Crisis: A Strategic Marketing Approach*. Wallingford: Cabi Publishing.

Buhalis, D. and Laws, E. (2001). *Tourism Distribution Channels*. London: Continuum.

Cateora, P.R. and Ghauri, P.N. (2000). *International Marketing: European Edition*. Maidenhead: McGraw-Hill.

Doganis, R. (2005). *The Airline Business*. 2nd edn. London: Routledge.

Doole, I. and Lowe, R. (2001). *International Marketing Strategy*. 4th edn. London: Thomson Learning.

Henderson, J.C. (2003). Communicating in a crisis: Flight SQ 006. *Tourism Management*. 24: 279–287.

Holloway, J.C. (2005). *Tourism Marketing*. 4th edn. Harlow, England: Prentice Hall.

Hudson, S. and Miller, G.A. (2003). The responsible marketing of tourism: The case of Canadian Mountain Holidays. *Tourism Management*. 26: 133–142.

Jobber, D. (1995). *Principles and Practice of Marketing*. Maidenhead, UK: McGraw-Hill Book Company.

Kotler, P. (1997). *Marketing Management: Analysis, Planning and Control*. 9th edn. Englewood Cliffs, NJ: Prentice Hall International.

Office of National Statistics (2007). *Travel Trends 2006: Data and commentary from the International Passenger Survey 2006*. ONS/HMSO.

Okumus, F. and Karamustafa, K. (2005). Impact of an Economic Crisis Evidence from Turkey. *Annals of Tourism Research*. 32(4): 942–961.

Ray, S. (1999). *Strategic Communication in Crisis Management: Lessons from the Airline Industry*. Westport: Quorum Books.

Sandhu, R. (2006). Analysis of the business environment and strategy for tourism. In Beech, J. and Chadwick, S. (eds) *The Business of Tourism Management*. Harlow, England: Prentice Hall, pp. 199–225.

Sheldon, P., Wöber, K. and Fesenmaier, D. (2000). *Information and Communication Technologies in Tourism*. Vienna: Springer.

Teare, R., Canziani, B.F. and Brown, G. (1997). *Global Directions: New Strategies for Hospitality and Tourism*. London: Cassell.

Wahab, S. and Cooper, C. (2001). *Tourism in the Age of Globalisation*. London: Routledge.

Wang, Y. and Fesenmaier, D.R. (2007). Collaborative destination marketing: A case study of Elkhart county, Indiana. *Tourism Management*. 28: 863–875.

Wilson, B. and Smallwood, S. (2007). Understanding Recent Trends in Marriage. *Population Trends*. 128: 24–32.

Key Resources and Links

http://www.nycvisit.com/content/index.cfm?pagePkey=57
http://www.cityofno.com/
http://www.city-data.com/us-cities/The-South/New-Orleans-Economy.html
http://www.nrs.co.uk/
www.tsa.gov
www.dft.gov.uk
http://www.dma.org.uk/content/home.asp
http://www.adassoc.org.uk/index.html
http://www.cap.org.uk/cap/
http://www.tradingstandards.gov.uk/
http://www.ofcom.org.uk/
http://www.asa.org.uk/asa/focus/background_briefings/Holidays+and+Travel.htm

USA

www.ftc.gov
http://www.ftc.gov/bcp/menu-ads.htm
www.marketingweek.co.uk

Consumer Roles
in Marketing
Communications

At the end of this chapter, you will be able to

- Define and describe the consumer behaviour process in tourism and hospitality and how it is changing.

- Understand the changing role of the consumer and the effect on marketing communications for tourism and hospitality.

- Identify the role of communications in the tourism and hospitality consumption experience and relate how advertising and promotion influence consumption.

Introduction

This chapter focuses on the roles of consumers and their behaviour processes which interact with and is affected by marketing communications. It is suggested that in line with other influencing factors outlined in the introduction to Chapter 3, consumers' behaviour impacts on the marketing function generally and the marketing communications strategies and tactics in particular. Also significant, in the context of marketing communications, are the ways in which consumers are influenced by media representations and marketing messages, and specifically how they interpret and evaluate information. A great deal of marketing research is directed at understanding consumers' attitudes towards products and services, and importantly for our discussions in this book, their attitudes and behavioural intentions towards an organisation based on their evaluations of the marketing and promotional messages received. This research also feeds back into the communication process described in Chapter 2 since research of this kind contributes to the organisation's communications dialogue with its consumers. This is becoming increasingly important, given the heavily mediated and information-rich nature of our world, as consumers may react in different ways to certain types of messages or media channels or sources. In the context of promotion and selling, organisations must understand what forms of messages customers react favourably to, and in order to do this they must *evaluate* the effects of their marketing communications campaigns, to ascertain what forms of promotion or communication work best and produce the desired results. In this chapter, there is a differentiation to make between consumer buying processes and how these interact with or are influenced by marketing communications messages as appropriate responses.

This research and feedback process is made problematic, however, because the pervasiveness of marketing communications delivered through integrated communications strategies often means that consumers are aware of brands through a variety of communications forms, including advertising; product placement; sponsorship; through partnership communications alongside other products; through public relations (PR) initiatives; informal, word-of-mouth sources; and through exposure to places through film and television, for example (see Prentice, 2004; Connell, 2005). This makes it difficult for everyone concerned to evaluate how and where and when a person becomes familiar with a brand, organisation or destination and to be exact about the effects certain messages have on an individual's conscious feelings or belief states. And so marketing communications and brand images commonly now appear in many previously uncharted aspects of people's lives. Cultural, artistic and music events, televised music concerts and festivals, educational events, school books, classrooms and services, it seems that no aspect of social life is immune from the potential for marketing communications.

Whilst consumers themselves actively buy into, or identify (or 'disidentify' – i.e. reject and distinguish themselves and their identities) with, certain brands, images, messages, organisations and people for a whole host of reasons. Although branding and brand communications strategies are dealt with in more detail in Chapter 7, it is important in this chapter to make the link between consumers and the attitudes and relationships towards brands. Modern consumers often act as advocates for certain products or places. Miles (1998) and Miller *et al.* (1998) argue that social identity is intricately entangled with the products we consume. Within the context of tourism research, many authors have made the links between types and forms of experience and consumption of place and social identity claims (*cf.* Desforges, 2000; McCabe and Stokoe, 2004). The impact of this often intense and emotive link between tourism and hospitality consumption and identity has the potential to make a pervasive impact on destinations, organisations and brands. The power of word-of-mouth communications and peer evaluations has also been mentioned. Therefore it is important that we understand how consumers influence and are influenced by marketing communications.

This chapter explores these relationships between consumers and their interactions with marketing communications through a brief analysis of consumer theory as a way to inform an understanding of consumers' attitudes to communications and response behaviour and their possible reactions to marketing messages. The chapter also outlines the process that consumers undergo in the context of what organisations need to know about consumers in order to frame their marketing communications. Organisations seek to select profitable customers and build meaningful and lasting relationships with them as a means to create better value from the relationship, greater profitability through decreased marketing costs and stronger competitive advantage. It is suggested that organisations see the best value in pursuing those customers who value their services, identify with the brand and the values of the organisation and actively create positive onward messages through word-of-mouth communications. This is predicated on a thorough understanding and knowledge of how the customers value the services, including knowledge of the benefits derived from the purchase and a knowledge of the processes which lead to the purchase and consumption of the service and thus the meaningfulness of the dialogue.

Illustration

In the case of hotels links between service-quality levels and prices charged for an overnight stay are often communicated through ratings systems. This allows consumers to differentiate between different classes of hotels. In arranging an overnight stay in Paris, France, there are a huge range of hotels from which to choose. At the cheaper end, the Pierre et Vacances City Residence's Porte de Versailles offers apartments sleeping two to six people from around 120 Euros per night, whereas at the more luxury end of the market, the Paris Ritz offers the Imperiale Suite' at a shade over 9000 Euros per night. The Imperiale Suite has two bedrooms so it could sleep the family (prices correct as per February 2007). The choices made in deciding whether to book a stay in the Porte de Versailles or the Imperiale Suite are not only constrained by matters of whether we can afford it or not, as some people are prepared to make sacrifices to be able to obtain some particular experiences. Also for some very special occasions, consumers are prepared to spend over and above their normal budget, such as a wedding. If consumers associate certain brands with a positive sense of identity, consumption of luxury hotels could confer prestige and thus meet status needs of some consumers. However, many consumers could perfectly afford to pay such high prices for a good night's rest, but would never choose to stay at the Paris Ritz because their attitudes, personality or purchase behaviours would not be satisfied by this consumption. There is usually a limit to the price people are willing to pay for experiential services, and trade-offs are made between price, quality and personal attitudes towards hospitality services and subsequent purchase behaviours.

Consumer Behaviour Theory

This section briefly details the main concepts underpinning consumer theory located in a consideration of the key disciplinary contexts from which these theories were developed. Consumer behaviour theory is derived from the discipline of psychology which perceives consumers as rational beings whose buying choices will reflect their relative utility in satisfying needs (Bull, 1991). In an early review of the consumer behaviour literature, Lunn identified that the theory had developed out of three theoretical approaches: (1) the *a priori* approach, where researchers had attempted to fit previously developed theoretical frameworks to consumer behaviour; (2) the *empirical* approach, which attempted to derive laws and knowledge from observations of patterns and regularities in behaviour (marketing research approach); and (3) the *eclectic* approach, which attempted to include the major strengths of the first two (Lunn, 1974: pp. 39–41). The earliest comprehensive model of consumer behaviour was that developed by Howard and Sheth (1969) in their treatise on the theory of buyer behaviour. The main characteristics underpinning consumer behaviour theory are briefly as follows:

- The focal point is the consumer, whose internal processes are viewed as a system.
- The core of the decision process is seen as matching products to consumers' motives.
- The choice criteria can be viewed from two standpoints: the extent that the product possesses certain attributes, and the value of the attributes to the consumer.
- Two crucial and related concepts are the 'product class' and 'evoked set of brands'. The product class is the set of brands that are broadly substitutable for motives, and the evoked set is the varying amount of alternative brands considered.
- Perceptual processes figure extensively, including arousal, directive, value of motives, ambiguity of commercial stimulus and perceptual bias.
- Emphasis on the importance of feedback in the process, where the purchase act and usage experience can inform predispositions.

(Adapted from Howard and Sheth, 1969; Lunn, 1974)

Howard and Sheth considered the dynamics of the buying sequence in terms of the extent of problem-solving (extensive, limited or routine) in the decision process. A key issue in consumer behaviour theory which is underexplored in the context of tourism and hospitality choice behaviour is that of 'confidence'. Howard (1974) says that 'confidence' is a central construct in explaining buyer behaviour. It is not an observable phenomenon but rather is an idealistic construct: 'Subjective certainty – his [sic] state of feeling sure – in making his judgment of the quality of a particular brand'. (Howard, 1974: p. 161).

The Howard–Sheth type is only one of a range of consumer behaviour models. Chisnall (1995) in his review of consumer behaviour models describes the variety of different types:

- logical-flow models, or decision process models
- monadic models
- psychoanalytic model
- perceived risk model
- 'black box' models
- subjective verbal models

East (1997) identifies three different paradigms in consumer behaviour: (1) the cognitive approach (purchases are seen as problem-solving decisions), (2) the reinforcement approach (consumption is learned behaviour) and (3) habit (the routine production of behaviour in particular contexts). The latter two equate to behaviourist perspectives on consumer behaviour. East argues that consumer behaviour paradigms can be ordered from an analysis of different types of consumption. He differentiates between important purchases, which are usually novel or infrequent purchases, therefore 'high involvement', such as holidays or cars (the cognitive). Repetitive consumption is where purchases are made again and again, such as supermarket purchases, therefore, 'low involvement' (the behavioural). And involuntary consumption, such as petrol for the car or banking services, is where we may not have much choice in the actual consumption of these goods, although there is usually a choice of brands (the behavioural).

The Cognitive Paradigm

East argues that the cognitive paradigm focuses on consumer decisions that rest on ideas, information, evaluation, and so from this perspective the manager can provide information and persuasion through the delivery of marketing communications.

Assael (1987) describes cognitive decision-making as a process involving

- need arousal
- information processing
- brand evaluation
- purchase
- post-purchase evaluation.

This approach assumes a systematic decision-making process in a linear fashion, which East (1997) argues limits the value of the approach, since it seems more suitable for one-off decisions rather than repeat-buying behaviour which may be undertaken with limited, consciously ordered cognitive thinking, such as spontaneous decisions or a serendipitous 'walk-by' decision to take a drink in a bar or café.

The Reinforcement Paradigm

The reinforcement paradigm focuses on the way behaviour is modified by the environment, whereby managerial control is achieved through changing the consumers' situation. This approach is less useful for explaining complex behaviour that is built on a variety of past experience.

The Habit Paradigm

The habit paradigm focuses on established patterns of behaviour, which are rapidly mobilised in response to relevant stimuli in the situation. Here, behaviour is understood in association with particular stimuli, which, once identified, can be used to elicit behaviour. All of these approaches could be effectively deployed to account for decision-making in certain tourism and hospitality contexts.

Consumer Behaviour and Tourism and Hospitality Services

However, there are real differences in the conceptualisation of consumer choice and buying behaviour in relation to tourism and hospitality products/services which need to be highlighted. Ryan (1997) states that tourism products are not typical of the usual consumer processes because they are not physical purchases, but rather the ultimate intangible service good. The consumer gains little of real benefit for what is essentially a major purchase apart from memories, photographs and souvenirs which in themselves may seem fairly superficial. However, some tourist experiences can contribute to a sense of self-development and self-identity as mentioned earlier in this chapter (also see Erb, 2000 and Elsrud, 2000). Unlike other major purchases, the consumer pays a substantial amount of money on trust or without really knowing what the experience will entail and what satisfaction will derive from it. Consumers spend a large portion of the year *anticipating* the holiday. They begin the selection, planning, information-gathering and saving process, as a way of seeing them through the dark months of winter.

However, these general principles are changing rapidly in the context of contemporary trends identified in Chapter 3. For some groups and social classes, travel, tourism and hospitality experiences are readily available, and there are some groups in society who are high-frequency users, highly mobile, experienced, confident and well informed. For these groups the mix of expectations, motives, anticipations and socio-economic constraints is likely to be very different from those in the lower social groups or with different demographic characteristics. Some people, such as successful entrepreneurs or sole traders, opt not to take all their holiday entitlement because of pressures of work and career aspirations, whereas others might forgo some holiday time in order to save up for a once-in-a-lifetime trip. In many other ways, individuals seem able to resist and challenge the preconceived ideas which have been developed to describe and account for their consumption behaviour of tourism and hospitality products/services and increasingly so in the globalised context, and so it is not possible to reduce to common generalisations the inner desires or motives of people.

Consumers and Markets for Tourism and Hospitality Services

A market can be defined as all those willing and able to purchase tourism and hospitality services. A market can include the existing customers of the organisation and also potential customers. An organisation needs to know how its services are positioned in the minds both of current customers and of the wider marketplace who may be interested in buying the services in the future (e.g. as they move through the life cycle or change in their attitudes to certain services) or in case the organisation takes a strategic decision to target different consumers groups in the future. The market and customer-base for the organisation is likely to be undergoing structural change all the time, in terms of gradual changes in attitudes or changes in socio-economic circumstances, even if at a very slow rate, and an essential element of the marketing function is to be aware of how these changes might affect the future competitiveness of the organisation (as argued in Chapter 3). Not only the customers and markets change in terms of their character, they might also change in terms of their attitudes towards the products and services the organisation offers, and so the relationship between the product and the market becomes apparent or obscured by these changes.

The concept of a product market assumes that the marketing communications is directed towards the development of sales in either a business-to-customer (B2C) or business-to-business (B2B) sense, for example, package holidays, flights, nights booked on the hotel, conference or exhibition space booked, restaurant covers booked. This might appear to contradict the argument made earlier about the inclusive nature of marketing communications covered in this book. However, the principle remains the same in either the private sector context as described earlier, or in the not-for-profit or public-sector environment. The messages created and delivered need to be oriented towards the needs and values of the target audience, and as such, whatever the goals or orientations of the organisation, the message needs to be directed towards the relevant publics. In this sense, organisations need to be aware of their target audiences even when the message is not a sales or promotion one, for example, in relation to reactive messages in response to media exposure or reassurance messages in connection with external events at destinations.

Generic versus Variant Service Markets

In defining service-market relationships, there is a need to distinguish between generic needs for tourism or hospitality services and the range of offers and variants which can be encompassed within that generic category. For example, a generic service category for tourism might be a package holiday, but within that there is a range of subcategories or service product classes; winter sun, summer sun, lakes and mountains, fly-drive, activity package such as safari holidays and so on. Each service class has a defined market which can be classed as the generic service product market for each class. If we take the generic service market for safari holidays, this can be further subdivided into service-type service-market to represent all the brands within this class. This would include perhaps all the destinations which offer safari holidays or all the international and/or national tour operators which offer competing packages to the market. Service variants may also exist within a service type, and so there may be a whole range of different types of safari service product in different destinations covering, for example, day safaris; 1–3 night short-break safaris; luxury safaris; budget safaris and so on.

Marketing Analysis

The ability to break down a market into more discrete market groups or segments is essential for an organisation to understand more about its customers, and management can perform a great deal of analysis on customers and markets within their service class or service-market category. Although segmentation strategies are assessed in more detail in Chapter 6, the point to make here is the relationship between the marketing planning and communications strategies and selection of target audiences. This type of marketing analysis is sometimes referred to as the market analysis–competitor analysis relationship and will typically look at the following factors:

- the total number of people in a population who may be able to purchase the products and/or services
- the total number of customers actually buying these types of products/services
- the size of your sales of your products/services relative to the competitors
- the relationship between your products/services offered to your competitors and your markets
- the ability of people to buy your offer over other types of products/services

The marketing function in which this analysis is undertaken feeds into the marketing strategy and planning development process. However, this is not a simple linear or ad-hoc arrangement and forms a fundamental activity of the marketing department which in turn helps organisations to create and/or tailor its marketing messages for specific and identified audiences. This customer/market analysis can be

Figure 4.1 Relationship between market analysis and communications strategies.

represented by Figure 4.1. Here the management and marketing information system is shown (providing a key data and research resource) feeding into the marketing planning and communications strategy process. Within this strategic process, markets are analysed, stakeholders are identified, that is, all those people who might have an interest in or influence on the development and communication of the service in the marketplace. From this, potential subgroups of customers can be identified and analysed which can then be narrowed down into customer segments around which specific and discrete marketing communications strategies can be built. Dialogue is maintained through the customer relationship management (CRM) function. CRM relates to the marketing orientation but involves all internal stakeholders of the organisation and requires a systematic and coordinated approach to understand the needs of customers and thus entails a great deal and variety of points of communication over a long period of time. This in turn leads to complete customer satisfaction at least in theory.

What the Organisation Needs to Know about Consumers' Behaviour

Consumers and organisations exist in what Fill (2005) states is an 'open system' (p. 142) whereby both can affect and are affected by external environmental factors which influence consumer behaviour and therefore affect internal individual processing of marketing messages. These influences are represented in this section and highlight the types of issues which organisations need to understand about their consumers and the markets in which they operate.

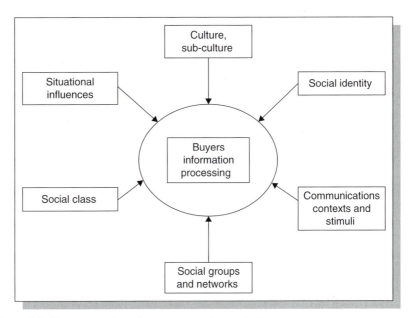

Figure 4.2 The open system of consumers and organisations.

In Figure 4.2 all aspects of the design, channelling and targeting of marketing communications must take into account that consumers are open to influence from a complex of sources, not just those of the organisation, including their cultural milieu, social class and background all of which impact upon the types of influential – 'groups' (peer groups) people interact amongst in their daily lives. These groups, local culture and an individual's social class are also influential in determining social identity. The communications context and situations influences refer to the external environmental conditions in which marketing communications is encountered.

In order for organisations to create messages which will be attractive to consumers, they need to understand who their target consumers are, and how they react to certain forms of message. They also need to know which media forms and channels are preferred by different market groups and how the system interacts with people's trust in messages through certain channels or media brands. These issues are also discussed in further detail in Chapter 8. The environmental conditions identified earlier can be translated into a set of questions the organisation can ask about its consumers and markets. Companies and organisations need to know the following information about their customers:

- Who – what type of person, their socio-demographic characteristics and situational influences.
- When – do people buy and when they receive and/or are receptive to the messages.

- Why – their motives for buying and also how they react to the messages through perception.
- What – their preferences, attitudes and beliefs about the services they buy and their purchase behaviour; also their reactions to marketing messages, the frequency of purchase and use.
- Where – the place they buy the products or receive the messages from.
- Which methods – they use to purchase the products/services.

Consumer Characteristics – Who?

Although segmentation strategies and the links between them and marketing communications are covered in detail in Chapter 6, this section details the concepts which underpin the approaches to specific and dedicated marketing campaigns. When analysing who are the people that make up the markets for our services, it is important to be able to analyse the broad socio-demographic characteristics of the customer base.

Demographics

Solomon (2002) defines 'demographics' as 'statistics that measure observable aspects of a population, such as birth rate, age distribution, and income' (p. 8). The importance of tracking demographic trends not only in relation to the customers to whom the organisation actually sells its products/services but also in the wider population cannot be underestimated, and Solomon argues: 'The changes and trends revealed in demographic studies are of great interest to marketers, because the data can be used to locate and predict the size of markets for many products.' (Solomon, 2002: p. 8). Therefore the more that is known about existing customers and how they correspond to broader demographic trends, the better organisations can target their marketing communications. It is important to know where they live (geographic dispersion) in order to define if many customers come from a particular region within the country, for example, or perhaps if we are dealing in largely international markets – perhaps many of our customers come from one or two major countries. There are regional differences in terms of culture and attitude which is likely to impact upon behaviours and attitude to communications, for example. Demographic details about existing customers are usually available quite readily if there is direct contact about them, and organisations can undertake research to check the broad socio-economic profiles of people within certain postcodes (zip codes) or demographic areas. Although postcode types of analysis are useful and a relatively cheap method of determining the broad spectrum of socio-economic profiles of consumers according to geographic dispersion, they are less useful in telling us about the types of people living in those areas and the detailed profiles of customers on a more nuanced and detailed level.

Socio-economic Characteristics

Other common methods for analysing socio-demographic characteristics include age profiling. Consumers of different age groups have very different needs and desires from tourism and hospitality services and they are likely to vary greatly in their responses to certain forms of communications. Gender is another common method of social classification and differentiation by gender is taken very seriously by marketers.

Another common method for segmenting the market relates to the employment status of individuals and households. This is often also referred to as social-class or income analysis. It is argued that people who work in similar professions or who have been brought up in similar social circumstances will to some extent share similar tastes in music, clothing, cultural attitudes and so on. Marketers are often interested in the readership characteristics of daily and weekend newspapers. Research in the UK has shown that younger people from all social groups read more tabloid newspapers, whereas older people from higher social classes tend to read more broadsheet (quality) type newspapers, for example. Another obvious way in which social class relates to consumer behaviour is in terms of disposable wealth.

Illustration

Businesses are developing more niche products and services to meet the needs of increasingly complex market groups, segments, based on socio-economic and demographic characteristics. Solo women business travellers are actively pursued by the hotel industry, for example, and marketing communications messages often aim to appeal to one or other gender depending on the type of service and who will decide and pay for the purchase. Recently, specialised marketing and promotion activities have been developed to appeal to the gay and lesbian market. VisitBritain was the first national tourism authority to develop a specific and dedicated communications and product strategy for the gay and lesbian market in the United States. Family structure also plays a very important role in the consumption characteristics for tourism and hospitality services. Families with young children often have less disposable income than students, older couples with no dependents, double income, no kids (DINKS) and so travel less distances, take fewer holidays and are likely to choose activities and holidays which will keep the children entertained. Younger people tend to attach less importance to personal safety issues and healthy lifestyles than older people and are influenced more by their peers and by celebrity endorsements. Older people tend to prefer more personal service, greater information and higher quality tourism and hospitality products/services. Marketing communications need to represent consumers' socio-economic and demographic characteristics in an appealing way so that targeted groups can identify and recognise their own social groups in the context of the consumer activity.

Roberts (2004) found from UK census data that those in social group DE (the low skilled, retired and unemployed in society) spent on average £2.68 per week on holidays, whereas those in the top social group ABs, consisting of professional and managerial incomes, spent on average £68 per week. Other methods include lifestyle analysis which is becoming very influential in terms of segmenting the market into smaller discrete groups. Lifestyles can differ even within similar gender, age and social groups. Lifestyle relates to the types of activities and interests we engage in our spare time, and so for tourism and hospitality, lifestyle is a crucial factor in determining the types of consumer patterns people exhibit.

Feelings, Beliefs and Values

In contemporary market-led organisations, there is a desire to know much more about the feelings, attitudes, beliefs, and values of consumers – their inner states, drives and desires. These issues are discussed in more detail in the following sections. Alongside this inner world of the consumers, organisations often would like to know about their preferences for certain types of products, their buying habits and intentions, their cycles of consumption and their frameworks for decision-making.

Decision-Making Units

A further relationship exists within the family decision-making unit, as different family members exhibit different approaches to tourism and hospitality decision-making and so will influence decisions in different ways, so that we know how and to whom we must pitch are marketing communications. For example, recent debate has focused on the ethics of targeting children with marketing communications messages particularly in relation to 'pester power' in holiday decisions (Evans and Moutinho, 1999) and current debates about rising levels of child obesity, healthy lifestyles and active targeting of children in marketing campaigns for fast food restaurant chains such as McDonalds (Euromonitor, 2001). In the context of tourism, advertising and other forms of promotion are often placed during television shows and other activities oriented towards children. This is purposeful since children will 'pester' their parents to take them for a visit to the theme park, book a holiday to Disney or to choose a certain type of fast-food chain. Television advertisements are then repeated or channelled or slotted within adult programming to ensure that the key decision makers, the purchases, the parents will be exposed to the same messages as the children.

Buying Centre Roles

These types of marketing communications strategies are examples of how communications are directed towards very particular roles within the family decision-making unit. These are known as buying centres, and each member of the centre can exhibit different types of roles. These roles are

- initiator
- influencer–evaluator
- gatekeeper
- decider
- purchaser
- user.

The key questions of who is responsible for the purchase are connected with those whose role it is to initiate, influence and persuade, and these are important factors which inform the development and delivery of marketing communications in which the tourism and hospitality industries are adept at understanding the dynamics at play in the family decision-making structure.

Decision and Purchase Characteristics – When?

Consumers undertake a cycle of consumption in their buying behaviour of tourism and hospitality services. Some of these services are purchased more frequently than others and so price and temporal constraints are important determining factors for consumers. If a person is busy with a demanding full-time job and a busy social life, they are more likely to want to eat and drink out and take advantage of hospitality services providers in their local area. Obviously, short breaks and especially longer holidays are consumed less frequently than evenings out, largely due to the cost of participation, but also because of the availability of time. This dynamic between time and incomes is crucial to understanding tourism and hospitality purchasing decisions. In the UK, for example, the main period during which holidays are taken are the summer months between June and September, but people begin to plan their holidays during the cold winter months after the Christmas season in January and February. This is changing rapidly, however, and many tourism organisations have noted a tendency for people to book later on in the cycle and put off their purchase decisions until the last minute. This has impacted on the tourism industry pricing structure, because the tour operators can no longer pre-block-book large numbers of hotel room and flight seats based on pre-orders from customers, the tour operators have changed their business model to have more flexible and responsive pricing. In the past, people could book ahead and pay more for their holiday than if they waited because the tour operators would have to sell off unsold holidays at the last minute to avoid perishability. Now, however, consumers often pay more the longer they leave booking. Knowing in advance when your customers are likely to think about planning for their holiday means that companies can tempt consumers or remind them about their products. Hotel companies often are least busy (in the northern hemisphere) in the period after the Christmas season in January and February and will often introduce sales promotion, discounting bed nights to try to stimulate demand. Consumers might be tempted with a bargain breakaway to help them over the long winter which would not impact too much on their decision-making behaviour in terms of their main holidays in the summer.

An organisation can do a lot to understand when customers buy their products and services by checking through their sales data; however, it is much more difficult to work out when consumers search for information, when they make their decision to buy and what influences those decisions, and so the timing of delivery of marketing messages through the communications strategy is extremely important particularly if it is a large and costly campaign.

Consumer Motivations – Why?

The next major aspect of information required by organisations and possibly the most important and difficult to understand is the question of why people consume the things they do. This is, of course, a question of motives. If the organisation understands its customers' motivations for buying their services and why they choose them over the competitors, then marketing communications can be used to stimulate new demand – extend the market – by telling other people who might share similar dispositions, attitudes or motives to the existing market as to the benefits and features of the experiences. Alternatively, communications can be used to remind existing customers how much they enjoyed – needed, were motivated – the services previously and so can be persuaded to repeat their purchase. Because it is more cost-effective (up to five times more so) to persuade existing customers to repeat purchase than it is to market to new customers, and easier to communicate to existing satisfied customers, understanding their motives, or how they benefited from previous consumption experiences enables the organisation to create the right type of message to connect with the customers needs or drives.

Motivation Theories

The study of motivation is a core aspect of psychology and it is complex and contested. In tourism, the issue of motivation has vexed academicians more than in hospitality. In this chapter, the concern is more with how motivation is connected with other psychological constructs and how those complex processes help organisations to understand their consumers and therefore work out how best to 'pitch' their marketing messages based on certain aspects of the target market's personal characteristics. Whereas questions of socio-demographic characteristics discussed earlier dealt with issues of consumers' 'external' social (more objectively classified) characteristics, this section deals with their 'internal' psychological processes. However, in this brief overview, the concepts are introduced which are then elaborated on the context of Chapters 6 and 7 on the design and planning of communications strategies.

Motivation refers to the processes that result in some behaviour, and it occurs when the body or the mind recognises that there is a need which could be satisfied. Solomon states that 'once a need has been activated, a state of tension exists that drives the consumer to reduce or eliminate the need' (Solomon, 2002: p. 102). Motivation theory as an idea underpinning action was operationalised as a set of 'needs' by Murray (1938) and gained currency after the work of Maslow (1943). Maslow's hierarchy of needs has been applied within the literature on tourism and hospitality consumer behaviour, and it is not necessary to explain all the details here apart from to state that the theory proposed that individuals progress in their needs through a five-stage hierarchy from basic human needs of food and shelter through to belonging and social needs, and concluding with the pinnacle of self-actualization. In social psychology, the major contribution to the theory of motivation for leisure and tourism is the work of Iso-Ahola (1980), who argued that individuals sought balance between intrinsic motivation (behaviour undertaken for its own rewards) linked to a level of optimal arousal (feeling states which directed behaviour in certain ways depending on the level of boredom or anxiety of the individual). In the context of tourism, Dann (1977) conceived the 'push' and 'pull' factors of tourist motivation as deriving from 'anomie' and 'ego-enhancement' rather than 'escaping' and 'seeking' dimensions driven by the individual's environment and stimulation levels (Iso-Ahola, 1980, 1982; Mannell and Iso-Ahola, 1987). Mansfield has argued against the apparent link between the 'escape' from a mundane or urban environment, coupled with a 'seeking' that is based on either destination attributes or a compensation mechanism on the basis of a lack of supporting evidence (1992).

Pearce (1993) developed the concept of a 'travel career ladder' that built on the notion that stages in the life cycle held value in determining the motivation for leisure travel (see also Holden, 2005). Pearce argued that at different stages of the life cycle, individuals were motivated by different factors that would influence their travel choices and decisions. Pearce later extended this analysis to claim that motivations can change within the one holiday experience. The main studies which proposed lists of essential purposes for leisure travel remain those of Krippendorf and Crompton. Krippendorf (1987) identified eight sets of reasons why people travel:

1. recuperation and regeneration
2. compensation and social integration
3. escape
4. communication
5. freedom and self-determination
6. self-realization
7. happiness
8. travel broadens the mind

A *going away from* motive (as opposed to seeking motive) connects all these motives, and Krippendorf argued that motives are personal and self-directed. Crompton (1979) similarly identified nine motives for vacation travel, seven of which he claimed were social-psychological, the remaining two being cultural motives (which were found to be relevant to particular destination attributes). The two cultural motives were novelty and education, and the seven social-psychological motives were

1. escape from a perceived mundane environment
2. exploration and evaluation of self

3. relaxation

4. prestige

5. regression

6. enhancement of kinship relations

7. facilitation of social interaction

Whilst Ryan (1997) accepts the view that experiences may be expressed in many different forms, the 'underlying' motivations, he argues, will remain few in number (p. 28). Ryan takes the Leisure Motivation Scale developed by Ragheb and Beard in 1983 as representing the continuing themes that emerge from an analysis of the research findings in tourism motivation and classifies them into four categories of motivational need:

1. intellectual need

2. social need

3. competence mastery

4. stimulus avoidance

It is clear that the tourism and hospitality industry routinely creates marketing messages which appeal to the motivational states or goal orientations of consumers and yet organisations also need to know how consumers process information internally and understanding how perceptions, identity and attitudes impact upon how messages are internalised.

Perceptions

Perception is a fundamental construct in understanding how consumers react to the world of marketing communications and stimuli. 'Perception can be defined as the process by which individuals receive, select, organise, and interpret information to create a meaningful picture of the world' (Belch and Belch, 2004). Consumers are being constantly bombarded with messages and sensory stimulations, some of which are filtered out and rejected and others are attended to more closely and are retained within the memory and enter into our stock of knowledge. The link between *sensations* and *perception* is made by Solomon (2002: p. 42), who states that sensations are the immediate responses of our sensory receptors, whereas perception refers to the processes by which the sensations are selected, organised and interpreted. The sensations consist of the sensory stimuli we receive as

• sights

• sounds

• smells

- tastes
- textures

These sensory stimulations can be incorporated into the marketing communications for tourism and hospitality products/services in many different ways. The visual is a primary way in which tourism destinations are experienced and consumed, for example, and so the use of visual imagery in the promotion of tourism places which evokes memories of warmth, peace, relaxation, the sound of the sea will stimulate memories of enjoyable holidays by the beach. Similarly, the use of images of well-prepared and deliciousfood in food and beverage hospitality marketing communications can often work to stimulate feelings of hunger. When exposed to certain messages at particular times or in certain places, we may become more aware of the message and the affect will be different.

Identity

As mentioned earlier, identity is an important construct in understanding how consumers react to certain messages. Self-identity refers to the beliefs a person holds about themselves – their attributes and values although there are many differing theorisations of identity within distinct disciplinary fields, and it is not possible here to provide real depth of analysis of these conflicting conceptualisations. However, it is important to state here that identity issues relate to the possible ways in which identity can affect the design and delivery, reception and interpretation of meaning of marketing communications. Therefore, it is important to note that in some theories, identity appears as fixed and stable and in others such as symbolic interactionism, individuals have many social selves which can be deployed in different social circumstances. It is clear that some aspects of identity would appear to be fairly stable, such as gender identity, and others are more fluid, such as professional identity which might change and develop with learning, changes in responsibility and so on. As far as this book is concerned, a crucial difference is that between the actual and ideal self. The ideal self is partly developed out of an individual's culture (their background and social milieu, the peer groups who are regarded highly) and refers to an individual's conception of who they would ideally like to be. The actual self is the realistic appraisal of those attributes and values we actually embrace. Marketing communications messages are often directed towards consumers' idealisations of themselves in an effort to convince them that consumption of the product/service will go some way towards realising their goals for themselves as a person.

Buying Behaviour Patterns – What?

This question relates to the types of things people buy, their consumer choice and buying-behaviour patterns. It also relates to a wider interest in consumers' attitudes largely because marketing communications seeks to either cement or change attitudes towards tourism and hospitality services or destinations. A great deal of research has been undertaken in terms of tourism decision-making process modelling since tourism decisions are conceived to be complex, high-involvement, 'shopping' (as opposed to routine) goods (*cf.*: Woodside and Lysonski, 1989). However, as we have already noted, the choice selection and buying processes are becoming less uniform. Many people now make their decisions based on the availability of cheap flights, and the decision process is consequently often less lengthy. Similarly, modern tourism consumers are more experienced, and (at least in terms of the middle classes in the advanced economies of the world) they are taking more trips of shorter duration each year. In the UK, a noticeable reduction in planning times and a shorter booking period have been witnessed, and the shopping nature of the buying process is also changing as people take more short breaks and shorter main holidays. However, this is not a universal trend, and obviously for long haul or special occasion trips, the buying-behaviour patterns still reflect the traditional modes and models.

Attitudes

However, of interest to marketing communications is how attitudes to places and services can be influenced. Attitudes are related to motivations, are presumed to facilitate social behaviour, can exist in relation to any object, and can be changed. It is here that marketing communications is often used in relation to its consumers. Organisations need to know how people feel in relation to their services or destinations, their attitudes towards them and how those attitudes could be changed if they are unfavourable. Attitudes are important because they are deemed to exist – they serve some function for the individual. And Solomon outlines four main functions:

1. *Utilitarian function* (related to basic principles of pleasure and pain; positive attitudes are formed towards products which provide a pleasurable experience).
2. *Value-expressive function* (attitudes which are related to identity and an individual's values. These attitudes form an important strand of research on lifestyles which look at how consumers' activities, interests and opinions express their values/identities as people).

3. *Ego-defensive function* (attitudes that are formed to protect a person against external threats or internal feelings).

4. *Knowledge function* (attitudes which are formed in response to the need for structure and meaning) (adapted from Solomon, 2002: pp. 197–198).

It is important to understand these functions, since if the marketer knows which functions the products serves – or put another way, how the product benefits the consumer – they can create messages which highlight these benefits. Attitudes are recognised as having three components:

1. *Affect*, which refer to the ways in which consumers feel about an attitude object

2. *Behaviour*, which refer to a person's intentions towards the attitude object (i.e. if they are likely to purchase)

3. *Cognition*, which refers to a person's beliefs about the attitude object, (Solomon, 2002: p. 200)

This is often called the 'ABC model of attitudes'. These three components correspond to a consumers' knowledge, feelings and intentions about a service. The ABC model works in different ways depending on the product/service, whether consumption is determined by rational or emotional decision-making and a number of other factors including the level of involvement in the decision-making. A simple example can be provided in that decisions to visit a fast-food counter for a burger are characterised by low involvement (in that the burger is relatively inexpensive and therefore does not require high level of investment in terms of problem solving or information and choice-selection criteria) and appeals to rational decision-making from a behavioural perspective (stimuli alert us to the fact that we are hungry and need to eat). An individual's attitudes towards decisions to buy a main family holiday are likely to be of much higher involvement (needing to ensure that all members of the family will be happy and satisfied with the decision), involve greater levels of cognitive processing (information search, processing of alternative destinations and tour operators, etc.) and so the attitude model will shift the hierarchy within the ABC model to reflect these differences. Again, in subsequent chapters, the process by which attitudes can be changed through marketing communications will be discussed in relation to strategies and communications planning.

Distribution and Access – Where?

This pertains to the points at which consumers access the services and also relates to how they access marketing messages. For example, it is vital to know the proportions and characteristics of consumers who search for and book their travel and hospitality services online, as opposed to, through a travel agent. It is also important to know how consumers hear about the services or destination. Since many organisations undertake a range of marketing activities and undertake different activities at different points in the cycle or season, they need to know which activities are preferred by customers through which channels at which times. Again this is achieved through research and data processing. As previously mentioned, organisations need to understand where consumers access the marketing communications and under which circumstances they reacted favourably in terms of the content of the message which in turn led to a favourable action or reaction, such as a purchase or some other desired action. As described in Chapter 3, organisations use a variety of tracking and evaluation techniques to assess the effectiveness of their campaigns.

Purchase Characteristics – Which Methods?

Organisations also need to know how people purchase services. Do they pay in cash or by credit card? For example, in the case of business travellers, do they ask secretaries or administrators to search and book travel and hospitality? Does the company pay in advance or do business clients pay their bills themselves? In terms of the marketing communications impacts, there is a need to know how consumers' book and the processes which underpin the booking and purchase process as this information can help identify the right audience to target with messages and also importantly the content of the message can be adapted to include information on payment terms or conditions or key points of purchase. Knowledge of any preferred methods of consumption will enable the organisation to tailor marketing messages which show affinity between the consumers and the organisation.

Summary

This chapter has provided a brief outline of the role of consumers in marketing communications. The chapter has argued that consumers can play an active role in the production of important word-of-mouth communication, and as such, organisations need to understand a great deal about how consumers react to their brands, what influences impact on the decisions they make about tourism and hospitality services and also how they react to the marketing messages distributed by the organisation. This last point highlights the importance of knowing consumers in a meaningful way that can contribute to the marketing communications process through dialogue and feedback. The chapter began with an outline of consumer theory which provided relevant theoretical concepts. It went on to discuss the relationships between customer, markets and marketing communications before going into a more detailed discussion on what marketers need to know about their customers and markets in terms of how analysis of consumers' decisions and contexts must be understood from the perspective of how the organisation aims to relate to and influence consumers' choices through its marketing communications strategy.

Discussion Questions

1. Describe the main processes underpinning consumers' decision-making in the context of tourism and hospitality services. Provide examples of the differences between the decision-making processes for tourism and hospitality consumption.
2. Explain how knowledge of consumers' external influences and internal drives and forces in the 'open system' of consumers and organisations impacts upon the marketing communications strategy of the organisation.
3. Evaluate the importance of identity to consumption decisions in tourism and/or hospitality.

Case Study 4: Virgin Trains, Winning Hearts and Minds with Emotional and Rational Messages

This case study focuses on how Virgin Trains overcame nationwide, deeply held, overwhelmingly negative perceptions about rail travel in the UK through a campaign which was designed to reach 'hearts' (through emotional engagement with trains as a form of transport) and 'minds' (reinforcing rational messages about the core aspects of the service) of the British public. 'By engaging the public with rail travel on a positive emotional level, we succeeded in making Virgin Trains the transport operator of choice in the UK', driving higher journey numbers, millions in incremental revenue and a high return on advertising spend (return on investment, or ROI) on the whole network and in particular on the strategically important West Coast line. Not only was this campaign a huge success in changing consumer perceptions of and attitudes towards rail travel, but it also delivered these changes in the face of severe competition from airlines operating on the same key routes (e.g. London to Manchester), a lack of any 'real' changes to services or core product (as the new Pendolino train stock had been in operation fully for 3 years) and in the face of the tragic London terrorist attacks of 7 July 2005.

According to Rail Passengers' council, 'By 2002, the public's verdict on the performance of Britain's railways could scarcely be more damning. After 5 years of Virgin involvement, the proportion of respondents who believed Britain's railways had deteriorated exceeded the proportion that believed they had improved by a ratio of thirteen to one. (You Gov survey for *The Daily Telegraph*). Passengers are at best jaded and at worst angry. They feel a sense of despair because the railways are now in such a mess.

Virgin had success with a campaign called 'New Beginning' in 2002, based on the new train stock, improved timetable and services. Awareness of the new trains and timetables had been raised and rational barriers had been largely overcome. The Cross Country route was performing well, with significant rises in passenger numbers following the campaign.

'However, the West Coast line was still failing to challenge other modes of transport, and the ultimate goal of rekindling public enthusiasm for rail travel was yet to be realised. Positive emotional engagement was still lacking, as demonstrated by the higher consideration afforded to airline operators and a lack of emotional proximity between the consumer and the Virgin Trains brand. In comparison to the plane and the car, the train still felt like the unglamorous, poor relation; a practical choice, but not a particularly sexy or exciting one. We wanted to encourage consumers to make an active, positive choice to take the train rather than driving or opting to fly – and to keep doing so over time. Virgin Trains wanted people to feel passionate about their trains; to reignite peoples' belief in the railway. It was time to behave like a true Virgin company; injecting some glamour and emotion into the brand.'

The aim of the campaign was to address 'deep-seated emotional barriers' despite a challenging environment including the following factors: the new trains had been operational for almost 3 years and had generated significant PR activity, and so there was no 'new news' story to help changing perception and behaviour; a highly competitive environment whereby other service providers offered heavy services between the major cities of London, Glasgow, Birmingham, Liverpool and Manchester (the main points on the West Coast line), including good road links via motorways providing significant opportunities for cost savings for consumers – as per Plate 4.1, showing National Expresses London to Manchester fares and examples of air schedules and prices.

Indeed, there were also found to be no less than five airlines servicing the London-to-Manchester route alone. These airlines were also offering heavy schedules, at competitive prices offering consumers real choices.

In terms of consumer behaviour, the West Coast route attracts a high proportion of business travellers, whose decision-making is less a function of price and driven more by the reliability, convenience and on board experience. Air travel in particular was seen as an enticing prospect for this market due to perceived punctuality and greater speed and

Plate 4.1 Examples of competitor's advertisements of services and prices.

comfort. The aim of the campaign was therefore to try and get existing users to switch rather than stimulate new demand on the route.

The importance of emotional affinity in driving preference has been well documented. In comparison to the glamorous airline industry and the close relationship between car and owner, we were on the back foot on this front. Years of underperformance from the nation's rail providers had left a legacy of deep-seated prejudice. Unless we addressed the emotional deficit, train travel would remain the poor relation to other modes of transport, and Virgin Trains would fail to reach their true potential.... [The new campaign] needed to engage people in the entirety of the train experience, and this would require an involvement-based strategy: a 'top down' approach, in comparison to our previous, 'bottom up' strategy centred on functional improvements to the service. Recognising that an emotive message without any form of rational back up could be perceived as an empty promise, we sought to underpin our campaign with a more rational form of communications.

The creative idea could be summarised as in Figure 4.3.

Emotional Messages

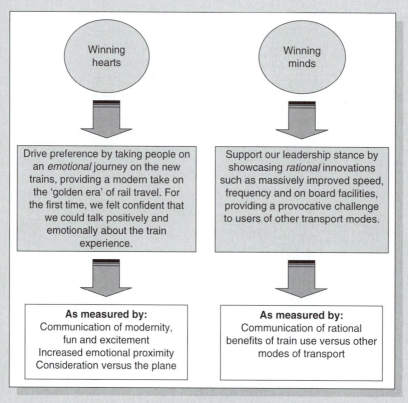

Figure 4.3 Emotional and rational communications drivers.

Plate 4.2 Still from the 'Return of the Train' campaign, featuring Lemon/Curtis in 'Some Like It Hot'.

Whereas competitors used 'anti-modal' advertising to deliver negative messages about the competition explicitly, this campaign sought to present rail travel in an overtly positive, confident, non-comparative manner.

'Our creative idea, "The Return of the Train", was a romantic celebration of the marriage of cutting-edge innovation with "golden era" train service'. This was achieved by interweaving clips from some of the most famous films which features train journeys, such as *The Railway Children*, *North by North West*, *Murder on the Orient Express* and *Some Like It Hot*, within the context of the modern Virgin Trains experience. These 60-second television and cinema advertisements sought to combine the romance of train travel with the excitement of the Virgin additions to the rail experience as shown in Plate 4.2.

The main television and cinema advertisements were extended by sponsoring a season of weekend matinees evocative of the 'golden age' theme on Turner Classic Movies channel and a film season at the Prince Charles Cinema in London. Interactive television also gave viewers the opportunity to continue their experience, adding emotion and involvement.

Rational Messages

The second strand of communication focused on three key rational messages that the new trains had brought to the West Coast line:

1. reduced journey times
2. higher frequency of services
3. better on-board services

These messages were tailored by specific location so that they were as relevant as possible to specific users at different points of the service. These were later replaced by more explicitly 'anti-modal' challenges to challenge users of other services head-on and were timed to coincide with another burst of the television campaign in early 2006.

Execution Strategy

National Television and Cinema allowed Virgin Trains to get closer to people's hearts and evoke a return to the golden age of train travel. 'Long spot lengths in this media showcased the creative work, and delivered fantastic levels of stand out and engagement.' It also meant that Virgin Trains could take their message into new media channels with an exclusive deal with *Total Film* magazine, explaining the making of the advertisements. Underpinning the emotive thrust of the campaign was a 'minds' strategy which sought to win consumers over in terms of evidence about how much the service had improved through the provision of 'hard facts'. Timetable and track improvement had come into effect, the new train stock had been rolled out, and whilst the campaign had to work on a national level, the real focus was on the competitive West Coast to make revenue opportunities a reality.

Detailed mapping, location and business analysis enabled the development of a detailed activity matrix which informed prioritisation. Proximity, type of message (speed, frequency, service) and the message itself were planned on a micro level, taking into consideration

- the estimated revenue and journey growth by station
- peak and off-peak load factors, by standard and first class.
- drive time around each key hub and the stations within this radius.

These tailored communications were designed to deliver the rational minds messages in optimum environments.

In situ, cheekier media prompted dissatisfaction with other modes of transport, such as the car; washroom panels at motorway services stations showed such messages as 'It only takes 2 shakes with Virgin Trains'; coffee-cup sleeves with 'Less time to grab a coffee'; drive-time radio to reach people in heavy congestion times; and truck rears on motorways with a 'Get a speeding ticket' message.

Interactive television highlighted the benefits of the train service and introduced details of the Pendolino train carriage itself 'the star of the ad'. Messages in the press 'underpinned the outdoor and radio activity and through the values of "hard facts" environments, gave further credibility. Online activity focused on core travel environments and consideration moments, delivering awareness and ticket sales'. Direct marketing (direct mail and email) allowed Virgin Trains to send tailored, relevant messages to current customers, building on the rational messages of the press and outdoor activity. Finally, in recognition of the importance of seamless internal communication, Virgin Trains members of staffs were sent an unusual 'campaign-briefing pack encouraging sneak-preview screenings of the new television commercial – complete with cinema-style posters and popcorn'.

How It Worked

The advertisement was seen and liked – Campaign-evaluation research showed a significant increase in both spontaneous and prompted advertisement awareness for both business and leisure users. Advertising enjoyment, saliency, involvement and persuasion scores were amongst the best ever seen. The campaign generated huge amounts of positive PR, with articles in numerous trade and national publications, whilst over the campaign period, negative PR around Virgin Trains decreased significantly. Visits to the Virgin Trains website went up by 43% over the campaign period, from 350,000 visits per week to 500,000.

The advertisement was communicated both rationally and emotionally – 'The Return of the Train' was designed to address emotional objections to train travel by communicating an emotive message with a rational underpinning. Evaluation research showed that emotional responses dominated and that rational messages were still communicated by the campaign, despite little references to product features.

People felt closer to the train – Emotional proximity is perhaps the best approximation for the extent to which Virgin Trains could be said to meet their objective of engaging consumers on an emotional level. Tracking suggests that this measure has moved strongly, most noticeably amongst the tougher business travellers.

Consideration improved – Attraction to using the train increased significantly over the campaign period amongst both leisure and business users.

Virgin Trains consideration improved versus other train operating companies – Opinions of Virgin Trains versus other train operators also increased significantly over the campaign period, again most noticeably amongst the business audience.

Consideration improved to the extent that we became the nation's favourite transport operator – 'At the end of the year, Virgin Trains overtook British Airways as the nation's most considered travel provider for the first time; a gap that has widened following a reprise of the campaign in January 2006. Likelihood to recommend also improved, from 77% to 85% amongst business customers and from 80% to 82% amongst leisure customers between January and July 2005.'

Journeys increased, including switching from plane – Overall journey numbers increased significantly over the campaign period when compared with the same period the previous year, despite the impact that the London bombings had on the number of people travelling. Airline volumes dropped during the period of the campaign. Market share for the train increased.

Source: Virgin Trains, *The Return of the Train: how Virgin Trains became the nation's favourite transport provider* by Lucy Howard, RKCR/Y&R and Claire Marker, Manning Gottlieb OMD. IPA Effectiveness Awards 2006 as published in *Advertising Works 15* (http://www.warc.com).

Learning Activity

- Discuss and evaluate how Virgin Trains challenged consumers' perceptions and attitudes towards rail travel.
- How did the advertising campaign work? Identify the critical success factors which you think were most important.
- Identify further consumer behaviour characteristics which could have been applied to this campaign (other than perceptions and attitudes).
- Identify what further arguments can be made in persuading consumers to choose rail travel over other modes of transport.
- Explain whether and how these arguments should be emotionally or rationally driven.

References and Further Reading

Assael, H. (1987). *Consumer Behaviour and Marketing Action*. 3rd edn. Boston, MA: P.W.S – Kent Publishing Company.

Belch, G.E. and Belch, M.A. (2004). *Advertising and Promotion*. New York: McGraw-Hill.

Bull, A. (1991). *The Economics of Travel and Tourism*. Melbourne: Aus. Longman Cheshire, Pty.

Chisnall, P.M. (1995). *Consumer Behavior*. 1st edn 1975. Berks: McGraw-Hill.

Connell, J. (2005). Toddlers, tourism and Tobermory: Destination marketing issues and television-induced tourism. *Tourism Management*. 26: 763–776.

Crompton, J.L. (1979). Motivations for pleasure vacations. *Annals of Tourism Research*. 6: 408–424.

Dann, G. (1977). Anomie, ego-enhancement and tourism. *Annals of Tourism Research*. 4: 184–194.

Desforges, L. (2000). Traveling the world: Identity and travel biography. *Annals of Tourism Research*. 27(4): 926–945.

Dumazedier, J. (1967). *Toward a Society of Leisure*. New York: Free Press.

East, R. (1997). *Consumer Behaviour: Advances and Applications in Marketing*. Herts: Prentice Hall.

Elsrud, T. (2001). Risk creation in traveling: Backpacker adventure narration. *Annals of Tourism Research*. 28(3): 597–617.

Erb, M. (2000). Understanding tourists interpretations from Indonesia. *Annals of Tourism Research*. 27(3): 709–736.

Euromonitor (2001). Marketing to children: A world survey.

Evans, M. and Moutinho, L. (1999). *Contemporary Issues in Marketing*. Basingstoke: Macmillan.

Fill, C. (2005). *Marketing Communications: Engagement, Strategies and Practice*. 4th edn. Harrow, England: Prentice Hall.

Holder, A. (2005). *Tourism Studies and the Social Sciences*. Oxon: Routledge.

Howard, J.A. and Sheth, J.N. (1969). *The Theory of Buyer Behavior*. New York: John Wiley.

Howard, J.A. (1974). Confidence as a validated construct. In Sheth, J.N. (ed.) *Models of Buyer Behavior. Conceptual, Quantitative and Empirical*. New York: John Wiley.

Iso-Ahola, S.E. (1980). *The Social Psychology of Leisure and Recreation*. Dubuque, IA: W.M.C. Brown.

Iso-Ahola, S.E. (1982). Toward a social psychological theory of tourism motivation: A rejoinder. *Annals of Tourism Research*. 9: 256–262.

Iso-Ahola, S.E. (1987). The social psychology of leisure. In Graefe, L. and Parker, S. (eds) *Recreation and Leisure: An Introductory Handbook*. State College, PA: Venture Publishing, Inc.

Lunn, J.A. (1974). Consumer decision process models. In Sheth, J.N. (ed.) *Models of Buyer Behavior: Conceptual, Quantitative and Empirical*. NY: John Wiley.

Mannell, R.C. and Iso-Ahola, S. (1987). Psychological nature of leisure and tourism experience. *Annals of Tourism Research*. 14: 314–331.

Maslow, A.H. (1943). A theory of human motivation. *Psychological Review*. 50: 196–376.

McCabe, S. and Stokoe, E.H. (2004). Place and identity in tourist accounts. *Annals of Tourism Research*. 31(3): 601–622.

Miles, S. (1998). *Consumerism as a way of life*. London: Sage.

Miller, D. *et al.* (1998). *Shopping, Place and Identity*. London: Routledge.

Murray, H.A. (1938). *Explorations in Personality*. New York: Oxford University Press.

Pearce, P.L. (1993). Fundamentals of tourist motivation. In Pearce, D.G. and Butler, R. (eds) *Tourism Research: Critiques and Challenges*. London: Routledge.

Plog, S. (1977). Why destinations why and fall in popularity. In Kelly, E.M. (ed.) *Domestic and International Tourism*. Wellesley, MA: Institute of Certified Travel Agents, 26–28.

Prentice, R. (2004). Tourist familiarity and imagery. *Annals of Tourism Research*. 31(4): 923–945.

Roberts, K. (2004). Leisure inequalities, class divisions and social exclusion in present day Britain. *Cultural Trends*. 13(50): 57–71.

Ryan, C. (1997). *The Tourist Experience: A New Introduction*. London: Cassell.

Solomon, M.R. (2002). *Consumer Behavior: Buying, Having, Being*. 5th edn. Upper Saddle River, New Jersey: Prentice Hall.

Um, S. and Crompton, J.L. (1990). Attitude determinants in tourism destination choice. *Annals of Tourism Research*. 17: 432–448.

Woodside, A. and Lysonski, S. (1989). A general model of traveller destination choice. *Journal of Travel Research*. 27(4): 8–14.

Key Resources and Links

World advertising research council (http://www.warc.com)
Institute of Practitioners in Advertising (http://www.ipa.com)
http://www.euromonitor.com

Part 2 of this book deals with the strategic context for marketing communications for tourism and hospitality and explores marketing strategy in relation to how strategic choices connect to communications strategies. Chapter 5 begins by examining the strategic marketing context. Here the focus is on the role of marketing within the organisational context, the links between organisational strategy and marketing communications strategies and how the integrated marketing communications (IMC) approach to marketing communications strategies is related to wider marketing and organisational strategy. Chapter 6 begins to analyse communications strategies and tactics in relation to meeting the needs of specific consumers through a discussion of how markets are segmented into subgroups which are then targeted through discrete marketing messages. Chapter 6 also outlines how services are 'positioned' through effective marketing communications in the minds of target audiences. Chapter 7, the last chapter in Part 2, outlines the role of marketing planning in the IMC strategic process. It explores the relationships between organisations and brand development strategies and management. The importance of branding was highlighted earlier and Chapter 7 outlines how brands are communicated to audiences in tourism and hospitality.

CHAPTER 5

Marketing Communications and Organisational Strategy

At the end of this chapter, you will be able to

- Understand the linkages between organisational strategy and marketing communications.

- Define the principles of services marketing.

- Explain a range of strategic choices available to tourism and hospitality organisations.

- Describe the concept of the value chain and how it relates to marketing communications strategies.

- Relate integrated marketing communications (IMCs) concepts to organisational strategy.

Introduction

Marketing communications is linked to strategic choices made by organisations. In Chapter 3, the links between the external environment of marketing and the function of the marketing department in relation to other functional areas of the organisation were briefly outlined. However, organisations have a range of choices to make in terms of their direction and orientation to the market or its customers. Some choices become more limited in the context of the tourism and hospitality sector because of the nature of the services as intangible offerings which were explained in Chapter 1. These choices influence the marketing mix for this sector, and therefore communications strategies and plans become direct representations of the strategic direction of the organisation.

Organisational strategy is concerned with the identification of a 'vision' for the organisation which is translated into a set of strategies giving direction to the organisation's activities (Johnson and Scholes, 1989). A vision can be defined as the viewpoint of the organisation about its ultimate reason for its existence. In this sense, the vision for tourism and hospitality services relates to an orientation to 'value'. Perhaps, the value orientation is to provide the 'best dining experience using only the finest locally produced ingredients', or the 'best value package holidays in the marketplace'. There is an intrinsic orientation to customer value in these statements. Therefore the vision provides the organisation with a direction which frames the activities of all departments and employees as these functions work towards delivery of the value. This includes marketing strategy and plans, and thus, marketing communications. In Chapter 3, it was argued that for marketing-led organisations, the marketing function is more than a set of tools to manipulate demand for the products and services: it plays an integrating role in shaping and directing the organisation's activities including the development and presentation of the brand. This chapter defines the links between organisational strategy and services marketing concepts. This is done in the context of an integrated approach to marketing communications. It is through the adoption of a customer focus and an integrated approach to marketing that the organisation can not only orient its activities to customer value but also it can seek to continually create and add further value to its customers and therefore meet and exceed its strategic goals, and so the concept of the value chain is described (Figure 5.1).

Organisational Strategy Formulation

It is important to remember that the marketing function is primarily constrained by the allocation of financial resources to achieve organisational

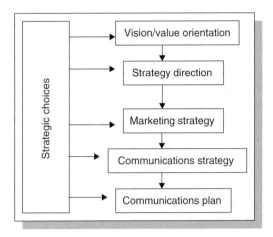

Figure 5.1 Organisational strategy and services marketing relationships.

goals and objectives (Tribe, 1996). As such, any marketing activity in which an organisation can participate is constrained by the ability of the organisation to commit a budget to the activity. Thus, marketing begins at the strategic level with the marketing director or manager who is responsible for matching up the strategic ambitions of the organisation to the resources needed to achieve them. The value orientation of the organisation informs the 'vision' and thus the choices for strategic direction. There are often difficult decisions to be resolved in terms of apportioning budget to different departments: production and operations; human resources and staffing; finance and research and product development; and marketing. Each needs to have the required resources which will enable it to contribute to the achievement of the organisational strategy.

Core to strategy development in any organisational context are the framing questions:

- Where are we now?
- Where do we want to be?
- How do we get there?

However, in many cases these questions might be reordered depending on the size of the organisation, the types of goals and direction to which it aspires and the stage in the organisation's life-cycle. In the case of an established organisation which has been slow to respond to gradual changes in the external environment which has left it out of step with current market developments, a reordering of these questions could include the following:

- How did we get here?
- Where do we want to be?
- How do we get to where we want to be?

Illustration

Organisational 'vision' must be appropriate to the market position occupied. A package tour operator, whose vision is to be the largest mass package holiday provider in the world, must be in a realistic position in the market to be able to achieve this goal. Although there is no reason in theory why any small package tour operator, for example, should not aspire to being the dominant player in the world market at some point in the future, there must be a sense of realism underpinning the vision in order for the organisation to have a firm grip on how this might be achieved. The issue is one of credibility as well as realisability. An unrealisable vision such as the one identified above for a small operator might result in the organisation losing sight of its current customers' needs as well as its value orientation to them, because the focus on a very long range strategic vision detracts from the delivery of services to customers. The current position of the company in relation to its direct competitors and its place in the market for the services is crucial to strategy development. Is the organisation a marker leader or market follower for example? What is its current market share, and what strategies led to it being in this position at this time? What opportunities and threats as well as external factors exist to enable the organisation to achieve its goals? Without a suitable organisational strategy, there is likely to be a loss of credibility with financial backers and other stakeholders.

In terms of the specific functions of marketing and how they articulate with the other functional management departments of the organisation, the marketing department contributes to the support of the organisation's vision and organisational strategy at a fundamental level in the following ways:

- Through the provision or commission of research, information and intelligence on the relative market position of the company in relation to its competitors, competitor analysis, market analysis and environmental scanning, product related research (i.e. consumer attitudes, preferences, buying behaviour and motivations).
- Through contributing to the development of the corporate brand for the organisation, which in turn feeds into the core strategic vision and values.
- Through the development of marketing strategies and plans, which incorporate targets to measure success either through key performance indicators (KPIs) or return on investment (ROI).
- Through the contribution to the evolution of an internal communications strategy.

- Through the ongoing evaluation of the systems and processes used in relation to the development of a customer focus for the organisation's activities, and to ensure that all the activities are oriented towards the creation of customer value.

The marketing function is one of the most important in the organisation, because it is through the marketing strategy and its communications that the organisation and its services are positioned in the minds of potential consumers, and because it contributes much of the research and analysis feeding into the organisational strategy. Some tourism and hospitality organisations, however, are too small to have separate departments or sophisticated strategies. Others rely heavily on conventional approaches to business where demand outstrips supply where the capacity or need to think strategically is not needed. The approach taken here is that for these organisations to be successful in the current era, a marketing orientation must underpin organisational strategy, one that is driven by the marketing concept that has been widely adopted in the sector. The marketing concept understands that organisations operate in a competitive and changing environment which can affect the organisations' ability to achieve its goals of meeting customer's needs and expectations profitably. Although this orientation to marketing is itself a strategic corporate decision, it is argued that the character and nature of tourism and hospitality services outlined in Chapter 1 requires a marketing orientation.

Marketing Orientation

A marketing orientation is a philosophical approach to marketing. It puts focus for all the activities of the organisation on meeting customers' needs and expectations for the service. At the root of this approach is a concern to understand as much about the consumers as it is possible to know: their motivations and buying behaviour characteristics; their preferences for and attitudes about the destinations, brands, products and services; their values and perceptions of quality and price relationships; their attitudes towards competing products and services; their cycles of behaviour. Many of these issues were detailed in Chapter 4. In this section, the focus is on how the organisational resources are focused and directed towards meeting the needs of customers and the creation of value.

Figure 5.2 shows customers' needs and expectations at the heart of all the activities of the organisation. Surrounding these are the extended seven elements (Zeithaml and Bitner, 1996: p. 25) of the services marketing mix – products (including product developments

Figure 5.2 The marketing orientation concept.

and innovations), pricing strategies, distribution, people, physical evidence, promotion and processes – together with the primary and support elements of the value chain (which will be outlined later in the chapter). These activities are in turn shaped by the organisation's stakeholders, strategic goals, vision and value orientation. The organisational decisions at this level provide strategic shape to the activities in the inner circle, but they are decisions which are oriented towards meeting customers' needs and expectations. The organisation must articulate its orientation to customers with its stakeholders including the wider media, shareholders, suppliers and competitors, trade associations, government and local administrative bodies where necessary and appropriate.

One example is the use of technology. Technology enables firms to manage business processes more effectively and to store information about customers' requirements, preferences or previous buying behaviour so that the organisation can manage its relationships with customers more effectively. Technological systems can also be used to introduce more flexibility into the planning and development of tourism packages, including flexible or 'fluid' pricing of products to stimulate demand and manage yields more effectively. It can also be used to communicate directly with customers or to increase the speed of response between customers and suppliers in the case of travel intermediaries and provide a wealth of consumer benefits (Buhalis and Licata, 2002). The extent to which the technology employed by the organisation contributes to meeting customers' needs, responding to their expectations and what they value from the processes, is dependent on the organisation having knowledge about what customers expectations are. In short, there is little point having a more advanced information communication technologies (ICT) system if this is not valued by customers and does not contribute to the delivery of the service required or impact upon demand and supply relationships. However, the use of technology to build relationships and communicate directly with customers has been a very successful application of ICT virtually in all tourism and hospitality organisations regardless of size and market orientation. It is without doubt that in many cases, the application of technology can also deliver cost savings which can be passed on to the customer. Therefore, technology can contribute indirectly to delivering customer value in terms of price reductions.

In this sense, a marketing orientation allows an evaluation of all systems, processes, actions and operations, plans and research to ask of them in what ways do they contribute to meeting customers' needs. Customers, then, are at the very centre of all the activities, operations and support systems of the organisation.

Competing Approaches to a Marketing Orientation

Of course, there are alternatives to a marketing orientation and change in the tourism and hospitality sector complicates the adoption of a marketing orientation in every case. Jobber (1995) recognises that production orientations or sales orientations are also common competing business philosophies. A production orientation can manifest itself in two ways: through a cost focus or production capability focus. Jobber states that in the former, the firm concentrates its activities on attaining economies of scale by producing a limited range of products in huge amounts, which provides quality control at low prices. In the cost focus model, consumers benefit from low prices and the organisation benefits from increased volumes of sales and a fairly standardised product range. In the latter, a capability-focused organisation, the emphasis is on the types of products which can be produced and putting in place an aggressive system of sales to make sure the products get sold.

Illustration

The production focus of the mass package holiday industry

In many ways, the production orientation system seems to represent accurately the approach adopted by the European mass package holiday industry during the 1960s through to the late 1980s. Sun, sea and sand destinations around the Mediterranean Ocean encouraged hotel development which would meet the demand for low-cost package holidays amongst the British, Scandinavian and Western European markets fuelled by the onset of the charter airline concept pioneered by Horizon Holidays in the 1950s (see Holloway and Taylor, 2006: pp. 50– 58 for a good summary). Hotels were built in high-rise, uniform blocks and resorts become indistinguishable from each other. Consumers did not seem to mind which country they were visiting as long as there was sunny weather, reasonable accommodation, beaches and entertainment facilities and low prices. This approach failed to recognise changes in consumers' attitudes as the markets matured, however, and an ever-increasing competitive arena against the difficult economic times of the early 1980s and 1990s put ever-greater squeeze on tour operator's profit margins. In some resorts hoteliers could not invest enough in the repair and maintenance of their properties, leading to downgrading of the destination product. Aggressive sales and marketing techniques were used based on reducing costs and 'dumping' cheap package holidays in the markets to shift capacity. Consumers rapidly turned away from poor quality resorts and shoddy service as their experience of package holidays grew and this led to a refocusing of many of the traditional sun, sea and sand resorts. Destinations had to invest heavily in resort infrastructure and tour operators and destination marketing organisations (DMOs) were forced to refocus their activities and reorient to a more sophisticated and quality conscious set of markets.

There are diverse models of business delivery in tourism industry, and it is clear that in the dynamic business environment, a marketing orientation is not a unified approach for all the organisations in the sector. Low-cost airlines and some chain hotels, for example, have adopted cost-focused orientations. The field of contract catering has conventionally applied a production-focused business model. The main differences between the two approaches in relation to package tour operations are presented in Figure 5.3.

It is clear that in many tourism and hospitality contexts, a production orientation or cost focus orientation is most suitable for the type of organisation. Often, however, contemporary organisations appear to

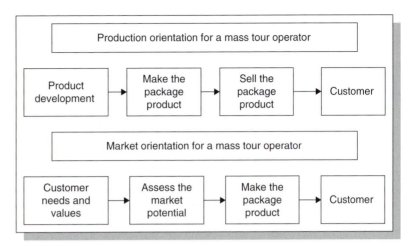

Figure 5.3 Production versus market orientation for a mass tour operator.
Source: Adapted from Jobber 1995: p. 8.

display a mixed orientation in that they have a production orientation or a cost focus as well as an orientation to customers. Since marketing is intrinsic to all businesses in the sector (because of intangibility, inseparability, perishability and heterogeneity) and tourism and hospitality services and operations are consumer-focused activities, a blended 'market-plus' orientation often seems the most apt description of the approach. One way of thinking about these types of organisational orientations is in terms of the services marketing triangle set of relationships.

The Services Marketing Triangle

Tourism and hospitality service characteristics were described in Chapter 1. The marketing issues which they create also relate to the strategic decisions of the organisation. In the not-for-profit sector, strategic goals are more likely to incorporate social and/or environment aims. Similarly in the context of public sector tourism organisations, strategic decisions on tourism development and marketing are directly linked to wider community development goals. The majority of organisations in this sector are for-profit corporations or firms. However, the concept of the services marketing triangle transcends the different orientations of organisations. It is a basic framework which links services marketing to the organisational and operational functions (Figure 5.4).

The 'services marketing triangle' highlights the relationships between organisations, customers and employees. This model identifies

Figure 5.4 The services marketing triangle.
Source: Wilson *et al.*, 2008: p. 19.

the important role of people in the delivery of services. It recognises that some organisations have used technology to replace some aspects of the service which were conventionally delivered by people. Examples include automated check-in services for airlines and hotels and also Internet-based intermediaries which have come to replace the traditional function of travel agencies. The 'services marketing triangle' shows the linkages between the groups responsible for developing, promoting and delivering the service. The service is positioned by Wilson *et al.* (2008) in terms of promises, recognising that for tourism and hospitality, what is offered is a promise of a type of experience. Although there are tangible elements, the core promise relates to the value orientation.

Enabling the Promise

The link between the management of the organisation and the employees (or technology) is conceived as 'enabling' the promise. Management is responsible for explaining and training employees about the nature of the service it wishes to provide to customers, because employees play a critical role in the production of the service. The orientation to service quality is defined through internal marketing communications. The management is responsible for delivery of consistent quality services through good strategic and tactical decision-making in relation to human resources, operations and marketing.

Making the Promise

The management engages in external marketing efforts in order to communicate a relevant brand image which is consistent with the internal marketing. This is referred to as 'making' the promise in terms of communication of quality and value. It is through this process of communication with customers that expectations are set – a promise of the service to be delivered. All forms of external communications with customers prior to the delivery of the service fall into this link between the management and customers.

Delivering the Promise

On the base of the triangle is what Wilson *et al.* (2008) refer to as interactive marketing, the delivery of the service. The delivery must match the promises made through the external marketing. Technology or other enablers and organisational decision-making must work to make the promise realised. A whole range of factors can impact upon the successful delivery of the promise, so it is important that organisations have plans in place to mitigate for service failure. An aspect of these plans might also be included in training of employees in their ability to respond to failures in the delivery of the promise. This is called interactive marketing because the delivery of the tourism and hospitality service forms an encounter (even if the encounter is through a website, there are still many ways in which the interaction with the technology plays an active role in the delivery of the service: functionality of the site, design and feel of the website, choice of words and images and so on).

There must be alignment between the three sides of the triangle so that what is promised from the external marketing matches what is delivered through the interaction with the service and the enabling activities of the organisation matches with what is expected of the service by customers.

Competitive Strategies

It is disingenuous to consider the orientation towards customers in isolation to the external environment and the actions of competitors, particularly, in the fierce competitive arena of tourism and hospitality services. Competition is not simply a problem for the private sector as destinations are increasingly operating within a competitive visitor environment. Ritchie and Crouch (2000) argue that competition between nations, regions, states and cities is growing rapidly as the latter recognise the importance of tourism and invest heavily in making improvements to destination image or attractiveness. In this section, different types of generic competitive strategies are discussed in relation to Porter's general theory (1980). This is a useful tool to assess the links between generic business strategy and marketing

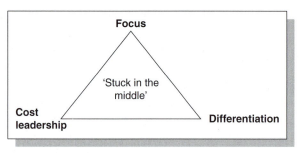

Figure 5.5 Porter's generic competitive strategies.
Source: Porter, 1980.

communications strategy, as clear links can often be made between the content of marketing messages and the overall positioning strategy of the organisation (Figure 5.5).

Porter identified that there are three main generic approaches to competitive strategy for organisations: cost leadership, differentiation and focus. A fourth category – being 'stuck in the middle' – can also be applied in a reflection that sometimes when organisations develop and grow in response to changes in the market and competitive environment over time, they find themselves in the middle of the road. This could result from mergers and acquisitions where the organisation has a number of strategic business units (SBUs) with 'inherited' strategic positions in the marketplace.

Cost Leadership

Porter argues that the cost leader in any market gains competitive advantage from being able to focus its energies on driving cost savings across all its activities which enable it to pass on these cost savings to consumers in the form of low prices. Often, companies which compete on the basis of cost leadership rigorously analyse and evaluate the cost basis of all their activities and aim to reduce operations costs and maximise efficiency savings and economies of scale to deliver the lowest possible cost to consumers. In the context of tourism and hospitality services, the two main types of businesses which have successfully adopted this generic strategy approach are the low-cost or no-frills airlines and fast-food restaurant chains on the hospitality bundle of services. However, these are not the only types of service providers who compete on a cost basis. In fact, much of the tour operations sector operates on a cost leadership strategy. Package holiday markets are saturated, destinations offering similar types of products in the mass package holiday market are abundant and external factors such as economic fluctuations in the generating and destination economies often impact upon the ability of destinations to compete for a very fickle and price sensitive market. Coupled with the fact that tour operators are continually negotiating with the other principals in the tourism supply chain, cost savings are always at the forefront of tour operators' business models.

Similarly, in the mass package holiday market, the intermediaries, travel distribution websites and travel agencies very often adopt a cost leadership marketing strategy, particularly at key times of the year when demand needs to be stimulated and/or pre-booked package holidays need to be sold due to considerations of perishability. Of course, low cost does not always lead to low price, and strategies must be adaptable and responsive to change in the markets depending on sales, competitor's strategies and margins at particular points in the season/cycle. However, Porter meant that a cost leadership strategy as a generic strategy should indicate an ongoing commitment to reduce costs and drive down the prices for products and services, and the low-cost airlines exemplify this type of strategy in the tourism industry. These companies make sure that every aspect of their businesses, including the messages, modes and types of marketing communications employed, reflect their focus on delivering cheap prices. The problem is that the market for low-cost airlines in some regions (such as Europe) is reaching saturation. High number of new entrants in the market coupled with the adoption of some aspects of the low-cost business model into 'conventional' standard carriers operations allowing for greater competition on ticket prices, alongside service quality, differentiated point to point air routes and, importantly, quality brand image in the communications strategies has resulted in a great deal of competition in the low-cost airline market. The extent to which this is sustainable will also be dependent on external factors including taxation policies on aviation which were outlined in Chapter 3, changing preferences amongst consumers with concerns for the impact of aviation on climate change, and economic stability in Europe.

The consequences for a cost leadership strategy on marketing communications are that messages tend to highlight sales promotions and emphasise communication of price or cost value. These types of strategies often necessitate lots of short-run campaigns using a variety of media channels to achieve wide coverage. Communications strategies for cost leadership are also often initiated in reaction to competitors' sales promotion campaigns.

Differentiation

One way in which organisations can shift consumers' focus away from price/cost issues is by pursuing a differentiation strategy. Differentiation refers to a strategic orientation to identify the points of difference between the organisation and its competitors. It relies on the identification of value relationships through quality of service in relation to the needs of customers and focuses on the identification of unique points of difference to create sustainable competitive advantage. This allows companies to shift the focus away from the price and to focus on delivery of customer value, which generates a comparatively higher price and often a better profit margin. Differentiation requires service providers to segment markets and deliver unique services to them, based on a complete understanding of what these customers value from the experience of the service. (Market segmentation processes are considered in detail in Chapter 6.) Another aspect of the term differentiation is that, by focusing on the needs and values of customers, the organisation is assumed to go beyond the levels of service offered by rivals and thus they are differentiated from the competition.

The benefits of a differentiation strategy are that the organisation needs to be close to its customers and recognise that needs are different for different types of users. This allows them the opportunity to create distinctive and valued services, thereby establish and retain loyalty and reduce marketing communications costs. Another benefit is that by moving away from a very narrow focus on cost control and therefore on competitor pricing strategies, the organisation can truly focus on meeting customer needs, and this is likely to result in higher levels of customer satisfaction, staff development and retention, and the benefits associated with prestige products and services. It is assumed that the adoption of this generic strategy will incur additional costs in creating its competitive advantage, in research and product development, branding and marketing communications, as well as in operations and delivery of the service. These investment and delivery costs must be recouped by sufficient levels of demand within the segments.

A major problem with differentiation as a generic competitive strategy is that services are often imitated by competitors. In the tourism and hospitality sectors there are differences here. It is not easy to simply change strategic direction from a cost leadership strategy to a differentiation strategy without major investment and the risk associated with (a) losing your original customers and (b) failing to win the competitive battle for each of the segments for which you are competing. However, new entrants into the market may find it easy to copy a differentiated strategy adopted in relation to certain segments, and considering the ease with which organisations can now operate in international markets; there are greater potential risks when an organisation with similar differentiation strategy operating in one international market enters into the competitive arena. Another potential problem with this approach is that differentiated service quality expectations could gradually become diffused across the whole industry and alters the nature of the price/quality relationship. Organisations need to continually add value and improve to keep pace with consumers' expectations to maintain the distinction of their products/services.

The consequences on marketing communications strategy in an organisation adopting a differentiation strategy are that the communications need to be high quality, and they need to be tailored for different market segments. The communications strategy often focuses on different elements of the services marketing mix such as the important role of people (the expertise of tour guides, the attentive and knowledgeable staff delivering the treatments and therapies in spa resorts for example) as opposed to sales promotional messages. Often, these organisations focus on communicating brand image in long campaigns using a single set of messages.

Focus

The focus strategy is also known as a 'niche' strategy. The focus strategy is adopted by organisations that are not able to adopt a cost leadership strategy or a differentiation strategy. The focus can mean a focus on a limited number of services to a broad audience, or a focus on a particular segment the market with a broad range of services. Based on the principle that it is more efficient to produce a limited range of products/services that are needed by many or by focusing on producing long-lasting relationships from a defined segment, the focus strategy allows organisations to concentrate their resources and create competitive advantage specifically for and within the niche of the service category/segment that they operate. If the organisation takes a focus approach based on reaching a wide market with a small number of service offerings, this is not the same as a cost leadership strategy. Similarly, if the organisation adopts a focus strategy in terms of a niche market segment focus, this does not equate to a differentiation strategy.

The difficulty in these contexts becomes then differentiating between a focus and the other two approaches since a focus can lead to market leadership in terms of cost/price, or to a differentiation amongst the segment group. A good example of this type of segment-based focus is Saga Group, whose focus on the over-50s covers a wide range of product and services, not least of which of course is the Saga Holidays product range. Saga have become the undisputed market leader in provision of services for the over-50s. However, a competitive strategy based on focus is often adopted by market followers or market nichers as opposed to market leaders.

As with the cost leadership and differentiation strategies, there are potential risks and problems associated with a focus strategy. The main problem being the potential for overreliance or dependence on one key market segment or product range which might become obsolete or fall out of favour with consumers. Some niche products exhibit rapid early growth and then fall out of fashion and may be prone to equally rapid decline. There is risk from international competition, or specialist niches may disappear in the long run as markets in tourism and hospitality naturally diversify and seek out new experiences. There may also be limited potential for growth, depending on the types of product or customer focus.

In terms of the consequences for marketing communications for a focus strategy often includes a 'broadcast' media approach using television and other broadcast media to send messages which are capable of reaching wide audiences either within the segment focus or in the wider market in terms of a service focus.

Stuck in the Middle

Porter argues that there is a danger of adopting a 'middle of the road' strategy, as this leaves the organisation with a limited control over its approach to the market and, importantly, the competitive position of the organisation. Being stuck in the middle might not automatically result in a loss of competitive advantage, but this is not a desirable state according to Porter: organisations which find themselves in this position need to engage in a strategic repositioning. In cases where organisations are stuck in the middle, marketing communications strategy might not effectively target the desired customers, the communications might not then reach the correct audience and messages might not communicate the goals and values of the organisation in its commitment to satisfying customer needs.

Generic Competitive Issues in the Tourism and Hospitality Sector

However, as noted above, each of the three main strategic directions has its own associated potential problems or weaknesses. In a highly competitive consumer market for discretionary spend, such as that for tourism and hospitality services, a focus on cost leadership, efficiency in operations and tight fiscal control is evident across the sector. Similarly, consumers are becoming more and more experienced and demand higher quality from their tourist experiences and, as such, organisations must work hard to differentiate and customise their products and services and communicate their values and commitment to the delivery of service quality in order to be competitive. Another generic issue is an orientation towards relationship marketing (*cf.* Fyall *et al.*, 2003). As mentioned previously, the hospitality industry has excelled at building loyalty through preferred guest or membership schemes (Palmer *et al.*, 2000). In some areas, however, consumers regularly eschew brand loyalty, although in others, brand loyalty is more commonplace. These types of attitudes and orientations of consumer markets are very different from those that typify the manufacturing sector, which Porter was describing, and yet the competitive strategies model allows for a detailed analysis of the choices available to organisations in their strategic direction.

The structure of the sector also impacts upon the types of orientation to the competitive markets. The fact that 'destinations' as opposed to the individual service organisations located therein can be the focus of consumers' choices, can effectively undermine the importance of strategic competitive orientation. However, this also places a fundamental importance onto the DMO in coordinating the marketing communications strategy at destination level and indeed for all aspects of quality (infrastructure and inward investment, destination branding development, relationships between the local government, public and private sector, etc.). The interconnected nature of the tourism industry in resort destinations is a prime example of this, and although individual businesses are dependent on the networks and partnerships they build and maintain with inbound tour operators in the generating markets, they are also highly dependent on the actions and support provided by the DMO and the complementary nature of services. In such cases, the DMO must represent the interests of all individual businesses within the resort destination. The individual organisational competitive strategies need to be independent of the DMO and yet also connected and joined up, and it is in this sense that marketing communications strategies need to be considered across a variety of stakeholder and interest groups. This can apply to any type of destination-based organisation including bars, restaurants and entertainment venues, casinos, hotels and other accommodation providers or the auxiliary tourism support organisations such as public transport, taxi companies, car hire firms, insurance and inbound tour operators and travel agencies.

Certainly in the case of very large multinational tour operations organisations such as Tui Thomson, a prominent European player, whose product portfolio is so broad and diverse that it is able to achieve economies of scale in management functions. This enables these organisations to compete on cost leadership in key service markets as well as being diverse enough to pursue focus and differentiation strategies to ensure a broad representation in the widest possible range of consumer markets.

Value Chain

A final strategic tool to consider in this chapter is that of the value chain. Porter developed the concept of the value chain in relation to a firm's competitive strategy. He argued that value could be created by the organisation for its customers through an analysis of all primary and support functions and activities. Essentially, the value chain analysis asks questions about what customers really value from the service. Then all activities are scrutinised to ensure that value is created and this process would lead to competitive advantage if the organisation were able to create more value than do its rivals. The value chain represents a customer orientation and a determined and systematic analytical tool to create value. It is particularly useful in tourism and hospitality contexts because of the focus on customer value.

In Figure 5.6, the value chain is applied to the services marketing mix. Although the 7Ps of services marketing will be discussed in greater detail in Chapter 7, it is useful to see here how the value chain can be related to tourism and hospitality services marketing.

Porter was writing about manufacturing industry but the same bundle of activities can be used to describe the production and delivery of services. He argued that the value chain consisted of five support activities: infrastructure (meaning, the organisational structure), human resources management (HRM), technology, procurement and marketing management. These support activities enabled the delivery of primary activities which consist of inbound logistics, operations, outbound logistics and after-sales services.

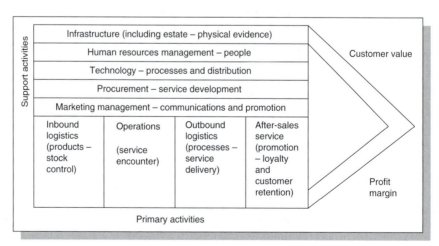

Figure 5.6 Value chain and the services marketing mix.
Source: Adapted from Porter, 1985.

Using the example of a restaurant, inbound logistics can be related to decisions about product quality and stock control. Stock control in a restaurant allows management to free up financial resources and develop more effective financial management. This may lead to decisions to improve the quality of the food and drink products which can create extra value to customers. This is linked to the procurement support function since buying decisions can also be linked to value creation. Decisions to source only locally produced meat and vegetable ingredients and organic produce can create extra value if this is desired by customers. The operations function relates to the delivery of the promise and connects with the HRM support function. Management must ensure that enough members of staff are available to meet demand at peak times and ensure that they are trained and empowered to deliver the correct levels of service quality. Value can be created through recruitment and training which is critical to the service encounter. Outbound logistics is linked to the concept of processes in the 7Ps of service marketing. Outbound logistics can be related to the systems and processes for managing customers through their experience of the restaurant, from initial contact, waiting times, delivery of the service in a timely way and so on. Value can be created to ensure a seamless service delivery process. These processes can be linked to technology. The use of electronic order pads in the restaurant or the use of wireless payment devices to speed up processes can create value from the outbound function.

After-sales service in the context of a restaurant include feedback surveys or comment cards, use of customer databases for promotions, the implementation of customer loyalty schemes, other strategies for customer retention and relationship management. These activities are linked to marketing management support functions and relate to the marketing communications strategy in terms of promotion. Customer value is created since it is more cost-effective to market to existing customers than it is to market to new customers. Sales promotions activities can deliver cost savings to customers.

In terms of infrastructure, this can also be equated to the estate, the physical infrastructure of the restaurant. This can include the amount of 'covers' – that is, the ability to increase and decrease supply within limits depending on the level of demand at key times (by opening up or closing off seating areas to enhance the dining experience or manipulate the 'atmosphere'). In relation to the 7Ps of service marketing, this can also be linked to the physical evidence of the restaurant. Physical evidence includes décor, fixtures and furnishings, lighting, ambience. These aspects of the physical 'servicescape' in the context of a restaurant can be changed to contribute to customer value creation.

The application of the value chain in driving competitive advantage which can be linked to services marketing strategies means that these elements of customer value can become the focus of marketing messages. There is a link here between the application of the value chain and a differentiation strategy.

Position in the Market

The type of competitive strategy adopted by the organisation is very much dependent on its position in relation to the market. This is determined by the financial and other resources (including communications networks), notwithstanding that competitive strategies can orient the organisation for future growth linked to the strategy decision frameworks discussed earlier in the chapter. Generally three types of position organisations can hold in the marketplace:

1. market leader
2. market challenger
3. market follower

Market leaders might use their market position to project their importance in the market place or to communicate their relative strength. *Market challengers* might use marketing communications to challenge or attack the market dominance of their rivals, whereas *market followers* and niche market players want to communicate to raid market share in particular locations or distribution channels or to communicate their differences from the rest of the pack.

Organisations can position themselves strategically for growth in terms of, say, market share, which is a strategy based on its current competitive position but goal driven. Needless to say, the strategies for corporate growth and development will impact upon the type of communications strategy required to achieve it. Intensive growth will require concentrated and concerted marketing across a range of different media employing a range of strategies, raising awareness amongst new target markets for example, or using new channels of distribution. Sales promotions may need to be considered to persuade people to try and to move people quickly through from awareness to taking specific action.

Communications strategies can be used to shift perceptions and attitudes of the public to reposition the organisation and capture market share at the same time as the case study on Virgin Trains shown in Chapter 4. However, the ability to pursue such an intensive and costly marketing communications campaign is similarly determined by the size and financial scope of the organisation. Market leaders in transport services such as the UK train-operating companies are not reliant on discretionary spending for all revenues, and resource allocations are different in that sector compared to the market leader for country house hotels for example. Similarly, organisations may aim to expand their share of the total market or undertake marketing communications campaigns to protect their market share in response to competitors' actions.

The key question that organisations need to address in their strategic decision-making regarding corporate and therefore marketing communications strategy is, Will it attract enough customers and convince them to buy in sufficient numbers at a price which will result in a significant ROI relative to the competitors' actions? Marketing strategies need to be consistent with broader corporate goals, meet the needs of the markets and targeted segments, relate to the range of other publics and stakeholders' information needs about the organisation, exploit the distinctive resources, competencies and product expertise of the organisation and yet be responsive to competitors' actions. Depending on size, scale, reach and capabilities of the organisation, the marketing function both directs and is constrained by the organisational strategy, and marketing communications strategy reflects the corporate goals, generic strategic approach and the relative competitive position.

IMCs as Strategic Choice

As outlined in Chapter 1, IMCs can refer to a number of different approaches to marketing. IMCs can refer to the integration of marketing across the organisation and thus as a pervasive and powerful driver of the support functions of the organisation. Alternatively IMCs can refer to the integration of marketing communications tools and/or messages across a range of different marketing channels. What is meant by this is that in planning a marketing promotional strategy, an organisation may decide to deploy a variety of communications channels to send a set of messages to its target audiences.

Conventional marketing viewed the separate elements of the promotional mix as separate and discrete functional methods of communications used to convey messages to discrete sets of audiences. Each communication tool was used to reach specific audiences with specific messages and as a result there was a fragmentation within the industry of specialist communications and promotional agencies dealing with PR, sales promotions and personal selling, advertising and so on. Fill (2005: p. 296) argues that IMCs emerged 'partially as a reaction to the structural inadequacies of the industry and the realisation by clients that their communication needs can (and should) be achieved more efficiently and effectively than previously.' The concept of IMCs can be seen as a reaction to this fragmentation in the industry but also as a proactive response to challenging competitive industrial environments and the fragmentation of advertising into different spheres of activity.

First, IMCs aimed at harmonising the messages across different types of communications tools. By adopting IMCs as a strategic marketing approach, a consistency of types of message, the words, images, brands and brand values, design and quality issues across all forms of promotion, selling and advertising channels, audiences would have a better understanding and recognition of the organisation and its core messages and appeals.

Types of media are becoming more and more fragmented with the widespread adoption of online media channels such as youtube.com and myspace.com, the proliferation of digital and satellite television channels and mobile telephony, the fragmentation of printed media titles, and together with audience fragmentation and direct marketing approaches, it is increasingly difficult to reach the desired target segments and so having integrated communications across different channels is seen to help overcome these issues and reinforce the brand appeal within the minds of consumers. The fragmentation of advertising and its spread into non-traditional areas of life outside conventional advertising channels present new opportunities for the promotion of tourism and hospitality products and services and also present potential problems in terms of saturation and consumers filtering out – disregarding – the core messages.

Secondly, IMCs ensures that all publics and stakeholders are informed of the organisation's core brand values, especially employees who should feel empowered to deliver the required service quality to customers. In tourism and hospitality this is vital to make sure that the service promises made through the marketing communications are effectively carried out by the employees. The clarity and consistency of message within the organisation can be delivered through internal marketing communications, training programmes, use of the organisation's chosen design, colours, branding in uniforms, internal mailing, payroll, memos etc. This is then easily transferred to external stakeholders, such as suppliers through billing and invoicing for example, to shareholders through the deployment of the core messages, design and so on in the annual report and other communications materials.

Therefore IMCs in itself can become a strategic choice which is deployed to achieve organisational goals in terms of service delivery, and in delivery of customer value. In this way, IMCs is linked to the strategic frameworks discussed earlier in the chapter.

Summary

This chapter has described the links between organisational strategies and marketing communications. Organisational strategy decisions have implications for the type of orientation to the market adopted.

A marketing orientation places the needs, expectations and values of customers at the heart of the organisation's business, takes an integrated approach to functions in the organisation and applies marketing philosophy and principles to all areas of the organisation's activities. However, there are a range of strategic choices available to tourism and hospitality organisations. Some of the strategic decisions are determined by the competitive market for these services. Porter's generic model of approaches to competitive strategy was outlined in relation to the impact each approach has on marketing communications. The concept of the value chain was also applied to the competitive strategy and linked to the main constructs in the services marketing mix. This showed how tourism and hospitality organisations can create, deliver and communicate customer value through marketing communications strategies.

Discussion questions

1. Define what is meant by marketing orientation and discuss how this applies to a tourism and hospitality organisation of our choice.
2. What is the relationship between generic organisational strategy and marketing strategy? Explain how marketing strategy is constrained by an organisation's strategic choices.
3. Assess how the services marketing triangle is linked to an IMCs approach.
4. Explain how the primary and support functions in the value chain can be translated into marketing communications.

Case Study 5: Visit Wales – UK Consumer Marketing Campaign 2005–2008

National DMOs must continually work to keep their destination brand image fresh in the minds of consumers. This is a challenge for small countries with a limited marketing budget. National destination marketing requires a great deal of internal coordination as well as a broad marketing communications strategy. To be successful, the communications must link directly to consumers' values, attitudes and motivations and they must be distinctive enough to stand out from the competition. Wales' UK consumer campaign for 2005–2008 has been highly successful. The campaign did not try to hide away from potential negative stereotypes about Wales as a country, particularly its reputation for poor weather. Instead the campaign has sought to specifically target groups for whom these factors are not obstacles. It also focused on the unique characteristics of Wales and in particular used humour in the campaign to represent a distinctly Welsh attitude and to connect to the values of the target audience.

Visit Wales UK consumer marketing campaign won many awards at the Chartered Institute of Marketing Tourism Interest Group (CIMTIG) campaign awards, including Gold awards for: Best Colour Press Campaign for 2005–2006; Best Use of DM for 'Mud' which also won Best Multimedia Campaign and Best Leisure television advertisement. Another Gold award was given for Best Colour Press Ad for 'Lobster', whilst 'Woolly Whites' won silver and 'Mobile' also won silver. The 2005–2007 campaign was clearly a winner with the tourism marketing professionals.

In January 2005, Visit Wales launched a UK Consumer campaign which was backed by a £6 million per annum budget.

The campaign aimed to portray the 'real' Wales by capturing the authentic sense of the place, people, culture and the true visitor experience. It is designed to reach and appeal to a wide range of potential visitors with a particular focus on 'Independent Explorers' seeking authentic holiday experiences.

Campaign objectives

Visit Wales set the following campaign objectives:

- To encourage reappraisal and positive impressions of Wales for holidays/breaks.
- To generate approximately 400,000 high-quality enquiries per year.
- To provide enquirers with effective sources of information, offers and booking opportunities to help them plan their holidays.
- To provide opportunities for tourism businesses/partners to promote their products via the campaigns.

The communications campaign included a series of four television adverts which were shown on ITV, Channel 4 and Channel 5 and selected digital channels in burst strategy over the three-year period. This was complemented by print adverts in national newspapers and magazines, online advertising and large volume direct response campaigns across the year.

The television advertising campaign consisted of four 30 second advertisements focusing on different aspects of adventure and activities holidays which were possible through a visit to Wales:

- 'Go Welsh' which according to the Wales government:

    The advert follows a family exploring Wales following signs in Welsh visiting many beautiful places. It highlights what makes Wales original and different in a straightforward manner with a little tongue-in-cheek humour. This makes potential visitors think of Wales as a refreshing place to visit that offers a real alternative to all other holiday destinations – an unexploited and imaginative experience.

- 'Mud' which featured a couple hosing mud from a mountain bike, whilst the narrative informed audiences that they were welcome to the wide open spaces and clean air, laver bread and so on, but that they were not welcome to take home Welsh mud, which is 'good mud'.
- 'Castles' featured two small children making a sand castle. The narrative explained how a sand castle is made, but then concludes that there is always someone who has gone one better, whilst the camera pans out to reveal a Welsh castle in the background.

- 'Reclining' featured close up of a woman relaxing in a hotel in front of a log fire, reading, sipping a drink and relaxing. The narrative explains all these actions and concludes that is a 'real activity holiday'.

The television advertisements were clearly humorous and represented Wales in a light hearted way which was sympathetic with English humour and sensitivities. The television advertisements were accompanied by 11 press adverts which showed different aspects of Welsh culture, landscape and a range of activity holiday ideas or themes.

The narrative which accompanies Plate 5.1 reads

As if the surfers don't have enough to fear with the vicious breaks to the north of Hell's Mouth. They've also got Llyn sheep to deal with. Wandering the three-and-a-half mile sandy beach. Watching. Waiting. Surfers needn't panic though. Local farmer Henry Hughes has been living here 38 years and can't recall a single sheep attack. Although their disinterest when you rack up a perfect cut back hurts a little.

The narrative which accompanies Plate 5.2 reads

Stunning, beautiful, outstanding and lovely. Some of the words Dylan Thomas didn't use to describe this view of Laugharne Bay, Carmarthenshire. He was more of a 'slow, black, crowblack, fishingboat-bobbing sea' type of guy. Just one of the descriptors from his famous play 'Under Milk Wood'. Penned from his shed, next to The Boat House below. It is amazing, but don't take our word for it. See for yourself and make up a few of your own.

Plates 5.1 and 5.2 show examples from the press campaign which represents unique images and associations with Wales. The Visit Wales campaign has a well-specified set of target market areas and types of consumer:

Target markets

Priority areas
Within a 2-hour drive time, the M4 Corridor, Midlands, North-West, Hampshire and the West Country. Television, press and direct marketing is upweighted in these areas.

Secondary areas
By airing our television adverts on satellite and digital television this provides a platform for us to reach a national audience. We also include advertisements in the national press and magazines.

Who are we aiming at?
We are evolving our targeting approach to segment visitors by their attitudes and motivations, rather than by simply using demographic factors. The campaign will reach a broad range of potential visitors but will focus on 'Independent Explorers'.

Who are they?
Independent explorers are in search of new experiences and places. They are slightly upmarket and tend to be adults aged 30 years and over. They shun the overcommercialised

Plate 5.1 'Great Woolly Whites' – Visit Wales's UK Consumer marketing campaign.

Plate 5.2 'Adjective Central' – Visit Wales's UK Consumer marketing campaign.

tourist honey pots. They are free minded, they do not follow the herd. They are free spirited, and they look for places that allow them to be themselves, that enrich them, that challenge them. They like to interact with the place to understand culture, to meet its people and to return refreshed and enriched.

What do they believe?

Attitude	'I am an optimist'
	'I consider myself to be a creative person'
	'Like to pursue life of challenge, novelty and change'
	'I have practical outlook on life'
	'I do some sort of exercise at least once a week'
Values	'I am interested in other cultures'
	'Important to respect traditional customs and beliefs'
	'We usually have family meals at the weekend'
Holiday	'I prefer holidays off the beaten track'
	'I like to take my holidays in Britain rather than abroad' or 'I enjoy planning holidays'

How many are there?

Within the UK there are potentially 7,021,000 people we could be attracting to Wales.

Can these be broken down further?

Family explorers	Independent Explorers + Children aged 5–15 years + 'My family is more important to me than my career.'
Independent explorers	Independent Explorers + 'I am interested in the arts' or 'I enjoy other cultures'
Active explorers	Independent Explorers + 'I enjoy activities on holiday', or 'I regularly take part in…'

The 2008 new *Wales View* magazine represents the culmination of the three-year campaign. The brochure is the lynchpin of the promotional activity for Visit Wales and through it, the organisation seeks to maximise Wales's exposure in the UK marketplace.

The campaign invites visitors to create their holiday 'talk-list' not 'tick-list' presenting a menu of the braver, more surprising elements to enjoy in Wales. Such as 'swapping cornflakes for seaweed' by having laver bread for breakfast or panning for the world's rarest gold.

The campaign will comprise of online and offline elements including

- 3.5 million leaflets inserted into quality broadsheets and selected consumer titles.
- Online advertising on travel and lifestyle websites
- Paid for search engine marketing
- 367,000 people on the Visit Wales database will be mailed the leaflets and a further 92,000 emails will be sent.
- 25,000 Wales View magazines will be sent directly to Wales 'fans' of which 10,000 will include a gift of a Sheep Poo Paper bookmark reflecting one of the articles in the magazine.

The campaign is targeted to generate 150,000 brochure requests for Wales View and the selection of marketing area guides and 100,000 qualified visits to www.visitwales.co.uk.

The theme is linked to 'green holidays' as below: **No Passports, No Planes**

Going green is at the heart of the 'Wales View' magazine, which is published annually by Visit Wales, the Welsh Assembly Government's tourism team. Opting for a holiday in Wales means that travel plans will be kinder and gentler all round. The magazine has top ten tips of how to holiday with a clear conscience. It features activities and events, places and heritage which are uniquely welsh.

Learning activity

- Visit the Welsh government tourism marketing website. View the television advertisements in the 2005–08 UK consumer campaign and download the campaign summary.
- Discuss Visit Wales' strategy for the UK consumer campaign, highlighting factors which you think contributed to its success.
- Discuss what type of competitive strategy, if any, you think Visit Wales has employed in this campaign. What are the competitor destinations for the UK independent explorer consumer?
- Evaluate which other markets might be attracted by Visit Wales UK consumer campaign.

References

Buhalis, D. and Licata, M.C. (2002). The future of eTourism intermediaries. *Tourism Management*. 23: 207–220.

Fill, C. (2005). *Marketing communications: Engagement, strategies and practice*. 4th edn. Harlow: Prentice Hall.

Fyall, A., Callod, C. and Edwards, B. (2005). Relationship marketing the challenge for destinations. *Annals of Tourism Research*. 30(3): 644–659.

Holloway, J. C. and Taylor, N. (2006). *The Business of Tourism*. 7th edn. Harlow: Pearson Education.

Jobber, D. (1995). *Principles and Practice of Marketing*. Maidenhead, UK: McGraw-Hill Book Company.

Johnson, G. and Scholes, K. (1989). *Exploring Corporate Strategy*. London: Hemel Hempstead Prentice Hall.

Palmer, A., Beattie, U. and Beggs, R. (2000). A structural analysis of hotel sector loyalty programs. *International Journal of Contemporary Hospitality Management*. 12: 54–60.

Porter, M.E. (1980). *Competitive Strategy: Techniques for Analyzing Industries and Competitors*. New York: Free Press.

Porter, M.E. (1985). *Competitive Advantage*. New York: Free Press.

Ritchie, J.R.B. and Crouch, G. (2000). The competitive destination: A sustainability perspective. *Tourism Management*. 21: 1–7.

Tribe, J. (1996). *Corporate Strategy for Tourism*. London: Thomson Learning.

Wilson, A., Zeithaml, V.A., Bitner, M.J. and Gremler, D.D. (2008). *Services Marketing: Integrating Customer Focus across the Firm*. First European Edition. Maidenhead, UK: McGraw-Hill Education.

Zeithaml, V.A. and Bitner, M.J. (1996). *Services Marketing*. New York: McGraw Hill.

Key Resource and Useful Link

http://www.new.wales.gov.uk/topics/tourism/marketing

Segmentation, Targeting and Positioning

At the end of this chapter, you will be able to

- Understand the links between marketing planning and effective targeted marketing communications.

- Define the segmentation, targeting and positioning process (STP).

- Evaluate competing approaches to segmentation of tourism and hospitality consumers.

- Relate the STP to tourism and hospitality services marketing mix.

- Describe the relationships between STP and marketing communications strategies.

Introduction

In Case study 5, it was shown that Visit Wales built their latest marketing campaign by orienting their messages towards 'independent explorers' as a discrete subset of the market. Although the campaign was focused in a geographic sense (people living within 2 hours' drive time from Wales), the focus of the messages was an orientation to people's values and attitudes as opposed to their age, position in the family life cycle or socio-economic status. Partially, the Visit Wales strategy was driven by a limited budget (making it impossible to undertake a large-scale international advertising campaign). However, the aim of the campaign was also to connect with the values of key groups in the overall UK consumer market for holidays which formed the group with the most potential for the Wales holiday market. This decision-making strategy is known as the segmentation, targeting and positioning (STP) process. Decisions concerning which groups of people in the total market form the core target audience of the organisation and the relationships to organisational strategy decisions were described in the Chapter 5. In order for marketing communications to be effective they need to be directed towards those people in the marketplace who are identified by the organisation as the main target audience for the messages. Otherwise marketing resources could be misdirected or fail to achieve the desired goals for the message. People's buying behaviour and characteristics are different, and it is unlikely that many tourism and hospitality services can satisfy all consumers in the market. Therefore, messages must convey appropriate cues to connect with particular groups of customers' values, in that the messages must position the service or destination in such a way as to make it attractive to specific target groups. This chapter focuses on the STP decisions and continues to link these management activities to the services marketing mix in terms of the impact on marketing communications strategy.

There has been a great deal of research in tourism on segmentation theory, strategies and techniques in a wide range of studies (Bieger and Lässer, 2002; Hsu and Lee, 2002; Klemm, 2002; Sung, 2004). In terms of hospitality research, the literature is less well developed and this is most likely due to the availability of data compared with tourism where visitor statistics is quite advanced. Dolnicar (2004) provides a review of tourism segmentation studies published in the *Journal of Tourism Research* during the past 15 years. Although Dolnicar identifies that most studies have adopted an *a priori* approach to market segmentation, she argues that combinations of *a priori* and *post hoc* methods will in the future lead to more original approaches to segmenting travel markets. The key assumption underpinning research on market segmentation is that sustainable competitive advantage can be gained through being able to match organisational capabilities to the potential needs and expectations of particular, well-defined groups in the market.

This chapter outlines the links between the STP process and marketing planning. It describes different approaches used to segment consumer markets in tourism and hospitality and links the STP approach to the extended services marketing mix, including the impact of STP on marketing communications strategy.

The Segmentation, Targeting and Positioning Process

Most authors writing on the subject of STP identify that it is a staged process consisting of three main activities: market segmentation, market targeting and market positioning (Figure 6.1). Within each of the stages is a set of actions. Once again, the importance of market research underpinning the market segmentation stage cannot be understated. Market segmentation and profiling research is a specialist function and this type of research is often contracted out to a market research agency. Before going on to define the activities of the three stages in detail, the links between STP and marketing planning which were outlined earlier in the book need to be highlighted.

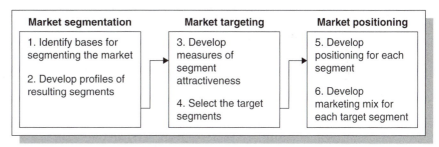

Figure 6.1 The segmentation, targeting and positioning process.
Source: Kotler *et al.*, 2006: p. 263.

Marketing Planning and the STP Process

In previous chapters the marketing planning and strategy development activities were outlined. The links between the external environment and the marketing strategy were made in Chapter 3. The importance of understanding customers and markets was described and related to marketing communications strategy in Chapter 4, and in the Chapter 5, links between organisational strategy and the competitive environment provided the context for an evaluation of how

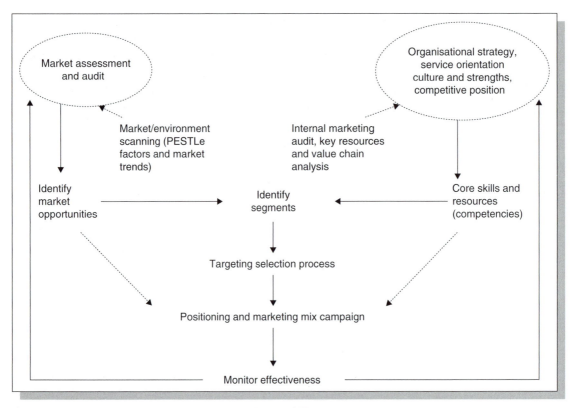

Figure 6.2 The relationship between marketing planning and STP.

marketing philosophy determines an orientation to consumers or markets. An organisation which does not plan its communications effectively will inevitably waste its time, financial resources and ultimately its market share if it does not create and deliver marketing communications which appeal directly to the intended audience. Thus there is a need for careful marketing planning which is based on a clear understanding of the customers, their needs and values and a judgement on how the services offered by the organisation meet those needs and values. Once this is known, the organisation can more effectively target those people with effective messages which actively position the services in relation to the needs and values of the group.

Figure 6.2 outlines the links between the marketing and directional flows in the decision process. This diagram expands on the marketing planning framework described in Figure 3.3 and focuses on the choices relating to market analysis and segmentation strategy. The model demonstrates that marketing planning begins with the analysis of the internal and external environment, including the PESTLe and market trends analysis described, respectively, in Chapters 3 and 4 and the value chain and competitor position analysis described in Chapter 5. The result of this activity is the identification of core competencies (skills and resources) and market opportunities. From this, a set of market segments can be identified which are then matched against the core competencies. Each segment is evaluated and the most suitable segments are selected. These become the target for the organisation which then makes any adjustments or modifications to the service and the marketing campaign is devised. The STP process is important in marketing strategy, because it allows the organisation to develop a tailored marketing mix package to meet the needs of a specific group of the market who share similar characteristics and needs. The final point in the sequence is to monitor the effectiveness of the campaign, which in turn feeds back into the next phase in the marketing planning cycle.

The level and type of segmentation process undertaken will vary considerably depending on the

- size of the organisation
- stage in the marketing planning process
- financial position of the organisation
- current market position.

Organisations may undertake market research into their current served markets and their target future markets at various stages in their marketing planning cycle. Organisations tend to review strategy at particular points whereupon new market opportunities present themselves, at other times, there may be some 'slack' in the marketing budget which allows some extra project work to be undertaken on customers/target groups to add depth to what is already known. And at other times, the organisation may commission research in an exploratory way to test and develop new segment opportunities. Market segmentation is a useful tool to identify new opportunities, creative segmentation might identify new emerging segments and this process can lead to service innovation. The segmentation process can therefore contribute to a competitive advantage and a differentiation marketing strategy.

Market Segmentation

Defining Segmentation

Market segmentation is the process of dividing up the total market (all the people the organisation can sell its products or services to) into identifiable, measurable and discrete groups who share some common characteristics or needs and whose attitudes or reactions towards communications messages about products or services might be similar.

Chisnall argues that market segmentation 'recognizes that people differ in their tastes, needs, attitudes, lifestyles, family size and com-pos-ition, etc.… It is a deliberate policy of maximizing market demand by directing marketing efforts at significant sub-groups of customers or consumers' (Chisnall, 1995: p. 264).

Kotler *et al.* (2006) relate the segmentation process to the develop-ment of marketing as a business practice, specifically the generic shift from a production orientation to a market orientation. They argue that conventional, early approaches to marketing adopted a *mass marketing production* orientation, whereby goods are mass-produced and distrib-uted and then promoted to all buyers. This was followed by *product-variety marketing*, whereby producers recognised that different people have different needs that vary over time and so subtly different prod-ucts can be designed towards satisfying these needs. These approaches evolved into a more *target marketing* orientation which is prevalent today. In a target marketing orientation, organisations identify discrete segments of the market and focus specifically on producing products and services tailored for their needs.

Bases of Market Segmentation

Common methods used to segment tourism and hospitality markets are by demographic, behavioural and psychographic approaches (Table 6.1).

Table 6.1 Bases of Market Segmentation

Demographic	Behavioural	Psychographic
Age	Motivation/purpose of travel	Personality
Gender	Frequency of use/purchase	Identity
Geographic region	Decision-making processes	Lifestyle (activities, interests, opinions)
Stage in the family life cycle	Benefits sought from the experience	
Education	Usage	
Race, ethnicity, culture	Attitudes, perceptions, values, beliefs	
Occupation or social class		
Sexual orientation		

Demographic Segmentation

Age and Life Stage

Age is the most commonly used form of segmenting markets. It is often very easy for tourism and hospitality organisations to classify their customers using age categorisations. Linked to this is the stage in the family life cycle – or party composition. Families with young children have very different requirements from a holiday than young singles, even if they are in the same broad age range. In restaurants, hotels and holiday environments, the extent to which different age groups and life stages can be accommodated together is variable. Sometimes, it is not possible to segment by age or life stage. The transport services are a case in point where different users with different needs have to coexist in one service environment. The package holiday market, however, is heavily age segmented. It is common for tour operators to package their offers based on age and life-stage variables because of the social nature of the experience. People want to share their holiday with others who will share their sense of values. The 'youth' package market as epitomised by '2wenties' or 'Club 18–30' generally want a party atmosphere to their holiday experience which would not sit well in a family resort. Tour operators aim to ensure that the accommodation they book corresponds well to the different age and life-stage segments of their customers. Older couples need peace and relaxation, families need fun and entertainment for the children, as well as family accommodation and it becomes possible to group people together with similar needs into particular hotels in the resort. Thus, even though many different segments intermingle in the space of the resort, their accommodation is geared towards their group needs.

Gender

Men and women have different tastes and values which are reflected in their choices and purchases of products and services. More and more people are beginning to want holiday experiences in 'friends groups'. These may be single-sex group holidays (for activities such as skiing trips, horse riding, walking, shopping or golf), for example. Gender is also useful in relation to buyer roles as in Chapter 4. This makes targeting of marketing messages which are based on gender an effective part of the marketing mix strategy.

Sexual Orientation

Sexual orientation is becoming a key segmentation variable as tourism and hospitality organisations – and destinations – realise that their offers may appeal distinctly to lesbian and gay audiences. Some destinations have a long association for attracting these groups: Sitges, and Mykonos in Europe for example, others prohibit same-sex relationships, such as some Caribbean and many African states. Lesbian and gay markets have been targeted as a lucrative market segment for tourism as the consumers are often high spenders, frequent users and adventurous.

Ethnicity and Cultural Background

Race and ethnicity is an important demographic variable because cultural norms and customs influence the types of food and food preparation, attitudes towards travel and holi-days, and destinations. Types of travel are also perhaps determined by ethnicity and culture as visiting friends and relatives or 'roots/genealogy' trips perhaps account for more travel behaviour.

Socio-economic Variables

These variables include occupation and income, education and social class. Social class distinctions and classifications differ by countries and regions of the world, but in general terms although it is quite easy to measure, the extent to which social class is a good predictor of behaviour is difficult to determine (*cf.* Zamora *et al.*, 2004). People in the same broad social category exhibit very different consumption patterns and tastes, lifestyles and values. Broadly speaking, however, people in lower socio-economic groups participate less in tourism and hospitality consumption than those in the higher categories. Middle class people travel most and are experienced and educated to work out the best way to access travel and hospitality services. One example is the use of youth hostels in the UK. McCabe and Foster (2005) undertook a national user survey of youth hostels in the UK and found that although this charitable organisation has a mission to help promote young, disadvantaged groups to access countryside experiences, the majority of users were middle class professional families. In the UK and in other countries economic prosperity has brought about a change in the number of people in the different socio-economic groups, and Figure 6.3 shows how the UK social class categorisation has recently been expanded to include new types of classification and occupation groups. The relationship between social class and income is also changing and together with life stage has an impact on the ability to participate in tourism and hospitality. For example, a family with one working parent and four young children is unlikely to be able to afford more than one main holiday per year even if the head of household is in a higher managerial professional income group.

Classification title	Description	Examples
1. Higher managerial and professional	This includes employers in large organisations, managerial professions and higher professional occupations. Higher managerial professions are those which involve general planning and supervision of operations on behalf of an employer.	Doctors Lawyers Dentists Professors Professional engineers
2. Lower managerial and professional occupations	This includes lower professional and higher technical occupations, lower managerial occupations and higher supervisory occupations.	School teachers Nurses Journalists Actors Police sergeants
3. Intermediate occupations	These are positions in clerical, sales and intermediate technical occupations that do not involve general planning or supervisory powers.	Airline cabin crew Secretaries Photographers Fireman Auxiliary nurses
4. Small employers and own account workers	Small employers are those, other than higher or lower professionals, who employ others and so assume some degree of control over them. These employers carry out all or most of the entrepreneurial and managerial functions of the enterprise.	Non-professionals with fewer than 25 employees, e.g. self-employed builders, hairdressers or fishermen. Shopkeepers – own shop
	Own account workers are self-employed people engaged in any (non-professional) trade, personal service or semi-routine, routine or other occupations but have no employees other than family workers.	
5. Lower supervisory and technical occupations	Lower supervisory occupations have titles such as 'foreman' and 'supervisor' and have formal and immediate supervision over those in classes 6 and 7.	Train drivers Employed plumbers or electricians Foremen Supervisors
	Lower technical occupations are technical jobs, which have some service elements in their employment contracts (e.g., work autonomy).	
6. Semi-routine occupations	The work involved requires at least some element of employee discretion/decision-making.	Shop assistants Postmen Security guards Call centre workers Care Assistants
7. Routine occupations	Positions with a basic labour contract, in which employees are paid for the specific service. Employee discretion/decision-making less relevant here.	Bus drivers Waitresses Cleaners Car park attendants Refuse collectors
8. Never worked and long-term unemployed	People in this category have never had an occupation or have been unemployed for an extended period and can therefore not be assigned to an NS-SEC category. "Long term" can be defined as any period of time but is generally 1 or 2 years. In the Labour Force survey it is 1 year or longer.	

Figure 6.3 UK social class categories.
Source: Population Trends, ONS: Autumn 2006.

However, social class is useful in terms of targeting marketing spend since social class is quite closely tied to media choices. People in higher socio-economic groups tend to read high quality, broadsheet, print media and are more likely to watch certain types of television channels, programmes and engage in particular types of cultural activity. Whilst it may be difficult to pin social class to behavioural characteristics, social class is useful to identify in relation to the marketing communications strategy selected.

Geographic Region

This segmentation approach is useful for tourism and hospitality marketers. This can be used in terms of pure geographic region, often in the case of airlines and airport authorities targeting whole populations within 2 hours' drive time of the airport, for example. Alternatively a combination of geographic and demographic – geodemography – can be used. For example, the majority of young, single professionals in the UK are based in London and the South East. People in the North East of England tend to have lower household incomes. This makes the targeting process more effective if criteria can be a combination of demographic and region-specific variables. In very broad geographic market terms, tourism consumer markets can be broken down by country and the United Nations World Tourism Organization (UNWTO) provides country by country assessments of market growth and decline based on the tourism satellite accounts (TSAs).

Although demographic segmentation is the most common form used by marketers, Jobber (1995) argues that demographics are of less impact than behavioural or psychographic variables since the ultimate purpose of a segmentation strategy is to identify similarities in behaviour amongst groups which are different than others, which can then feed into the marketing mix. Demographic information is still needed alongside behavioural or psychographic variables (as in the case of Visit Wales in Case study 5) because it is necessary to profile key geographic and demographic characteristics of the segments and to be able to direct marketing communications geographically, so that they can effectively appeal to those segments within specific geographic regions of a country.

However, demographic characteristics are often used as the primary basis from which to then develop behavioural segmentation variables. This is because behavioural segmentation techniques can entail high level of involvement and complex research and therefore can be expensive. Behavioural techniques are very important, however, since people can vary considerably within demographic profiles. Profiling of consumers in this way helps to direct the marketing communications strategy in that clear choices can be made in the types of channels used, the content of messages in terms of the language, colours and images used and also in ensuring that the messages reach the correct audiences.

Illustration

Club 18–30 might build up a descriptive profile of their target market as young men and women aged between 18- and 25-years old, mainly living within urban centres of the UK, with a medium to high proportion still living in the parental home, either in full-time education or employed in junior routine, semi-routine or technical positions such as in call centres, retailing, industry, trades or services. These people are likely to have quite high disposable incomes living in rented accommodation or in the parental home with few long-term financial commitments. They will be mainly heterosexual, gregarious and extrovert, enjoy nightlife, entertainment and to be influenced by fashion, the media and celebrity. They will watch youth-oriented television programmes, read tabloid newspapers and weekly magazines, interested in listening to radio and music, watching and participating in sports and activities. They will be medium to heavy users of the Internet, and heavy users of mobile phone services. They are likely to have a positive attitude towards new mobile phone products and interactive services, and sign up to youth-oriented Internet media sites and programming, be interested in computer gaming and computer-based social forums. They will also enjoy active nightlife and going out and are likely to be moderate to heavy consumers of alcohol and tobacco products. They will be fashion conscious and will take advice from immediate reference groups, peers, mainly friends, in their choice of holidays. Although they are frequent users of nightclubs and bars and will travel to enjoy these leisure pastimes at home, they are likely to be occasional users of Club 18–30 holidays. They will enjoy the fun, liberal and social orientation of the Club 18–30 experience and will be looking to make new friends and perhaps sexual partners. The cycle of activity is likely to be quite short, perhaps three or four purchases before they move on in their preferences for holiday types and service providers.

As mentioned in Chapter 2, the socio-economic and demographic composition of societies is not static, but constantly evolving at a slow pace. Some segmentation variables can change at a more rapid rate, however, and certainly in conjunction with developments in the spread and use of information communication technologies (ICTs), which was also outlined in more detail in Chapter 2, information about and attitudes towards new destinations or products and services in the tourism and hospitality sector can rapidly disperse throughout a group of the society. New segmentation opportunities then constantly present themselves. However, in practice, most organisations simply do not have the resources to continually monitor or identify new segmentation opportunities or to review their currently served segments to identify any structural shifts away from the targeted group(s).

Behavioural Segmentation

Benefits Sought from the Experience

In Chapter 4 motivations for consuming tourism services were discussed in detail. In the context of segmentation approaches, motivations can be linked to benefits sought from the consumption experience. Benefits segmentation looks at the reasons why people buy in the market and is fundamental to tourism and hospitality because of the need to know what people value from their experiences in what is a discretionary spending category. Holiday makers value 'total relaxation' and 'authentic experiences' from their holidays. Business travellers value seamless service, speed of service processes, access to wireless technology and so on. If the organisation can identify the fundamental benefits that certain users value then this can provide them with the basis to reorient their products to meet these value requirements.

Defining Service Benefits

Kotler identifies that products can be categorised into the following three levels which can be used as an analytical tool to define and assess differences between competing products in the same product category group.

1. *Product benefits*: They are perceptions of how the consumption experience meets consumers' needs and values, including concepts of customer satisfaction and contributions to positive self-image through consumption. This might equate to the 'core' product concept. At the heart of the holiday experience is a set of values which are met through the service encounter. These may be defined in any number of different ways: 'ultimate luxury', 'paradise', 'total pampering', and 'cheapest flights'.

2. *Product attributes*: This refers to the tangible features of the service including elements of the 'servicescape', the physical evidence and also including specifications, design, branding and/or 'packaging'. The tourism and hospitality product attributes can be equated to the tangible features which contribute to the 'production' of the benefits. Comfy pillows and mattresses, branded bathroom products, flat-screen televisions and CD players with complementary CDs in hotel bedrooms can all be classified as tangible attributes which together can meet benefits sought by consumers for a relaxing nights' rest.

3. *Marketing support services*: This refers to the additional elements such as after-sales service, guarantees, complaints handling, rights and redress, customer loyalty schemes and relationship marketing and management strategies. These can also contribute a great deal to the perception of benefits sought. The degree to which consumers want to associate with brands through affiliation to a frequent flyer programme or preferred guest scheme can meet some status needs.

For many tourism and hospitality services the delivery of the service forms a vital function of differentiation and is critically linked to benefits sought and the service attributes (tangible features). Take for example transport service providers such as airline, ferry or train companies. One aspect of the service delivery might include the timing of the services, punctuality. This can be an important benefit for business and leisure users and a company's record on punctuality of departure and arrival of its services may be used to position a product through marketing communications depending on whether the company thinks this aspect of their service provides competitive advantage. Similarly the level of service quality, staff to customer ratios, training, orientation to customisation in the service is often used as a competitive positioning strategy in the context of five-star luxury hotels as part of the benefits sought by consumers in terms of prestige or status conferment or as aspects of the quality of the service delivery as an attribute of the core product.

Attitudes, Perceptions, Values, Beliefs

Attitudes, perceptions, values and beliefs are strongly linked to behaviour (Jobber, 1995). These types of segmentation analyses contribute to an understanding of how particular groups view services in the marketplace. A good example of this is the market for backpacker travel experiences. The backpacker market can be segmented in terms of their perceptions and beliefs about the world around them including attitudes to politics, the organisation of society and attitudes towards other cultures.

Decision-making Processes

Decision-making factors were discussed in Chapter 3, but in the context of segmentation strategies, purchase behaviour is another method of categorising markets. Issues covered in terms of decision-making behaviour are in relation to brand loyalty, risk, adoption of new innovations as well as choice criteria and selection variables and so on. Specific communications can be tailored to groups targeting them on the basis of these characteristics.

Usage Patterns/Frequency of Use

Purchase occasions and usage are also critical aspects of segmentation variables for tourism and hospitality services. Special occasion users have different values to frequent, heavy users of hotel and/or restaurant services. It is unlikely that tourism services can be categorised into heavy users in the same ways although some business travellers are very heavy users of tourism services. It is likely that in the case of hotels pre-defined segment categorisations are likely to be employed depending on the type of use and the type of consumer (e.g. leisure, business, convention, special occasion, overnight, short break, long term, restaurant, banquet, events and meetings and bar).

What is clear is that hotels are very good at developing marketing communications which are targeted very clearly according to usage groups. Some hotel chains are able to use ICTs to profile their customers in terms of personal preferences such as pillow type, types of newspapers ordered, special dietary requirements and room preferences.

Psychographic Segmentation

Personality and Identity

These types of approaches are useful for tourism and hospitality services because of the inherent link between consumption of these discretionary services as an expression of self-identity or as an expression of individualism or other aspect of personality. Marketing communications based on status and on personality characteristics is prevalent in many tourism and hotel chain marketing strategies. Consumers' participation in certain leisure activities becomes an expression of their identity and can be transferred to their travel behaviour. Travel in itself becomes an expression about who we are and how we would like to be seen by other people. This is particularly useful in relation to niche market behaviours in travel, such as adventure holidays and sports and activity holidays. But it can also relate to brands, particularly where brands take on a public personality. An example of this is branded restaurants and hotels. The name Ritz in the context of hotels is synonymous with the rich and famous. Consumption of the Ritz as your hotel of choice says something about your personality.

Lifestyle

Lifestyle segmentation is a common method of segmentation of tourism and hospitality markets according to activities, interests and opinions. The problem is that they tend to be quite general, and marketers are continually coming up with new types of descriptors for lifestyle segments as they undertake sustained market research with consumer groups. However, lifestyle segmentation strategies can contribute a great deal to the development of the marketing mix as it can add depth to the profile of segments which, in turn, can be used as the basis for the creation of detailed and appropriate marketing communications (see Case study 6 on South Africa's segmentation of the UK consumer market).

This type of approach generally tries to link consumer choices, habits and pastimes to generate lifestyle types. In the previous illustration profiling, the Club 18–30 user, many details on the interests and activities were also highlighted. Additionally, political opinions could be mentioned, attitudes towards change, work–life balance are all aspects of lifestyle. The extent to which people are conservative, forward thinking, interested in green issues, trendsetters, concerned for social justice, pleasure-seeking, interested in experiencing culture, listening to music, interested in films, tolerant can all be considered. Bigne and Andreu (2004) used emotional state to segment tourists at leisure attractions. They found that those experiencing greater pleasure and arousal showed an increased level of satisfaction as well as more favourable behavioural intentions, meaning loyalty and willingness to pay more.

Target Marketing

Once an organisation has identified a range of possible segments within the market, it begins the targeting process. As highlighted in the modified Figure 6.1, this consists of developing measures of the attractiveness of the segments and selection of the segments to target. This process is a re-evaluation of the segments and the profiles matched against the core competencies and resources (what the organisation actually offers from the service or the experience) to identify which are the most attractive segments to target.

Criteria for Assessing Segments

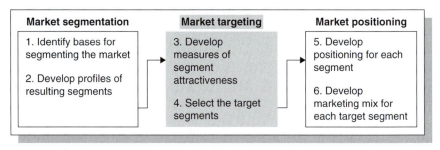

Market segmentation	Market targeting	Market positioning
1. Identify bases for segmenting the market 2. Develop profiles of resulting segments	3. Develop measures of segment attractiveness 4. Select the target segments	5. Develop positioning for each segment 6. Develop marketing mix for each target segment

In developing the measures of attractiveness of each segment it is useful to deploy criteria against which the organisation can assess the contribution that each segment of the market could potentially deliver. These criteria can be defined as a series of questions to ask of the segment

- Is it attainable?

This means that the segment profile really exists outside of the market research agency or marketing department responsible for identifying it. To be attainable, the segment must be a discrete group and the people in the segment must recognise the characteristics, likely to be a mixture of both demographic and behavioural and feel as though the segment profile actually describes them and they identifiably belong to such a characterisation.

- Is it measurable?

This means it is possible to collect data about them using conventional market research methodologies and datasets. This is a question relating to the ability to conduct research to assess the viability of the segment (see next question) and also that it is possible to reach the group with marketing messages.

- Is it large enough?

This is not only a standard question relating to the size of the proposed segment, but also a possible indicator of the longevity and viability of the segment and allows the organisation to consider the product life cycle in relation to the segment.

- Is it defendable?

This is a question of the extent to which the segment is an appropriate target group for the organisation at this particular moment in time (considering that the organisation might have produced a service/product for which the market is yet to be ready and/or for which the segment has yet to realise the profile). The question helps the organisation to check the STP process against the strategic goals and aims.

- Is it sustainable?

Related to a previous question on size of the segment, this question focuses on the potential of the segment to yield profits over a specific period of time. This can be either the long-term viability of the segment or the short-term where the return on investment (ROI) is sizeable.

Targeting Criteria

Middleton and Clarke (2001) suggest five main criteria that must be applied to any segment if it is to be usable or actionable in marketing:

1. Selected segments must be distinctly identifiable by criteria such as purpose of visit, income, location of residence or motivation. In other words, there must be clear boundaries between the segments.
2. The criteria used to distinguish between segments must be measurable via marketing research data. If the segment cannot be measured, it cannot be targeted.
3. The projected revenue exceeds the full cost of designing the marketing mix to achieve it by margins that meet the organisation's financial objectives.
4. The chosen segments reflect the inseparability of production and consumption for tourism and hospitality services, and measures are put in place to recognise or manage the potential for conflict of interest and potential for complaint.
5. In this context, assessing the extent to which segments contribute either positively or negatively to the environmental mission of the organisation or destination.

Self-selection

From the consumers' point of view, the segmentation process cannot hide the fact that we all see ourselves as individuals with our own idiosyncrasies and so we will not necessarily affiliate ourselves to the types of segmentation exercises outlined earlier. However, in some cases, individuals do wish to ascribe to groups, particularly where they see a clear interest in their own interests or in cases where group membership is important to the activity. For example, belonging to a club or society like a football-supporters club is useful for obtaining discount tickets to matches, and if the club organises overseas match tours then it is probably preferable for supporters to book travel, accommodation, transfers and match tickets in one package through the club as opposed to making an individual and independent booking.

A recent television advertisement in the UK for the online travel services comparison service http://www.travelsupermarket.com described what the service actually does, i.e., compares the prices of thousands of companies' services at the click of the mouse. The benefit to the consumers is that they can use the service to specify their personal requirements for a holiday package or separate flight and hotel, and the website will compare products. The service offered is akin to the traditional travel agency intermediary service, yet undertaken through a website at a time and place of the customer's choosing. The core message is one about the value to the consumer

> *Choosing this service means that you will get the widest choice of package holidays available on the market.*

The distribution channel is important to consumers, the ease with which they can access the service from home or office computer, and price or value are not emphasised in the message. We can assume that consumers may search for package holidays based on low price but there may be a range of other values and needs required from a very wide target market comprising a great many different segments. The core message of travelsupermarket's advertisement is about making life easier for all people, as using this one site helps to cut through the clutter of holiday information on the web. This represents an undifferentiated segment strategy reaching the widest possible audience and hence requires a mainstream television campaign.

Market Positioning

The product positioning process consists of making any fine adjustments to the service offering in the light of research conducted in the marketing planning process and then the creation of an 'image' of the service which meets the target market values. This position can be made up of the core competencies or the specific value requirements of the target group. For each target segment, adjustments are made in the marketing mix.

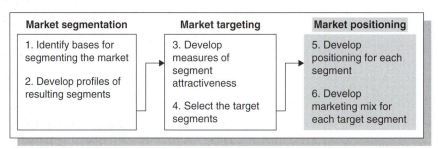

Market segmentation	Market targeting	Market positioning
1. Identify bases for segmenting the market 2. Develop profiles of resulting segments	3. Develop measures of segment attractiveness 4. Select the target segments	5. Develop positioning for each segment 6. Develop marketing mix for each target segment

Market positioning in this sense relates to the place the service occupies in the minds of the consumers. Because consumers are continually referring back to product evaluations when they come into contact with new messages about products and services, they classify them according to what they already know about these and related, competitor, products. The marketing communications strategy is based upon these positioning statements about the image of the service in relation to target market values and needs. It is in this way that products are positioned both by the organisation and by consumers when they come into contact with the marketing messages of the organisation. The most important thing is that the position articulated by the company through its internal and external communications strategies corresponds with the position the brand, product or service occupies in the minds of the recipient audiences of those messages.

In product marketing, goods are often positioned in terms of the technical features and quality of the materials, packages, design and so on. Tourism and hospitality service offerings differ in this respect from many other forms of product or service offering. This is largely due to the importance played of the additional services marketing mix elements in the positioning process.

In the context of tourism destination marketing organisations (DMO), however, positioning can be based on the physical qualities or attributes of the destination which includes consideration of all the touristic resource types:

- culture and society (including food and drink, pastimes and dress, tradition, work, leisure and social organisation, but importantly also attitude towards strangers and hospitableness of the society)
- heritage (including built and natural heritage, archaeological or industrial, cultural)
- wildlife (including marine, birdlife, farming as well as flora and fauna)
- climate (including the lack of rain, abundance of sunshine, correct balance and [lack of] extremes, heat, cold etc.)
- landscape and physical attributes (including mountains and lakes, beaches and seaside, countryside and nature, cityscapes and architecture)

This is generally because in each destination the DMO must communicate the diversity of attractions to appeal to a wider set of market segments (depending on the size, scale and nature of the DMO area) and must communicate something of the core attributes or benefits of the whole region.

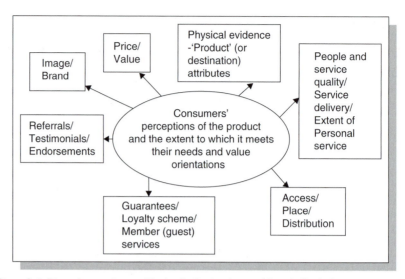

Figure 6.4 Bases for service positioning in the tourism and hospitality industry.

In reality, service providers can attempt to position their products and/or service offerings according to any aspects of the services marketing mix (see Chapter 7). However, there is little point in trying to position the product according to any of these aspects of the service unless it is valued by the target customers.

In Figure 6.4, the extended services marketing mix is linked to bases on which organisations can create a differentiated position for their products/service offerings. The image/brand can include destination image as well as the image of the organisation or product. The price/value dimension relates to the value of the product to the consumer relative to the prices and values of other similar products, services and destinations. Referrals, testimonials and endorsements relate to the promotion aspect of the market mix. If a destination is visited by film, television or music personalities, the destination then becomes the focus of media coverage which is not in the control of the organisation and yet can add much value to the image and/or promotional development of the place. Similarly, peer groups, family and friends routinely pass on messages about their consumption of hospitality organisations like restaurants, bars and hotels and this 'objective' source of information about the place or the service can be a useful basis on which a destination or company positions itself. Physical evidence or the destination resources or the design and specification of the hotel, restaurant or nightclub are commonly used to position tourism and hospitality services and places, as are the people (service quality and delivery) aspects. Finally, membership services, loyalty schemes, service guarantees as well as distribution channels and access can be used to differentiate a product from competitors.

Importance of Market Segmentation

The aim of segmentation is clearly to maximise the return on the organisation's investment in marketing and to ensure that tourism and hospitality services meet selected customers' needs, values and expectations. But as mentioned previously, the STP process can lead to a fundamental repositioning of the products and services and ultimately organisational strategy in some cases. Significantly, market segmentation works on the basis that only in very exceptional circumstances does marketing communications need to try to reach the whole of the market. Since advertising space is expensive and since there is a proliferation of media forms and channels and a great deal of fragmentation of audiences across these, the financial risks associated with market segmentation strategies are very high.

Today's advanced consumer market economies are characterised by

- pervasive mediation within the realms of everyday life
- product placement and sponsorship of television and film programming
- celebrity endorsements
- blurring of distinctions between marketing communications and other information (e.g. advertorials).

Organisations need to find out

- how effective their marketing communications are
- how people respond
- which media channels were most effective
- what is the ROI for marketing spend.

Consumers actively filter out unnecessary information and seem to make rapid judgements as to the relevance of messages to them personally. This makes segmentation important for successful product positioning and to ensure that the desired responses to marketing mix (including communications) strategies are elicited.

Segmentation Options

There are a number of different approaches to segmentation. The ones chosen will affect the approach taken to the organisation's marketing communications strategy as follows:

- Single segmentation (concentrated marketing)

Here a single basis of segmentation is chosen which allows the organisation to concentrate its marketing, sales and promotion activity in particular, focused ways. One example might be the Saga group of products, including Saga Holidays, which uses a single point of segmentation, the over 50's age group market, as the focus of the marketing mix and communications strategy. This market segment is growing and the 1950s market for tourism is a mature and high value market. Another smaller and more emerging market segment example might be the single-traveller market. In the UK, specialist tour operators have emerged in the recent years which have recognised the importance of the single-unattached traveller market. Examples include Solo's Holidays (http://www.solosholidays.co.uk/) and Friendship Travel (http://www.friendshiptravel.com/). These organisations offer specially designed marketing mixes specifically aimed at the singles market. In the UK, single occupancy households have been the fastest rising form of new living arrangements in the past few years and demand has partially fuelled the housing boom. High divorce rates, career aspirations amongst women and more people opting out of parenthood are some of the reasons for this growth and there are still many barriers for people in a range of different groups to travelling on their own. Mintel produced a report in 2001 entitled 'Singles on Holiday – UK' outlining the potential for this market segment.

- Selective segmentation (differentiated marketing)

In the case of selective segmentation, the organisation has different points of segmentation and different products on offer, but a clearly differentiated marketing strategy. An example here might include Page and Moy which offers a range of different products to different segment groups, Cruise products, last-minute package holidays and adventure trekking products to name just three, which can clearly be targeted at separate market segments. However, the marketing messages also emphasise a number of points of similarity such as an enduring attention to quality service whatever the type of travel product chosen, and their pedigree as a quality tour operator, so that there is clearly a focal brand and common points to differentiate the organisation from competitors (http://www.valuetour.co.uk/).

- Exclusive segmentation (undifferentiated marketing)

In an undifferentiated marketing approach to exclusive segmentation (all the people in the market for a type of product are potential customers) the same marketing communications are deployed very widely across a number of different media channels to target the widest possible group of travellers. One example here is First Choice, the second largest package holiday provider in the UK, which although, like Page and Moy, offers a range of different travel products, the marketing mix and communications strategy employed is universal (http://www.firstchoice.co.uk/).

Issues in the Segmentation Process

In an ideal world, particularly from the marketing perspective, each customer is unique and special and should receive personal service or a unique, authentic experience. In some cases this ideal may be realisable, particularly in the regions of the world where labour costs are low and there is a highly skilled labour market. But in most tourism and hospitality organisational settings, the focus is on grouping segments of the market and creating a level of service and differentiated products for the group level, which is mainly driven by operational constraints.

Of course no one fixed rule can be applied to all situations and all forms of market segmentation approaches exist within this industry. Mass segmentation approaches are used to target many people within markets based on a standardised product/service offering. Hotels and restaurants and the physical attributes of tourism destinations are to a large extent 'fixed' stock, in that there is a limit to the extent they can be changed and adapted to suit different markets and segments. It is common to see that destinations as well as restaurants, airline operators, hotel chains and visitor attractions have a number of different market segments to which they may communicate directly, with distinct messages to each. Once a strategic orientation has been developed and implemented within an organisation, for example in relation to competitive strategy, such as cost leadership, this in some way determines the type of market segmentation strategy which needs to be adopted. Low cost airlines business model depends on high volume of sales, and thus the ability to appeal to a very large market with broadly similar values and so mass segmentation is most appropriate.

Similarly, it is difficult for a destination to change its image from say a mass, package destination appealing to a holiday market to a niche market focus. The strategic orientation of the DMO is to represent the broader industry in which it is contained in the region or resort and often DMOs promote the region in a mass segmentation approach. Of course, the industry encompasses enormous variety of organisations, as previously outlined, and there are increasingly sophisticated techniques used from segmenting and targeting markets as we will see in following chapters so it is possible for organisations to adapt their approach to markets and to use a variety of segmentation strategies at different stages of the life cycle or in response to changes in the market. For example, if a low cost airline opens up a new route from a major source market to a destination which had previously relied exclusively on the packaged holiday market, then this will open up new opportunities to add different segments to target.

The key decisions to be made in terms of the segmentation strategy adopted centre on the ability of the organisation to attract a number of different segments and its capacity to absorb different groups in one physical space. This may be more or less of a problem in the case of DMOs, depending on the size and scale of the resort and the types of activities undertaken therein. A common cause of conflict between different user groups is in the case of national parks or countryside/nature reserves. Although parks may be very large in geographical area, the actual touristic use can be concentrated in relatively small visitor areas. In some national parks the presence of other user groups can impact upon people's enjoyment and visitor experience, but this is less easily managed by the marketing and organisational departments of the national park authorities. In other types of organisation the physical space may be much smaller, but the management of different users can be so carefully planned that different user groups are not aware of each other. This may be the case in hotels and/or event venues.

However, if the organisation focuses too narrowly on only one key segment, there are a different set of considerations. The organisation might be so focused on the needs of one core segment that it knows and understands much more about the users profile than any competing organisation, yet such a focus might mean that they are less aware of structural changes affecting the segment, or more general changes in demand for the services and products. The most important solution to such issues is to compromise to make sure that the organisation has enough segments that it is not over-reliant on one core group, but not too many that it cannot reconcile the needs of the different segments and fails to accommodate diverse groups' separate needs and consequently fails to deliver complete satisfaction.

Summary

This chapter has outlined the key principles underpinning the STP process. It has defined the bases for segmenting the market and shown how segmentation is linked to the marketing communications strategy through the services marketing mix for tourism and hospitality. It argued that although demographic segmentation variables appear as the predominant methods in tourism and hospitality, the psychographic and behavioural approaches were most suited as segmentation methods for these services because of the relatively high involvement in decision-making and the discretionary nature of the services. The chapter went on to evaluate the different methods of segmentation

linked to consumers' characteristics. The STP process was linked to the marketing planning and effective targeted marketing communications strategy. Segmentation, targeting and positioning was identified as a key step towards developing an effective marketing communications strategy. Multivariate approaches to profiling consumers were explained and linked to the development of market positioning and communications. The chapter concluded with a discussion on issues in market segmentation.

Discussion Questions

1. Describe the main steps in the STP process.
2. How does the segmentation process relate to other tasks in the marketing planning and strategy development process for tourism and hospitality?
3. Why is it important to segment the market for tourism and hospitality services?
4. Who positions tourism and hospitality products, services and destinations? Why does this impact upon the marketing communications strategies chosen?

Case Study 6: Segmenting the UK Long-haul Market to South Africa – Profiling 'Positive Convertibles'

South Africa Tourism (SAT) is the tourism marketing organisation of South Africa.

This case study is taken from South Africa Tourism's Marketing South Africa in the UK. First Edition 2006. www.southafrica.net/research and www.southafrica.net/trade.

SAT identified that the UK long-haul outbound market is one of the largest and most lucrative tourism markets in the world. South Africa currently captures 4% of the UK long-haul outbound market (*Source*: UK Travel Trends, National Statistics, 2004; Monitor Group Analysis) but has seen a significant increase in UK tourists over the past decade to over 450,000 in 2004. In terms of importance to SAT, the UK market is the largest and most valuable international market with almost double the numbers of Germany, which is the second largest market. SAT undertook extensive market research on buying behaviour, channel structure of the tour operations sector in the UK and also on the segmentation analysis which underpinned its approach to the UK market.

Segmentation

Defining the Relevant Market

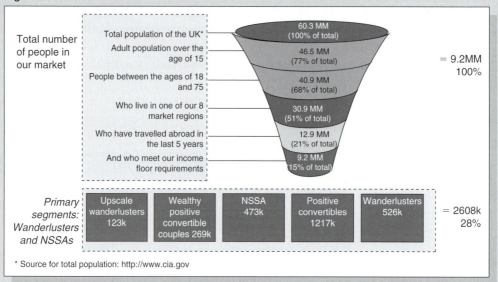

* Source for total population: http://www.cia.gov

Source: Marketing South Africa in the UK, First Edition 2006.

SAT identified that 2.6 million UK residents met their target segment criteria (representing 28% of the 9.2 million people in the UK who are aged between 18 and 75, live in one of the eight market regions in the UK, have travelled abroad in the past 5 years and who meet the income requirements for a visit to South Africa).

Within this 2.6 million group, SAT was able to identify five key market clusters:

Upscale Wanderlusters = 123,000
Wealthy positive convertible couple = 269,000
NSSA = 473,000
Positive convertibles = 1,217,000
Wanderlusters = 526,000

This case study focuses on the 'positive convertibles' since these are the largest segment in terms of numbers of people and potential conversion rate. It must be noted that SAT's full report provides an analysis of all five clusters and that the focus on 'positive convertibles' in this case study does not reflect SAT's own priorities.

Positive Convertibles: Segment Overview

Segment Size	
Percentage of market	13.3
Number of People	1216.5k
Per person travel	
Spend per annum	£2330

Conversion Challenge

Awareness	72%
Positivity towards South Africa	56%
Interest in going in next 2 years	48%
Plans to go in next 18 months	17%

Demographics

General Characteristics

• Average age	39.9
• Married/living with partner	48%
• Children <18 at home	0%
• Top region(s)	
– South east	27%
– London	18%
– Scotland	16%

Social Characteristics

• House hold Income p.a. ('000s £)	
– <50	70%
– >50	19%
• Higher education	55%
• Working full time	90%

Information Sources

Top Five Sources (General)

• Word of mouth	48%
• Brochures	34%
• Television travel shows	18%
• Internet	18%
• Travel agents	17%

Purchasing Behaviour Purchase Channels (Total Accommodation)

• Chain travel agents	27%
• Independent travel agents	26%
• Direct	14%
• Internet travel agents	8%

Reasons for TA Usage

• Provide destination information	70%
• Offer best deals	20%

Past/Future Long-haul Travel Frequency of Vacations
- Average number of vacations 1.72

Future (Next 18 Months) Score of 1–7
- USA 4.4
- Caribbean 3.4
- Australia 3.4
- Mexico 2.9
- Thailand 2.9

Trip Reason and Activities

Trip Reason (Top 5)
- Get away 65%
- Relax 59%
- Get some sun 54%
- Spend time with partner 32%
- See specific place 31%

Main Activities in South Africa (Top 5)
- See mountains 84%
- View wildlife 84%
- Admire natural beauty 78%
- Meet South Africans 73%
- Relax on beach 72%

Importance of Associations

Average of Score of 1–7
- Natural wildlife experience 6.29
- Authentic travel experience 5.38
- All year round travel 5.17
- Rest and relaxation 5.04
- Historical and cultural experience 4.89
- Value for money 4.75
- Welcoming people 4.51
- Easy to get around 4.22
- Safe and secure environment 2.78
- Too 'cheap' to be acceptable 2.76

Perceptions of South Africa

Positive (Average of Score of 1–5)
- Good weather 4.5
- All year-round destination 4.2
- Plentiful wildlife 4.1
- Luxury safaris 4.0
- Welcoming to tourists 3.6

Negative
- Crime   4.1
- AIDS   4.1
- Politically unstable   3.7
- Apartheid   3.6
- Expensive to fly to   3.0
- Not ideal for family holiday   2.9

Positive Convertibles 'Consumer Portrait' Key Themes: Purchase and Usage Environment

Demographics
- Between 30- and 49-year-olds, with an average age of 40.
- No kids under 18 living at home.
- Half are married, but more likely than other segments to be single (42%).
- Almost all work full time, and there are many business travellers.
- 55% have a university education.
- Not as likely as others to live in urban areas.

Past Travel Profile
- Have only travelled short haul in the past 5 years.
- Generally take one holiday per year, and it is likely to be in the summer or autumn.
- Very likely to be influenced by brochures, travel television shows and teletext.
- Spain, France, Cyprus, Greece and Italy are the most popular holiday destinations.

Interest
- Not as interested in visiting someplace new on holiday and not concerned about going to a place where friends/relatives have not been.
- Not as likely as others to have a particular type of holiday in mind when planning.

Awareness
- Not as worldly as other segments.
- More likely than others to hear negative things from expatriates in the UK.

Desired Experience
Travel Desires
- Most likely to take holidays to get away and get some sun; not likely for the purpose of spending time with a spouse.
- Nice and sunny weather and good value for money are the two most important factors when choosing a holiday destination.
- On past trips, dislike packages and organised tours – almost all want to organise their own arrangements.

Potential Travel to South Africa

- If travelling to South Africa, interested in visiting the mountains and seeing wildlife; not as interested in special interests, adventure sports or battlefields.
- For a trip to South Africa, would want everything organised for them – receptive to self-drive trips and organised tours.
- Not likely to want to visit South Africa in complete luxury.

Purchase and Usage Behaviour

Behaviour Profile

- Quick decision-makers: many likely to make a reservation and take the trip all within a week of the origination of thinking about it.
  - Most wait 1–2 months after making the reservation before taking the trip.
- When gathering information, likely to use Internet search engines and Internet travel agents.
  - Not as likely as others to use brochures, travel agents, travel operators or travel magazines.
- Most holidays last either 1 or 2 weeks.
- Very likely to travel with a friend or groups of friends; also likely to travel alone.
  - Not likely to travel with a spouse or significant other.

Spend

- 70% spent under £750 for their last holiday.

Channel

- More likely than others to book flights with Internet travel agents and teletext.
- Average use of independent and chain travel agents for booking purposes.

Beliefs and Associations

Channel

- Unlikely to feel travel agents are very useful.
  - Do not believe best deals are found with travel agents.
  - Not likely to have a relationship with a travel agent.
- As do not use travel agents, generally also less likely to use brochures found in travel agencies.
  - May use brochures to get ideas about destinations, but unlikely to book packages.

South Africa

- Perceptions of South Africa
  - Likely to believe South Africa is a year-round destination and has good weather.
  - Similar to other segments, most of the negative associations are with AIDS and crime.
  - Greatest concerns about travelling to South Africa are the ease of getting around, safety, and perceived expense.
- Barriers to visiting South Africa include a priority for other destinations as well as not having enough time to see enough of the country.

Competitors

- Most positive opinion of Australia, but same level of positivity to South Africa as to Thailand and Kenya.
- Versus South Africa
  - Australia is safer, recommended by others, and more likely to have great weather/beaches and to be relaxing.
  - Thailand is recommended by others and has an interesting culture, but South Africa is easier to get to and has a great deal of sunshine.
  - Kenya is very similar to South Africa, but has better safaris. South Africa has great weather/beaches.

Positive Convertibles Consumer Portrait Story

Not a Long-haul Traveller

Like all good Brits, 40-year-old Nigel loves his holidays. In the past 5 years, he has managed to go on holiday each year. He has only travelled to European destinations though. Travelling someplace far away sounds like something he would really like to do, but if he goes, he wants to make sure he has enough time to really enjoy it. He probably should go since he does not have kids, but with work, it is hard to find the time to do that sort of thing. He is happy going to Spain or France though – they are popular, easy to get to and his friends and relatives go there too. There is just always so much information about them too – in brochures, on travel television shows and on teletext.

Looking for Sun on His Summer Holiday, but Not a Package Holiday

Nigel's top priorities for a holiday are to get away and get some sun. Just this week, he bought a ticket on Ryan Air to the south of France. Since he has been many times before, he feels like it is OK to book last minute. He saw a late summer deal on the Internet for £29 seats each way. What good value for money! He told his mates about it too, and they plan on travelling together this weekend. He probably could have gotten a package holiday to France – after all, that is what most people do. Nigel has taken package holidays before, but has not had great experiences. Besides, he really does not like the high street travel agents – it just seems easier to do it himself. Since he has been to France many times before, he feels like he knows what he is doing. As he drives into work each day from the suburbs, he thinks about how great it will be to get away from the awful British weather for a week and go to a sunny destination. There is a lot on the Internet about accommodation in Toulouse, so he is trying to find a way to book it soon. If nothing works out, then he'll probably just find something when he gets there. He enjoys organising his holidays, and it feels really good to have some control over the process. If he didn't know the destination very well though, he might consider a package. It would probably be good to have everything arranged if he were going to travel long-haul, for example.

South Africa Sounds Great, but So Many Places to See, So Little Time!

There are lots of places he'd like to visit on holiday and has specifically thought about South Africa. What a different experience that would be compared to his usual holiday! He knows some people at work who have been there on holiday, and they say great things. He once knew a guy from South Africa who talked a lot about the crime though. Overall, it sounds like a pretty cool place. It would be fun to go on a safari or see the mountains. If he were to travel there though, he'd want to have enough time to see it all. Nigel would also need some more time to plan, compared to the recent France holiday. Since he hasn't been before, he could also probably use some help with the arrangements. He wouldn't want to pay too much – no more than £900 for a week. It is not like he has to travel in complete luxury, but it would definitely be a splurge from his usual summer holiday. And, maybe his friends would want to go too…?

Source: Marketing South Africa in the UK, First edition 2006.

Learning Activity

Work in groups to design a poster or make a television commercial (30 seconds) using digital video recorder or radio commercial (30 seconds) using digital audio recording equipment. The focus of your communication should be a marketing campaign for SAT (the national tourism organisation, not a tour operator) based on the segmentation profile for 'positive convertibles' outlined earlier.

Think about the types of images (pictures) and copy (narrative) you would use. Assess how useful the consumer profile is to your decision-making?

Identify possible channels for your poster (printed media, billboard posters, etc.) or radio or television channels you would use to target the segment. In addition, think about the main geographic catchments of this segment, which geographic regions do you think are most valuable to target your media campaign?

Think about the types of ways in which your message connects to the values and beliefs of positive convertibles. Your message should be realistic, believable and credible.

References and Further Reading

Bieger, T. and Lässer, C. (2002). Market segmentation by motivation: The case of Switzerland. *Journal of Travel Research*. 41(1): 68–76.

Bigne, J.E. and Andreu, L. (2004). Emotions in segmentation: An empirical study. *Annals of Tourism Research*. 31(3): 682–696.

Chisnall, P.M. (1995). *Consumer Behavior*. 1st edn (1975). Berks: McGraw-Hill.

Chisnall, P. (2004). *Marketing Research*. 7th edn. New York: McGraw-Hill.

Dolnicar, S. (2004). Beyond commonsense segmentation: A systematics of segmentation approaches in tourism. *Journal of Travel Research*. 42: 244–250.

Doole, I. and Lowe, R. (2001). International Marketing Strategy, London: Thomson Learning Ltd, p. 295.

Hsu, C.H.C. and Lee, E.-J. (2002). Segmentation of senior motorcoach travelers. *Journal of Travel Research*. 40(4): 364–374.

Jobber, D. (1995). *Principles and Practice of Marketing*. Maidenhead, UK: McGraw-Hill Book Company.

Kotler, P., Bowen, J.T. and Makens, J.C. (2006). *Marketing for Hospitality and Tourism*. 4th edn. Upper Saddle River, NJ: Pearson International.

Klemm, M.S. (2002). Tourism and ethnic minorities in Bradford: The invisible segment. *Journal of Travel Research*. 41(1): 85–91.

Middleton, V. and Clarke, J. (2001). *Marketing in Travel and Tourism*. 3rd edn. Oxford: Butterworth Heinemann.

McCabe, S. and Foster, C. (2005). *YHA User Survey*. Unpublished report for the Youth Hostel's Association (England and Wales).

Mintel (2001). *Singles on Holiday – UK*.

Sung, H. (2004). Classification of adventure travelers: Behavior, decision making, and target markets. *Journal of Travel Research*. 42: 343–356.

Zamora, J., Valenzuela, F. and Vasquez-Parraga, A.Z. (2004). Influence of household origin and social class on choice of rural vacation destinations. *Journal of Travel Research*. 42: 421–425.

Key Resources and Links

http://www.solosholidays.co.uk/
http://www.friendshiptravel.com/
http://www.valuetour.co.uk/
http://www.firstchoice.co.uk/

Marketing Communications Planning

At the end of this chapter, you will be able to

- Describe and apply the links between marketing communications planning and set communications objectives.

- Relate the processes of product development and branding to the communications strategic process for tourism and hospitality.

- Describe the application of the marketing communications strategy in differentiating tourism and hospitality products and services.

- Understand communications campaign planning.

- Apply evaluation techniques for marketing communications strategies.

Introduction

In this chapter, the focus is on the links between decisions regarding marketing communications planning and how these translate into choices for the marketing communications mix. Marketing planning decision-making is taken in the context of product policy decisions for target market segments. As such, organisations must decide their branding strategy, product portfolio, pricing and commitment to quality in relation to specific target markets identified through the segmentation, targeting and positioning (STP) process in Chapter 6. This chapter describes the strategic decisions which direct promotion and communications decisions on product positioning and branding, as a context for the discussion of how these feed into the marketing communications plan. The steps in marketing communications planning are outlined, including objectives and goals for the campaign, the marketing communications mix decisions and types of media strategy decisions. This planning process is outlined in Figure 7.1. This chapter discusses the different aspects of the communications plan, including implementation and evaluation. This process links with the marketing

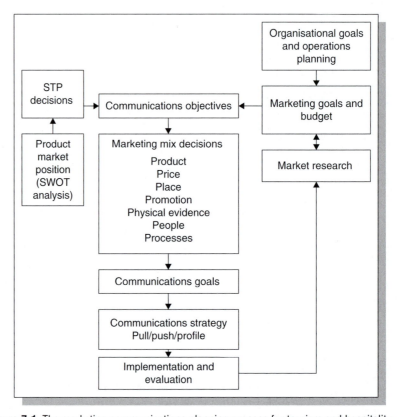

Figure 7.1 The marketing communications planning process for tourism and hospitality.

planning process outlined in Figure 3.3 on page 56, and also with the relationships between the STP process and marketing planning outlined in Figure 6.2. In this chapter, the focus is on the marketing mix decisions and the marketing communications mix. In Chapter 6, it was argued that different marketing mixes were required for each market segment. Here, these frameworks are drawn together in relation to the marketing communications plan.

Marketing Communications Planning

Fill (2005: p. 333) defines a marketing communications plan as being 'concerned with the development and managerial processes involved in the articulation of an organisation's marketing communications strategy'.

It has already been established that marketing communications is concerned with saying the right things to the right people at the right time. Preceding chapters have taken the reader through the processes of research, information and intelligence-gathering which feeds into the development of the marketing strategy and planning decision-making frameworks. The organisation has made its strategic decisions on its overall marketing strategy in relation to products and target segments of the market. In previous chapters the various types of communications approaches were discussed in relation to the varying types of information requirements, including for the private sector, but other types included, for example, the need to respond to adverse media coverage of a destination or to provide specific information about travel advice due to weather problems affecting travel. These situations often require rapid responses to counteract situations which arise in an unplanned way, usually relying on press and public relations (PR) activity together with promotions to ensure that planned marketing activities are compatible and maximised. This type of communications activity falls outside of planning. These types of communications are discussed in Chapter 9.

This section deals with the practical steps involved in the marketing communications plan which can be adapted to respond to a range of different situations. The majority of organisations will consider marketing communications as planned activities designed to achieve strategic goals and aims.

Conventional marketing approaches tended to take a production orientation to plan and develop communications strategy. For the tourism industry, this generally centred on the production of brochures (Wickes and Schuet, 1991) for tour operators; leaflets, posters, films and booklets for destinations; and for the broader industry, a range of seasonal advertising campaigns targeted at key booking stages in an annual cycle (for the Northern European markets, directly after the Christmas holidays). Even though these conventional forms of communications planning cycles still predominate, they are changing. This is due to the changing nature of the marketing and advertising industry, changes in consumer behaviour, responsiveness needs from communications activities, coupled with a general fragmentation of media sources outlined in earlier chapters, a more general shift towards a market orientation is evident in the marketing strategy development. The role of planning is therefore more prominent.

Marketing Communications Plan Context

The effectiveness of any marketing activity wholly depends on the level of attention given to the research and development activity which underpins the communications spending. Larger organisations in the sector understand the need for strategic research on customers' perceptions, images and attitudes towards the brands, particularly considering the influence of general media coverage of places, and knowledge of media activity which is outside the control of the organisation in the context of tour operators, hotel companies and other private and public sector operators. These organisations aim to track changes in market share religiously, always seeking to understand the fundamental reasons for changes in their market share.

Marketing Communications Context

This refers to the considerations discussed in previous discussion in Chapters 5 and 6, whereby the organisation sets its immediate and long-term goals for itself in terms of market share and position for products/brands and markets. The marketing environment surrounding the organisation is also important, and the extent to which the organisation is focused towards meeting customers' values and needs for the service determines the use of marketing research and an integrated approach to marketing communications.

Market research on the chosen market segments must also include an analysis of the communication needs and drivers for these target markets, the types of media they rely on or prefer, the strength of word-of-mouth recommendations to decision-making, the types of purchase-behaviour patterns, the key buyer decision roles which will all feed into an analysis of what the communications plan needs to achieve. In the context of a tourism destination, for example, the destination marketing organisation (DMO) will need to understand the levels of awareness amongst the target market segments to understand how to position its marketing communications to them as was identified in case study 6.

If there is a high level of unaided awareness amongst a market segment, then the communications strategy does not need to orient towards the provision of basic information about the destination but might focus on reminding and/or trying to stimulate the target segment into action, into moving the consumer into a search for further information, so that the destination moves into the consideration set of possible destinations alternatives. If, however, there is a low level of unaided awareness of the destination, the type of information provided by the organisation might be oriented towards developing awareness of the attributes and benefits of the destination. The type of communication channels chosen by the organisation might also reflect the differences in information needs, as well as preferences and attitudes towards various information sources amongst the target groups.

However, the marketing communications context is not simply an analysis of the part of the marketing plan that deals with customer and market research, but also consists of a consideration of the context in terms of broader marketing objectives and strategy, the timing of any campaign within the cycle of activity, any changes in terms of the budgetary situation in the run-up to the promotional campaign or changes in the external environment since the agreement of the marketing plan. The marketing communications context draws on the marketing plan and environmental auditing analysis, but it is also more focused on the context of the organisation in relation to its markets, and its targeted customers and their needs for information about the products and services of the organisation.

SWOT Analysis

Market assessment using the SWOT framework is an analysis of the *s*trengths, *w*eaknesses, *o*pportunities and *t*hreats in each market. Strengths and opportunities are identified through the analysis of internal core competencies (core aspects of the services, the value dimensions in which the organisation excels) matched to competitor analysis and market opportunities identified through the STP process from Chapter 6. Weaknesses and threats are identified through the analysis of the external environment (see Chapter 3) and the competitor analysis. This analysis might include the following:

- sales, by volume and value
- market share broken down by product category
- profitability

- levels of brand awareness
- new product introductions/product removal
- expansion/contraction of distribution

This analysis needs to be realistic rather than a set of ideal goals for each of the segments. At this stage it is useful to differentiate the different scales and goals of organisations in the overall industry. At the national level of the National Tourism Organisation, the scale of SWOT analysis for different key markets will undoubtedly be very complex and detailed. In regional or small enterprises, the scale of SWOT analysis undertaken in relation to different markets will be much less complex. Decisions at this stage also focus on the degree to which and the points at which the organisation competes on price competition or non-price dimensions including product quality, new product development, advertising and promotion, people, processes and physical evidence.

Communications Objective Setting

Objectives are concerned with questions of *what* is to be achieved by the communications. Objectives should be well defined and achievable and should give specific target figures in terms of sales volume, market share, hits to the website or numbers of people able to recall and recognise the organisation or place. Marketing objectives examples include

- sales/turnover/market share
- market position
- loyalty/repeat business
- image
- awareness.

Strategy addresses questions of *how* objectives will be achieved by the communications. Strategy identifies target market segments, product/service marketing mix variables to be deployed, positioning strategy to be adopted and marketing communication channel strategy decisions.

Formulating Objectives

Good Objectives

- Good objectives can be converted into specific actions and activities for the organisation.
- They will provide direction and purpose to the marketing communications strategy and a clear brief for a marketing agency.

- They can help identify and establish longer-term priorities for the organisation.
- They can enhance the accountability and control of the marketing budget allowing the organisation to evaluate performance and return on investment (ROI).

Generally, all such marketing objectives are estimates or targets of performance based around strategic goals. A discussion on the success of such objectives and critical factors of success or failure of marketing and/or promotional campaigns is beyond the scope of this book. As mentioned previously, there are often wider considerations which affect the success of campaigns including political issues, and in many cases, the financial situation of the organisation and its ability to commit resources to marketing strategies and campaigns are related to wider market supply and demand balance. However, it is important to note that marketing strategies do fail and can have major negative effects on the performance of the organisation.

Poor Objectives

- Poor objectives are often vague in terms of specific details or targets.
- They are not linked to customers' values or orientations, particularly in relation to differences between cultures.
- They show a lack of awareness of how the organisation is perceived by its customers and other stakeholders.
- They fail to recognise the current and future external market environment conditions.

However, if marketing communications are undertaken in a planned and systematic way, then the risks associated with this activity will be minimised.

Integrated Marketing Communications Objectives

As discussed previously, marketing communications objectives are not solely directed towards the achievement of sales growth or market share position and may be directed towards a number of different corporate, marketing or communications objectives or a mixture of all three, depending on the strategic objectives of the marketing plan. A re-branding and re-positioning of strategic objective will necessarily entail a great deal of coordinated marketing communications activity providing information about the new brand logo, themes and values to the desired audience which is directed towards raising awareness and providing information. This might include an emphasis on PR and advertising. However, in so doing, the communications will also tie together messages about the organisation's vision and brand values, and it may also connect these types of information-pull strategies with a sales-promotion objective, pushing the communication through the intermediary channels and driving sales. Hence, the objectives for this type of marketing communications campaign are complex and involve corporate, marketing and communications functions.

The Marketing Mix for Tourism and Hospitality

The services marketing mix has been outlined briefly in earlier chapters in relation to strategy development, consumer behaviour and communications theory. It was also discussed in relation to STP processes in Chapter 6. According to Wilson *et al.* (2008) services marketing mix consists of the familiar concept of the 4Ps which is extended to 7Ps for the services industry:

- product
- price
- place
- promotion

- people
- physical evidence
- processes

Each of these aspects can be incorporated into the communications mix strategy. However, the specific techniques of the promotions mix will be addressed in detail in Chapters 8–10, including how people, physical evidence, and processes can be incorporated into the communication of differentiation through promotion and advertising. The concept of place – distribution strategy – relates more to the channel strategy decisions (which are discussed in detail in Chapter 8 and so are not covered here). And the generic strategies of differentiation, cost leadership and focus were also discussed in detail in Chapter 5. This section addresses briefly how product decisions and branding strategies can articulate with communications objective and strategy.

Product Strategies

Product Portfolio Analysis

Many larger tourism and hospitality organisations or destinations have a range of products in a 'portfolio' and it must analyse them differently according to each product market. The organisation carefully assesses what each product offers to the markets, including defining why people buy these products. This will indicate the current strategy. Product Portfolio Analysis developed by the Boston Consulting Group (BCG) analyses the current size and market position of each product in a company/destination portfolio. The purpose of this model is to allow the company or destination to compare the performance of each of its products. Holloway (2004: p. 39) describes how this could be used in the context of a tour operator where products are assessed according to sales volume (revenues generated) and market share, and stage in the product life cycle relative to the leading competitor. This type of BCG matrix could also be applied within a hotel setting where the relative revenues generated by different departments can be analysed. This would provide strong directive 'steer' in determining the focus of the marketing communications strategy. For example, in the case of a hotel which have a very high performing food-and-beverage department but an underperforming conference and events or overnight accommodation department, strategic decisions need to be made about what products to promote to which market segments to develop the business.

Product Strategy Decisions

Standardisation/Adaptation Strategies

1. *Straight extension*: This represents a global strategy, taking the same product and the same promotion and communications strategy to a new market. An example of this would be the marketing of resort destinations to successive markets as core markets wane and decline. Resorts in the advanced Mediterranean tourist markets have successfully extended their products to new emerging markets over the last 10–15 years as successive markets have fallen out of favour with the standardised product offer across many country resort destinations.

2. *Communication adaptation*: This strategy represents a decision to take the same product and communicate it differently with the aim of opening up the product to new markets segments. This is a strategy that has also been applied by the sophisticated resorts of the Mediterranean.

3. *Product adaptation*: This strategy represents a decision to make slight changes to the product to meet local conditions or to meet changes in market segment expectations.

4. *Dual adaptation*: This strategy decision represents changes to both product and market/communication.

5. *Product invention*: This strategy represents a decision to diversify completely and to develop a completely new product with an intention to meet the needs of a new market. In the context of tourism and hospitality industry where new market segments are emerging all the time, rapid changes in trends within key developed markets are identified alongside social and cultural, lifestyle trends.

Figure 7.2 shows Ansoff's product–market matrix applied to service offerings. The diagram represents the core choices the organisation must make in relation to its markets for its services and the types of services it may develop in the future in relation to its core competencies.

Market penetration is the choice made when a company or organisation aims to challenge its competitive position through the deployment of new marketing communications strategies. To penetrate the existing market with its existing services, the organisation has recognised a relative weakness of its position and market share, in the light of positive growth in the market for its services overall. It may choose to select a new marketing communications agency to try and capture new or recapture lost market share.

Market extension is required when the organisation identifies through its market research that there is a significant interest in its existing services from newly identified market segments, and the organisation chooses to target these new markets with its services. Service development is chosen as a strategy in those existing markets where there is a generally favourable reaction to the company, and existing customers are targeted with different products within the product range offered by the company. In a diversification strategy, the organisation chooses to develop new products for new market segments.

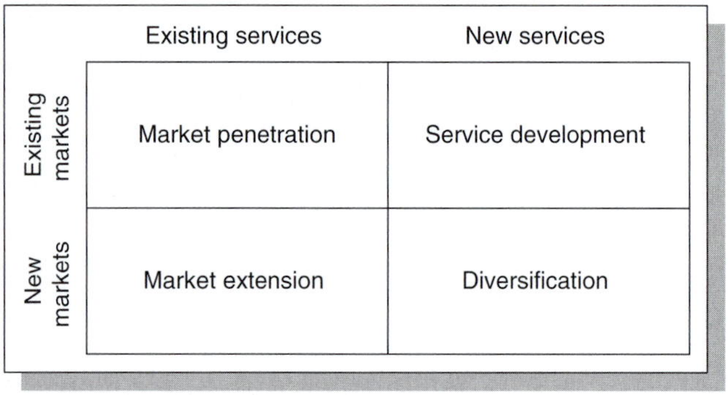

	Existing services	New services
Existing markets	Market penetration	Service development
New markets	Market extension	Diversification

Figure 7.2 Ansoff's product–market matrix applied to services.

Product Formulation Decisions and the Communications Strategy

A *product* in tourism and hospitality can be defined as

> Any services, experiences of places and/or use of facilities which are offered to a market for use or consumption to satisfy the needs and wants for hospitality and travel.

For a place, service or experience, or facility to be offered for market use, it must be planned for consumption in a particular way, including plans to promote and/or otherwise communicate messages about the product. Organisations and destinations have to be aware of the needs and values of the customers and really understand how they benefit from purchase of the product. Medlik and Middleton (1973) identified that the product includes the complete experience from the time the tourist leaves home to the time they return. This has been even more complicated in recent theorising, in the relationship between anticipation, experience and how some tourist experiences are integrated into long-term narratives of self (Parinello, 1993; Wearing and Wearing, 2001). As identified in Chapter 4 on consumer behaviour, the organisation needs to be aware of the relationship between consumption of services and social identity and higher level social needs. And Holloway (2004: p. 129) argues that "Getting the product right is the single most important activity in marketing."

In Figure 7.3, the core product is at the centre of the offer to the customer. This might be the overall 'experience' they expect from the company or the destination. For a special-occasion user of a luxury hotel

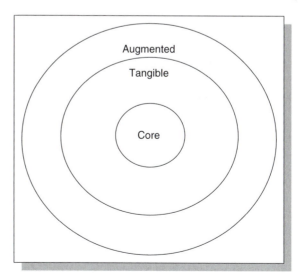

Figure 7.3 The three levels of the product.

with excellent leisure, health spa and sporting facilities, the core product might be the sense of complete indulgence and luxury. The tangible elements of the product act as a facilitator for this type of experience to be realised. This might include the physical features of the hotel's facilities such as the pool, sauna, gym, treatment rooms, bedrooms, reception desk, restaurants, bars and public areas such as shopping facilities which make up discrete product categories of the hotel in their own right. The tangible elements also include other aspects of the physical evidence of the hotels 'servicescape', including the specification of the facilities, décor and quality of the furnishings and facilities (such as pillows, duvets and towels). The augmented product includes all the additional service dimensions including the ratio of staff to customer, the quality of training and delivery commitments of the services, the presence of qualified and trained personnel to deliver the health, leisure and fitness aspects of the product. The augmented product also includes additional services offered such as after-sales support, loyalty-scheme membership, administration and the nature and level of relationship formed.

The tangible and augmented dimensions of the tourism and hospitality product environment enable the core product to be realised or achieved and thus form a crucial role in the packaging and design aspects. The organisation or destination needs to have in mind an idea of a core product for its various consumer (target) segments and knows how to package and present the tangible and augmented product elements to create the core product.

In Chapter 6, the relationship between markets, segmentation and consumer motivations and needs was related to the process of positioning the product in the mind of the customers. This process is often achieved through product branding and brands make up a core aspect of the marketing communications strategy and mix.

Illustration

Three Levels of Product for easyJet

Core product – cheap, convenient, reliable and consistent transport (flight) services between the routes offered by the company.

Tangible features – routes and destinations, plane stock, personnel, brand name (suggests carefree attitude, friendly and informal service, convenience and 'easy'), design (informal, fun) and colour scheme (bright orange), fast processes (no tickets, no seat allocations) associated with the brand.

Augmented – service at check in desks, informal processes of check-in and embarkation/disembarkation, convenient Internet booking service, 'add-ons' such as car hire and hotels.

A range of factors must be taken into consideration in product formulation decisions, which can be identified as follows:

- service
- quality
- range
- brand name
- features and benefits

Whereas previous chapters have dealt with issues of service quality, and product benefits and features, this section focuses on brands and brand communication issues.

Branding

The American Marketing Association defines a brand as a 'name, term, sign, symbol, or design, or a combination of them intended to identify the goods and services of one seller or group of sellers and to differentiate them from those of competition' (Kotler and Gertner, 2002: p. 41). Brands have become a powerful means by which organisations communicate ideas about their products, services or values to audiences. The importance of branding to tourism and hospitality is critical since the features of these products and services are generally easy to copy, and so companies rely on their brand image to differentiate themselves from competitor products and services.

Branding has been used very successfully in the hotel market since Conrad Hilton established Hilton Hotels as being a name which was synonymous with guaranteed service quality for business travellers around the world. Hotel brand loyalty has become as important as airline brand loyalty in very highly competitive markets. These two sectors of the industry are particularly well suited to branding since risk and uncertainty impact on consumer choice for both sectors. Whereas for destinations and food and beverage outlets, it is easy to envisage a desire for experimentation and both could be positioned as lower-risk decisions (or where potential benefits outweigh possible risks), hotels and airlines both create images which emphasise security, reliability, trustworthiness and dimensions of quality assurance. Thus brands have a value which goes beyond their surface value as the identifying name, logo or design of an organisation. They have an emotional and social value and so the relationship between the communicative power of brands and the marketing communications strategy process cannot be understated and is linked to the extent that they establish a brand personality with which people can readily associate and identify (Cai, 2002; Pitt *et al.*, 2007).

Destination Branding

Brands can become icons in their own right (Aaker, 1997). People can become brands. It makes sense therefore that places such as tourist destinations can be subjected to the branding process (see Kotler and Gertner, 2002; Morgan and Pritchard, 2001). Indeed, it is clear that some places can be subjected to a process whereby an image is created, constructed and represented – communicated – to a market, whereas other countries or places become identified or associated with a set of ideas, images and myths over a long, historic process of accumulation and transmission. The difference is the self-conscious decision to communicate certain aspects of a place and its culture to an audience in a manner which makes a particular set of associations between place and people possible via different channels such as the Web (Williams and Palmer, 1999). The difficulty in distinguishing between places which attempt to brand themselves in a deliberate way with those that are not is exacerbated by the fact that in creating brands, countries or places often refer to those more organically formed and distinct images, associations and myths which define or otherwise characterise the place in question.

It is also important to note that the destination image or brand is not formed entirely out of images of the natural environment or people. Indeed, in the case of many destinations the iconic associations and images are tied to the physical built environment. New York has an iconic skyline and the Statue of Liberty; Paris has the Eifel Tower and Arc de Triomphe; and London has Big Ben, Tower Bridge and the Houses of Parliament. Gilmore (2004) notes the central role that skyscrapers play in the iconography of cities denoting modernity, accomplishment and competition. But these iconic built environments change, and so do the associations. For New York, the 'ground zero' site of the World Trade Centre Twin Towers has become a world-recognised iconic symbol of the city, encompassing the strength of character and determination of the city's people. The London Eye visitor attraction and Sir Norman Foster's 'Gherkin' have, as additions in the very recent past, become intrinsic elements of the contemporary London skyline, together with the re-developed Turbine Hall (an old power station on the South Bank which was previously 'invisible' in the images of London) as the Tate Modern art gallery. These buildings symbolise the economic power of London, its role as a world-class visitor destination and its cultural capital as one of the world's most important centres of popular modern art. They don't necessarily replace the traditional iconic buildings of London in promotional material but add more depth and quality to the overall positioning of London as one of the world's most attractive and important centres.

Plate 7.1 'Totally London' – Branding London.

The Visit London logo, for example, encapsulates the idea that London is a modern, vibrant cultural centre. The use of the words 'Totally London' (Plate 7.1) provides a contemporary feel, but draws on the distinctiveness and traditional elements through the styling of the font and design representing London street signs. Being 'on' refers to being turned or switched on, active, non-stop, exciting, jam-packed with a full programme of arts, entertainment, cultural and visitor experiences. Being 'on' is represented by the use of red colouring for the letters. The wording 'totally' implies that everything is encapsulated within: it is *the* place to be, a place with a buzz. It also suggests that the website is the place where you can explore everything that's going on. Visit London have created a brand image for London out of the fabric of the name itself. This strategy relies partially on the recognisability of the city's name which is then infused with a set of connotations about the place, drawing on traditional reference points but given a radical and slightly edgy, contemporary twist.

Whereas in the past close-up shots of Big Ben might have been used to represent London, together with red phone boxes, images of the police in their distinctive uniforms, or the guards at Buckingham Palace, in recent communications, emphasis is now placed on the modern.

The role of destination branding is vital for a destination marketing partnership organisation to help the individual businesses they represent achieve their goals. At the level of destinations, this process is concerned with the communication of a set of ideas and images about the place to the targeted audience. There has been a large body of research work undertaken in destination image formation processes (see the following for the main theoretical developments: Gunn, 1988; Um and Crompton, 1990; Chon, 1991; Echtner and Ritchie, 1991; Baloglu and Brinberg, 1997) which focuses on consumers' processes of becoming aware of and developing an image of destinations, and the various factors they take into consideration in selecting destinations in terms of attributes. The purpose of this section is not to delve into this literature but to highlight the processes and mechanisms used in the development and communication of ideas, images and symbols of destinations.

Illustration

Destination Branding: How Marketing Makes a Country Stand Out

Country and region brands are everywhere, each vying for attention in a crowded market of 250 countries and thousands of regions. Chic, sensational, sparkling and incredible – these are, respectively, the brands adopted by Thailand, Brazil, Korea and India. New Zealand's '100% Pure' slogan, in use since 1999, focuses on the country's unspoilt beauty, while 'Uniquely Singapore' seeks to set the island apart from its Asian neighbours. Two main approaches to country branding are evocative and informative. The former aims to reach into consumers' emotions, while the latter aims to educate. 'Love Cyprus' aims for the former, whilst 'Croatia: the Mediterranean as it once was' aims for the latter.

Berg said, 'Croatia was a new country in 1991 and it wanted to get across the fact that it was undamaged by the war and that it was not a tacky, mass-market destination. The slogan was also important in helping position Croatia geographically and culturally as part of the Mediterranean, rather than being vaguely in the east somewhere'.

Japan wants to promote the old and new with its 'Cool Japan – Fusion with Tradition' campaign. 'The aim is to make people aware that Japan is much more than geisha, sumo, temples and Mount Fuji', said Kylie Clark, PR manager for Japan National Tourist Organization. 'The aim of the campaign is to diversify the types of travellers going to Japan. It is hoped that by highlighting Japan's cool attractions we will get more young couples, professionals and families visiting'.

With so many country brands competing for consumers' attention, there is a tendency for messages to merge together in a swirl of words and phrases. 'It can be an expensive, time-consuming process,' said Representation Plus managing director Alison Cryer. 'It requires the whole country to embrace the concept of developing and communicating the brand values. It also needs to be promoted rigorously – all too often a new brand can just be a logo without any meaning.'

'Branding involves is all about differentiation and creating a clear proposition that can be adapted for varying audiences', she said.

Source: Adapted from http://www.travelweekly.co.uk/Articles/2007/11/08/25792/destination-branding-how-marketing-makes-a-country-stand.html accessed on 8 November 2007.

Hotel Branding

Brands can become the product, they should symbolise the value, service quality orientation or the distinct qualities of the place or organisation. The Taj Hotels, Resorts and Palaces predominantly in India, has come to symbolise the ultimate in luxurious hospitality in India, impeccable service, authentic design and magnificent properties. The Taj group began with the Mumbai Palace and Tower over a hundred years ago and now has 77 properties in five continents, but mainly in India and South East Asia, boasting private jet and luxury yacht services for its guests; the company's commitment to the delivery of the finest service has become synonymous with the brand (see http://www.tajhotels.com). The company name and its associated symbols such as the font style and flower design which is transposed into the dot of the letter 'j' denote quality, peace, calm and harmony.

The incorporation of the words 'Hotels, Resorts and Palaces' conveys the range of luxurious properties held by the group. The words alone create a symbolic association with luxury. This ensures that in marketing communications some things can be left un-stated, such as prices or guarantees. If in tourism and hospitality the product is largely the values or benefits derived from an experience, then brands can play a powerful role in symbolising those benefits and values through recognisable associations.

Illustration

For hotel chains, brand name and image must symbolise and represent the commitment to service quality of the organisation. A large hotel chain like the American-based Starwood holds a number of different hotel brands which are designed to meet the different needs of a diverse range of customer market segments, including Sheraton, Four points by Sheraton, St Regis, 'W' Hotels, Westin, Luxury Collection, Le Meridien.

The range of hotel brands offered by the Starwood group (www.starwoodhotels.com) is tipped towards the more exclusive, upscale, luxury and business markets, with the Westin brand serving the three star business and leisure markets. Whereas the French Accor group of hotels (www.accorhotels.com) aim to capture a broader cross-section of available market segments with a larger portfolio of brands, the overall emphasis is on the budget leisure and business markets. Similarly in terms of the geographic markets served, whilst Starwood offers hotels which are predominantly in North America with some additional hotels and resort properties in Asia, the Accor group of hotels offers a more global reach of its brands with over 4000 hotels in 90 countries on five continents: Sofitel, Novotel, Mercure, Suitehotel, Ibis, All Seasons, Etap, Formule 1, Red Roof, Motel 6, Accor Thalassa.

However, in many organisations, branding is used alongside specific references to products and also to other elements of the marketing mix, including price, place, promotion, people, physical evidence and processes. The following chapters return to address these interactions between other elements of the marketing mix. The following section describes the marketing communications planning process.

Marketing Communications Strategy

An integrated marketing communications approach dictates that all forms of organisational communication should adhere to and reflect the corporate or organisational goals and values. Thus not all forms of communication will necessarily be directed towards potential customers. Each set of stakeholder communications requires specific messages which can be coordinated and represent the organisation accordingly.

The main communications strategies are

- push strategies
- pull strategies
- profile strategies.

Push and pull strategies relate to the directional thrust of the communication through the marketing channel, directly targeting end-users (potential customers, business-to-business [B2B] clients, etc.) by either 'pulling' them towards contact with the organisation or 'pushing' the communication towards intermediaries, such as destination marketing partnerships, tourist information centres, travel agents and tour operators. Profile strategies are less related to the achievement of direct action or sales and can include those communications directed towards internal and external stakeholders as well as performing a supporting strategy function for push and pull strategies. Therefore, a range of strategies can be employed simultaneously in the case of a new product launch or a strategic drive to raise or change an existing profile of a country, region or organisation. Re-branding initiatives involving a shift in values or orientations to customers or a change of name and/or design and styling often requires a concentrated profile strategy which can be tied to sales promotion, personal selling, PR and a concentrated push strategy.

Push Strategy

Push strategies refers to the channel network for products and services. Therefore, a push strategy involves communications directed towards intermediaries as mentioned earlier. As the role of the tourism distribution system has come under scrutiny over recent years with the move to independent booking and direct marketing and selling of tourism and hospitality products, the role of the traditional intermediaries has been sharpened. Indeed the value of face-to-face communication through personal selling in travel agencies and through exhibitions and fairs has, although not without a great deal of pressure, proved resistant to the forces of direct marketing through the Internet. Tour operators, hoteliers and transport providers which form the 'principals' in the distribution channel chain create package products and offers which are pushed down through the intermediary channel. The value of adopting this type of strategy is in the network of the travel agency or the destination marketing partnership/organisation (through tourism information centres) and its position in the minds of the customers as a trusted and reliable source of good advice. Thus, the intermediary can add value to the products through the services they offer to customers. Therefore, push strategies often are B2B channels of communication and therefore personal selling. Travel trade fairs and exhibitions such as the World Travel Market in London every November or the ITB in Berlin every March represent a type of push strategy, where destination countries and tour operators can vie for business and inform, remind, persuade other businesses to take action. The core message of the communication needs to be articulated accordingly, and personal selling must be supported with appropriate printed or other supplementary communications.

Pull Strategy

Pull strategy tends to be directed towards end-users and the provision of a message designed to inform, remind or persuade. It aims to pull people towards taking some specified action. Examples could be to visit the travel agent, call a telephone number to order a brochure, log onto a website or contact the organisation by mail. Therefore pull strategies aim to produce or stimulate some specified action from consumers and 'pull' them into the distribution channel for the organisation. Pull strategies are often also used in conjunction with a particular type of promotional activity such as a price discount or incentive (sales promotion), but in the case of tourism and hospitality products, there is a strong emphasis placed on reminding customers about the organisation or a destination at defined times during the season. Thus, the frequency of purchase and the timing of the main holiday, event or festival season provide a requirement for dedicated types of communications strategies at different points in the annual cycle.

Profile Strategy

Profile strategies include integrated corporate communications across a range of channels and activities. Profile strategies are concerned with the maintenance of the corporate image to all stakeholders. In relation to the present context, the main ways in which a profile strategy is employed include those communications to employees, suppliers and other external stakeholders in the form of newsletters, e-mail updates and briefings but can also include annual reports and corporate strategy documents, billing and financial communications, policy and lobbying briefing communications. In terms of the main profile strategies largely applying to destinations is the need to monitor and respond carefully to media reports and stories, which can often arise outside the control of the destination marketing partnership/organisation and have an adverse effect on markets or need to be exploited to maximise opportunities.

Communications Mix Decisions

The content and delivery methods (in terms of media channels) chosen should be directed towards the information needs of the targeted audience, as this will inform the type of strategy employed in terms of pull, push or profile, or combinations of them. For many larger tourism and hospitality organisations, a mixture of different approaches will be tied to a larger-scale campaign, but for smaller and medium-sized organisations, the type of approach is more limited. The size and scale of the organisation also constrain the level of resources that can be deployed towards various types of media channel. The cost of television (TV) advertising is prohibitive for many organisations and inappropriate in terms of being able to focus on the specific target market.

The style and content of the message is also considered as this will inform the type of media channel chosen. Questions about the basic design, core message, the type of response required, the type of appeal, either rational or emotional, the mix of copy and image, should be identified, since the direction of the communication mix will dictate the types of information provided for each targeted group. For example, a bold and provocative set of images may provide the focus of a pull campaign using outdoor billboard and bus shelter advertising directed towards consumers, which may be complemented with a more detailed set of communications and promotional material utilising the same images or drawing on the same messages delivered via a push strategy through relevant intermediaries. The more detailed information may include price discounts, sales promotions or incentives, for example.

Marketing Communications Evaluation and Control

The evaluation and control aspects are an essential component of the marketing communications planning process. Without evaluation of the communication, there will be a gap in the communication process as a two-way dialogue. One of the most important issues for marketers is to assess the effectiveness of the advertising or other communications strategies on the consumers' awareness. However, as mentioned earlier, it is often not easy in the context of tourism destinations to distinguish or attribute awareness to the promotional material of DMOs. Mercille (2005) argues that although tourism marketers assess the effect of advertising on destination image, it is less common to measure the effects of media representations on destination image. He found that there is congruence between tourist's images of Tibet with media representations, for example. Similarly, in assessing the effectiveness of advertising compared to publicity in tourism, Loda *et al.* (2007: p. 263) argued that in today's media-saturated environment, it is even more important to understand how consumers are influenced by different media representations. They found that tourism marketing effectiveness could be increased if we understood the relationships between advertising and publicity. They argued that publicity generally outperforms advertising, that advertising's effectiveness could be improved if preceded with publicity, that publicity is less effective when it follows advertising and that campaigns must be planned well in advance.

One of the most popular forms of monitoring the effectiveness of advertising in the context of tourism is the conversion method (see Woodside, 1990; Woodside and Dubelaar, 2003; Kim *et al.*, 2005). This approach generally focuses on evaluating individual's responses to advertising campaigns within the context of evaluating the extent to which the advertising intervention had an effect on destination awareness, visitation and visitor expenditure. Although these methods are contested, they are widely used to assess the effects of advertising.

Control concerns the monitoring of the success of the communications campaign in terms of the achievement of stated objectives for ROI, market share or sales growth, or recognition or awareness levels increases. Evaluation can also include the more generic feedback on the messages themselves and the extent to which the message was received and interpreted in the manner in which it was intended by the target audience. This information is then fed back into the planning process to inform the development of future marketing planning development.

Summary

This chapter has outlined the main tools used in the development of a marketing communication plan. It was argued that it is crucial for organisations to have a clear set of goals and strategies for products and markets which will enable them to identity and determine the direction and thrust of the marketing communications messages. SWOT analysis provides organisations with a tool to determine the potential of future product market opportunities which can be matched against the core competencies, the key resources of the organisation or destination. These analyses form the basis for the identification of strategies for product development, branding and positioning. These values underpin the development of core messages, ideas and ideals to be communicated to the targeted audiences, which are in turn incorporated into the process of determining the marketing communications objectives and channel strategies. These are undertaken through the marketing communications plan which was outlined as the key process in devising a marketing campaign. The following chapters detail how marketing campaigns are implemented through the marketing communications mix.

Discussion Questions

1. Outline the main tools used in the development of marketing communications objectives. How can each contribute to the implementation of a marketing communications plan?
2. How do tourism and hospitality products become brands? Why are brands so important in marketing communications for these types of products and services?
3. Describe how SWOT analysis is used to underpin the development of marketing strategies in relation to products and markets for the tourism and hospitality sector.
4. Evaluate the need for clarity and accuracy in the development of marketing communications messages for tourism and hospitality. Outline the main priorities for organisations in developing their marketing communications plans.

Case Study 7: Thomas Cook's Campaign for an Extra Holiday Puts 'Clear Air' between Them and the Competition

Thomas Cook's 2008 campaign has seen the UK tour operator take a different path to its traditional marketing strategy. The strategy which began on 26 December 2007 features a number of distinctive and innovative elements to try to capture market share by differentiating itself from the competition (namely TUI Travel) and striking a chord with the British public's values and opinions.

Thomas Cook bank holiday campaign hits the streets (by Michelle Perrett: 15 January 2008).

Thomas Cook's campaign calling for an extra UK bank holiday has hit the streets with its teams donning uniforms and megaphone calling for support.

The electioneering team has issued a call to Brits to sign up to its petition, which now has 180,000 signatures, in the cities of London, Newcastle, Birmingham, Bristol and Glasgow. Thomas Cook has also undertaken some research as part of its 'Vote for an Extra Bank Holiday' campaign revealing that more than a third of Brits think a new bank holiday should be introduced to mark St George's Day.

'The Thomas Cook campaign for an extra bank holiday has really captured the public's imagination, but whilst St George's Day has come out as the lead contender it's not really a day for the whole UK to celebrate,' said Simon Carter, executive director of marketing at Thomas Cook.

'Perhaps it would be more appropriate to have a more unified day, not just for England but the whole of the UK, such as the number two favourite Remembrance Day or the Queen's Birthday.'

http://www.travelweekly.co.uk/Articles/2008/01/15/26391/thomas-cook-bank-holiday-campaign-hits-the-streets.html

As the TravelWeekly article shows, the campaign is focused around a campaign for an extra public holiday for Britain. Thomas Cook identified that British workers have the fewest number of public holidays in Europe (apart from Romania which at 7.5 days beats Britain by half a day). The campaign has generated a great deal of media and press coverage and has received support from the Fabian society and a national TV show GMTV has launched its own campaign for an extra public holiday in aid of the armed forces. Presenters on the show have raised the issue in an interview with Prime Minister Gordon Brown. The lobbying campaign that aimed at gathering signatures on a petition has reached over half a million (at 14 March 2008: http://www.thomascook.com/content/free/day/homepage.asp?intcmp= hp_07promo_vote). Thomas Cook aims to lobby MPs to call an Early Day motion in the House of Commons, and according to Thomas Cook they already have the support of around two-thirds of all MPs (http://www.travelweekly.co.uk/Articles/2008/01/07/26309/tho-mas-cook-bank-holiday-campaign-reaches-100000-signatures.html). The campaign is tied to a multi-million pound advertising push featuring TV, press, radio and online advertising as well as 'guerrilla marketing' through the street lobbying highlighted earlier, which gradually shifted in emphasis to adopt a more conventional message about destinations and holidays as the market hits peak booking times: Carter said, 'The peak time for sales is around January 14–19 and that's when we'll make the transition and alter the message accordingly'(http://www.travelweekly.co.uk/Articles/2007/12/26/26228/thomas-cook-calls-for-extra-british-bank-holiday.html). The advertising is also accompanied by a sales promotion strategy offering a 'free day' with every holiday of 14 nights booked through any of its brands. The company is also giving all its employees an extra day's holiday. Carter argues, 'Why should we wait for the Government to take action – we value our employees and think they deserve that extra day off. And if it's good enough for our staff – why not for all Brits?' (see Plate 7.2).

The use of a campaign which does not specifically focus on selling holidays but invites customers to become emotionally involved with the company is clearly intended to differentiate Thomas Cook from its competitors as Marketing Director Simon Carter argued in an interview with TTG Live in late December 2007 that the campaign will put 'clear air' between itself and TUI Travel (http://www.ttglive.com/NArticleDetails.asp?aid=9437). The point of the campaign was to remove confusion between Thomas Cook and its rivals by doing something stunning and unique and to focus on emotion rather than price, create a strong story which has a life after the campaign came to an end in February 2008. Carter also highlighted that holidays now compete for consumers' aspirational spending. 'If the customer is walking down the high street with £1000 in his pocket, he could buy a flat-screen TV, a sofa or a holiday. And if they see an inviting window display, they will go to that store before mine. So we must have an exciting proposition and message'. In other words, Thomas Cook must broaden its perspectives on how it views the competition, which must include non-travel consumer goods (http://www.ttglive.com/NArticleDetails.asp?aid=9425).

Plate 7.2 Thomas Cook's 'Campaign for a free day' poster.

Learning Activity

- You are working for a tour operator in the UK specialising in 'soft' adventure holidays aimed at the 55–65-year-old, middle-class couples market. You have recently developed a new package for Kenya offering part-beach, part-walking safari tours.
- Devise a marketing communications plan for this new product, detailing the main aims of the campaign, the marketing objectives and the communications channel strategy chosen. Justify your choice by referring to how you would position this product for the market.

References and Further Reading

Aaker, J.L. (1997). Dimensions of brand personality. *Journal of Marketing Research*. 34(3): 347–356.

Baloglu, S. and Brinberg, D. (1997). Affective images of tourism destinations. *Journal of Travel Research*. 35(4): 11–15.

Cai, L.A. (2002). Cooperative branding for rural destinations. *Annals of Tourism Research*. 29(3): 720–742.

Chon, K.S. (1991). Tourism destination image modification process: Marketing implications. *Tourism Management*. 12(1): 68–72.

Echtner, C.M. and Ritchie, J.R.B. (1991). The meaning and measurement of tourism destination image. *Journal of Tourism Studies*. 2(2): 2–12.

Fill, C. (2005). *Marketing Communications: Engagement, Strategies and Practice*. 4th edn. Harrow, England: Prentice Hall.

Gilmore, F. (2004). Brand Shanghai: Harnessing the inner force of people and place. In Morgan, N.A., Pritchard, R. and Pride, R. (eds) *Destination Branding: Creating the Unique Destination Proposition*. 2nd edn.. Oxford: Elsevier Butterworth-Heinemann, pp. 169–184.

Gunn, C.A. (1988). *Tourism Planning*. New York: Taylor and Francis.

Holloway, J.C. (2004). *Tourism Marketing*. 4th edn. Harlow, England: Prentice Hall.

Kim, D.-Y., Hwang, Y.-H. and Fesenmaier, D.R. (2005). Modeling tourism advertising effectiveness. *Journal of Travel Research*. 44: 42–49.

Kotler, P. and Gertner, D. (2002). Country as a brand, product and beyond: A place marketing and brand management perspective. *Journal of Brand Management*. Special Issue on Nation Branding, 9(4–5): 249–261.

Loda, M.D., Norman, W. and Backman, K.F. (2007). Advertising and publicity: Suggested new applications for tourism marketers. *Journal of Travel Research*. 45: 259–265.

Medlik, S. and Middleton, V.T.C. (1973). Product Formulation in Tourism. *Tourism and Marketing*. Vol. 13, Berne: AIEST.

Mercille, J. (2005). Media effects on image: The case of Tibet. *Annals of Tourism Research*. 32(4): 1039–1055.

Morgan, N. and Pritchard, A. (2001). *Advertising in Tourism and Leisure*. Oxford: Butterworth-Heinemann.

Morgan, N., Pritchard, A. and Pride, R. (2001) *Destination Branding: Creating the Unique Destination Proposition*. Oxford: Elsevier Butterworth-Heinemann, pp. 40–56.

Parrinello, G.L. (1993). Motivation and Anticipation in Post-Industrial Tourism. *Annals of Tourism Research*. 20(2): 232–248.

Pike, S. and Ryan, C. (2004). Destination positioning analysis through a comparison of cognitive, affective, and conative perceptions. *Journal of Travel Research*. 42: 333–342.

Pitt, L.A., Opoku, R., Hultman, M., Abratt, R. and Spyropoulou, S. (2007). What I say about myself: Communication of brand personality by African countries. *Tourism Management*. 28: 835–844.

Selwyn, T. (ed.) (1996). *The Tourism Image: Myths and Structures*. New York: John Wiley.

Um, S. and Crompton, J. (1990). Attitude determinants in tourism destination choice. *Annals of tourism research*. 17: 432–448.

Wearing, S. and Wearing, B. (2001). Conceptualizing the Selves of Tourism. *Leisure Studies*. 20(2): 143–59.

Wickes, B.E. and Schuet, M.A. (1991). Examining the role of tourism promotion through the use of brochures. *Tourism Management*. 12(4): 301–312.

Williams, A.P. and Palmer, A.J. (1999). Tourism destination brands and electronic commerce: Towards synergy. *Journal of Vacation Marketing*. 5: 263–275.

Wilson, A., Zeithaml, V.A., Bitner, M.J. and Gremler, D.D. (2008). *Services Marketing: Integrating Customer Focus across the Firm*. First European Edition. Maidenhead, UK: McGraw-Hill Education.

Woodside, A.G. (1990). Measuring advertising effectiveness in destination marketing strategies. *Journal of Travel Research*. 29(2): 3–8.

Woodside, A.G. and Dubelaar, C. (2003). Increasing quality in measuring advertising effectiveness: A meta-analysis of question framing in conversion studies. *Journal of Advertising Research*. 43(1): 78–85.

Key Resources and Links

http://www.asa.org.uk/asa/adjudications/
http://www.accorhotels.com/accorhotels/index.html
http://www.visitlondon.com
http://www.starwoodhotels.com/

http://www.ttglive.com/NArticleDetails.asp?aid=9425

http://www.ttglive.com/NArticleDetails.asp?aid=9437

http://www.travelweekly.co.uk/Articles/2008/01/15/26391/thomas-cook-bank-holiday-campaign-hits-the-streets.html

http://www.thomascook.com/content/free/day/homepage.asp?intcmp=hp_07promo_vote)

http://www.travelweekly.co.uk/Articles/2008/01/07/26309/thomas-cook-bank-holiday-campaign-reaches-100000-signatures.html

http://www.travelweekly.co.uk/Articles/2007/12/26/26228/thomas-cook-calls-for-extra-british-bank-holiday.html

http://www.travelweekly.co.uk/Articles/2007/12/26/26228/thomas-cook-calls-for-extra-british-bank-holiday.html

Part 3 focuses on concepts and strategies for implementing marketing communications in tourism and hospitality organisations. It does this through an examination of the marketing communications mix. Traditionally, the marketing communications mix has been split into 'above the line' (conventional non-personal, intervention-based mass media advertising) and 'below the line' (sales promotions, public relations, etc. which do not make an overt play for consumers' attention through advertising). This balance is changing in favour of 'through the line' communications which employ a range of tools in the mix often including direct marketing methods. Chapter 8 begins with an examination of advertising strategies. It defines advertising and assesses the value of advertising in the current communications environment. This chapter outlines a range of applications of advertising in informing consumers about tourism and hospitality services. It also discusses how advertising messages should be constructed to appeal to the target audiences. Chapter 9 then looks at the range of alternatives to advertising in the communications mix, including personal selling, public relations, direct marketing, events and exhibitions and sponsorship. This chapter also contextualises these discussions within the current communications challenges for tourism and hospitality organisations. Because of the impact of Internet technology and the diffusion of broadband Internet service provision across the globe, e-communications are discussed separately in Chapter 10. Here the value of Internet advertising is discussed together with a description and assessment of different forms of media content available through the Internet. The chapter concludes with a discussion of user-generated content for tourism and hospitality organisations. Peer-to-peer e-communications forms an exciting and challenging medium and is akin to word-of-mouth communications and provides a useful focus for the discussion on future issues in marketing communications which concludes the book in Chapter 11.

Advertising Strategies for Tourism and Hospitality

Learning Objectives

At the end of this chapter, you will be able to

- Understand, define and evaluate the role of advertising in marketing tourism and hospitality products and services.

- Evaluate a range of applications of advertising to the provision of information about tourism and hospitality products and service.

- Understand the range, functions and specific features of tourism and hospitality advertising.

- Recognise the role of advertising in the communications strategy process for tourism and hospitality.

Introduction

This chapter describes a range of advertising strategies and approaches which are relevant to a cross section of the tourism and hospitality sector. Other factors determining the nature of the advertising message are also outlined. The chapter begins with a definition of advertising and a discussion on how advertising works as a communication tool. This discussion relates back to the issues outlined in relation to communication theory and consumers' behaviour in Chapters 2 and 4. Different types of advertising are considered and key trends in the development of advertising platforms are discussed. Strategic decisions concerning available advertising strategies are described. Particular focus is given to the types of media and relevant strategies. The chapter compares and analyses how advertising messages are constructed for different purposes and audiences.

What Is Advertising?

The Institute of Practitioners in Advertising (IPA) defines advertising as 'The means of providing the most persuasive possible selling message to the right prospects at the lowest possible cost'. This represents a highly practical and profit-oriented view of the role of marketing communications through advertising messages. This definition highlights the crucial role that advertising plays in an organisation's strategy to drive sales growth. However, this book has demonstrated that the role of organisations varies very greatly in tourism and hospitality, particularly when taking into consideration the quasi-political motivations of destination marketing organisations (DMOs), whose role is to promote the local region for the benefits of the whole of the society rather than specifically to drive 'sales'.

Similarly, the effect of advertising in relation to direct impact on sales growth is very much contested in the marketing literature generally and in the tourism and hospitality literature in particular (Loda et al., 2007). 'Strong' and 'weak' theories of advertising effects can be applied in different situations in this sector. Thus a broader view of advertising needs to be applied to cover all aspects of the rationale for, and motives of, advertising for organisations in this sector.

> Advertising is a specific form of marketing communications which is concerned with bringing information about an organisation, its products and services, or any other messages to the attention of the market.

> Advertising can take a variety of forms and should be targeted directly at desired audiences; it has been selected through the STP process

described in Chapter 6. Advertising is not synonymous with 'promotion,' because many messages delivered through advertising are concerned either about providing information and creating awareness of the organisation, its channels of access/distribution or about otherwise informing or reminding the markets about the organisation through the provision of appropriate information, as discussed in Chapter 3. The trends towards DIY holidaymaking and the adoption of independent booking via the internet for travel and hotel services especially have also created a shifting focus in terms of the message content of traditional forms of advertising for tourism and hospitality, towards creating awareness of websites, informing markets of the benefits of using Internet sites for booking and comparing prices and products and also for persuading, through promotional strategies, the markets to purchase through the web.

Thus the examples and cases used in this book suggest that the direction of advertising messages in the present context has taken a shift in terms of

- greater fragmentation in terms of use of media channels
- growth in pull strategies (to drive consumers towards certain actions)
- greater interactivity in advertising messages
- increase in use of personal endorsement (by celebrities or 'ordinary' users)
- more innovative media strategies.

Although a few case studies in this book (Case studies 4 and 7 for example) have highlighted how communications strategies have sought to engage consumers on an emotional level as opposed to rational thought processes, it is probably true to say that most tourism and hospitality communications appeal at the emotional level, even those which are driven by a price/value message.

How Advertising Works

Similar to the theories of buyer behaviour outlined in Chapter 4 (Figure 2.8 in particular) and also the 'buyer readiness states' concept outlined in Chapter 2, it is clear that advertising seeks to connect with consumers' needs at a specific time, to provide consumers with appropriate cues for behaviour which anticipate their needs for services through the provision of stimuli or communications messages. However, the 'hierarchy of effects' model can be applied to show how advertising must move people through a series of steps or states, in order to ensure the appropriate behaviour or action is achieved.

Morgan and Pritchard (2001) argue that successful advertising must take consumers through a six-stage process which draw on the hierarchy of effects model and usefully relates to the types of strategic orientation to the organisation's message.

Stage 1   *Awareness* – particularly in the case of new products or services or a recent rebranding exercise.
Stage 2   *Comprehension* – once aware of the product or brand, customers need to be familiarised with the benefits of purchase or product attributes.
Stage 3   *Acceptance* – potential customers need to be sure that the product or experience will serve their requirements and needs.
Stage 4   *Preference* – potential customers must feel sufficiently sympathetic towards the product or service and place it towards the top of their 'consideration set' of alternative products, services or experiences.
Stage 5   *Purchase* – the customer buys the product.
Stage 6   *Reinforcement* – the customer feels reassured that their decision was correct and that the effects will be or were positive. The time issue is important since the advertising might continue on after the purchase of the product but prior to the actual consumption phase.

The focus of advertising should, then, be directed towards elicitation of particular types of response including

- *the sales response* (whereby price is the key message to stimulate action)
- *the persuasion response* (whereby the advertisement message is powerful enough to change attitudes towards a product or brand)
- *involvement response* (whereby customers empathize with the product or brand)
- *the saliency group* (like persuasion, but where advertising attempts to relate the product or brand to consumers identity or social, cultural and socio-economic characteristics, so that they identify with the values of the brand/product).
(Morgan and Pritchard, 2001: pp. 14–16).

This last aspect of advertising is particularly relevant in relation to current marketing theory about the nature and power of brands (see Chapter 7). The primary purpose of advertising in current markets (for established brands) is not exclusively to increase sales, but to improve consumers' attitudes towards brands over the long term. Many marketing theorists argue about whether advertising is 'strong' enough on its own to impact on sales immediately. Partially this is because advertising is an impersonal type of communication. But also it is because advertising has a variety of different possible functions. 'Weak' theories of advertising are based on

- awareness
- trial
- reinforcement.

Consumers are made aware of products and services through advertising, which can be useful in order to prompt a trial or to provide some reinforcement after an initial purchase. The main purpose of advertising in this approach is to increase awareness of, and defend, brands. Advertising also works to position the brand to the relevant target audience. In Chapter 6 segment profiling was demonstrated as one way in which organisations can create an idea of the target consumers through narrative and images, feeding directly into the advertising brief.

It is important to note, however, that 'strong' and 'weak' theories may apply in different tourism and hospitality services. The hierarchy of effects model often assumes a rationalised decision-making process/framework for consumers, whereas as we have noted, tourism and hospitality decisions are dominated by emotional decisions. Tourism decisions comprise a complex set of different service providers, and as more people book their travel and accommodation independently (as opposed to a package booked through a tour operator) different conditions and states might apply to distinct sub-decisions in the process. And whilst some commentators argue that these models only work with 'high-involvement purchases' (Hackley, 2005) – and tourism in particular has conventionally been categorised as a 'shopping' or high-involvement purchase – this is rapidly changing as more and more experienced consumers with access to credit cards and the Internet make more spontaneous travel purchase decisions.

Fill (2005) argues against this type of essentialising processes either in terms of the ways in which advertising hopes to effect changes in the minds of the consumers or in relation to the promotional strategies of organisations. He argues that there are three main streams of objectives for promotional goal setting:

- marketing goals (achievement of sales of the product to consumers)
- corporate goals (issues relating to market share or volumes of sales, profitability and revenue)
- communication goals (relating to the image, reputation and attitudes of stakeholders towards the organisation)

(Fill, 2005: p. 370).

He argues that all these issues are identified (derived) from the analysis of the current situation and should be directly traceable back to the marketing plan. For various reasons, many organisations fail to reconcile the synergies or differences between promotional goal setting with wider communications strategy or even fail to set promotional objectives at all.

Hackley (2005: p. 34) argues that in any case, there are differences between 'strong' and 'weak' advertising appeals. For many shopping purchases like cars, holidays, a new watch, which are purchased infrequently, advertising needs to consistently remind audiences of the brand's relevance to them, that it is current and successful, rather than continually aim to stimulate sales with a strong sales-oriented promotion. This can easily be related to destinations and to large tour operators and hotel chains. At certain times of the year, like at peak holiday booking times in the seasonal cycle, the messages created might shift towards more strong appeals to purchase.

Hackley discusses another generic model which has been applied to purchase decisions –the *think–feel–do* model. Here, the cognitive component of advertising is linked to thinking. The advertisement must convey key messages concerning attributes of the place, experience or product. However, most messages also include appeals to the more emotional, affective elements of decision-making, feeling, through the use of appealing visual imagery, colours or people engaging with places or activities in a way which produces an empathetic response, a feeling of shared identity. 'Doing', the conative component, refers to appeals to action, either an appeal to persuade a purchase or to motivate action. Most advertisements include elements of all three, combining both rational and emotional messages with a call to action.

In Chapter 4 the process of consumer behaviour and decision-making were outlined in greater detail, but in this part, the purpose is to relate to the specific aspects of design which correlate to the types of feeling states, emotions and motivational forces through the advertising message.

The IPA issues advice that warns of overestimating the power of an advertisement. Although advertising does work, it should not be seen as coercive, but the message should aim to persuade the audience of the benefits and value of taking action in respect of the message. The advertisement must be delivered through the appropriate medium so that it can be seen by the target audience and also that it must be seen over a period of time. Organisations should not expect their advertisement to have an immediate impact; rather, it should aim to provoke interest in the issues, messages or promotions conveyed to a receptive audience over a period of time, and so organisations need to plan for a consistent message over a specific period of time, often related to a period of sales promotion. A single advertisement may be overlooked or forgotten, and so the campaign must stay in the mind or measures taken to remind the audience of the messages.

The IPA also argues that competitors also advertise, and recent advances in technology and the fragmentation and competitiveness of the advertising marketplace mean that competitors can react quickly to a message or promotional campaign. Being innovative in terms of the manipulation of the marketing mix (pricing strategy, product/service innovation or brand) or specifically in terms of an innovative and creative advertising campaign can have a positive impact on sales and market share and can also be readily copied by competitors. So organisations need to be aware of how competitors are advertising their products and services and how that affects the way in which the target audiences react to the advertising.

The main issue is to try to make the advertising stick in the minds of the target audience. Truly great advertising has the potential to create a wider impact by becoming newsworthy in its own right and to create interest through word of mouth and/or reaction from a much broader set of audiences, as was demonstrated by the shocking advertising campaign for Club 18–30 which was discussed in Chapter 2. This results in positive long-term benefits for the organisation as long as the reaction is not negative.

Media Strategies

The term 'the media' is often used to refer to mass communication classes that have the capability to reach an exceptionally wide audience – this is called 'broadcasting' and is predicated on an undifferentiated, multi-segment marketing strategy. Broadcasting strategy is contrasted by its corollary, 'narrowcasting' which assumes that media classes can be used to target narrower segments of the market in a more focused and directed sense. However, as previously mentioned, broadcast media have become very fragmented: there has been a proliferation and diversification of television channels, newsprint media and radio stations, together with the development of new, more ambient forms of media (a range of outdoor and interactive media, including mobile poster displays/billboards, petrol pumps and parking tickets). Furthermore, the associated fragmentation of audiences has led to more narrowcasting approaches being adopted. However, the principles of broadcasting media types are that large numbers of people can be reached within a short space of time. Generally there are three types of media strategy: mass media, targeted and 'mixed strategic' approaches (those that use both mass and targeted approaches). As the names suggest, mass strategies allude to mass media types (*media class*), whereas targeted media suggest a more selective approach (*media vehicle*).

The media decisions for advertising strategies are dependent on

- which consumers are targeted
- the total numbers of people in the segment
- their habits in respect of usage of different media
- the purpose and objectives of the strategy
- the available budget.

The Range of Advertising Channels

It is important to note that advertising is not simply or solely concerned with television and radio and other broadcast media. Indeed, the structure of the tourism and hospitality industry – with a large proportion of small and medium-sized businesses, a small proportion of large multinational organisations, together with regional and national DMOs – means that only few organisations can afford the high prices of production and high media costs of television and radio advertising. Aligned to the resource constraint issues are the marketing communications objectives discussed in Chapter 7.

The Advertising Association (AA) lists the following types of advertising channels (http://www.adassoc.org.uk/):

- directories
- magazines
- national newspapers (display or classified)
- regional or local newspapers
- television or in the cinema
- commercial radio
- poster advertising
- direct mail
- exhibitions
- merchandising and point of sale
- sales promotion
- sponsorship
- Internet
- mobile communications

Some of these channels will be discussed in other chapters with more details. Internet advertising, online and mobile communications are the subject of Chapter 10. Issues and strategies involving sponsorship, sales promotion, exhibitions and direct mail will be discussed in Chapter 9.

Tourism and Hospitality Media Channels

In addition to the list of general advertising channels listed earlier, there are distinct ways in which tourism and hospitality organisations advertise their products and services.

In the case of resort-based hospitality or visitor attractions, for example, it is common to use leaflets or flyers to promote competing venues for bars and nightclubs and restaurants. These are distributed on busy shopping and/or culture streets or quarters of the city or resort. These forms of advertising are particularly important for spontaneous decision-making and to raise awareness of promotions or current events.

When planning a tourism advertising campaign, the organisation must consider the types or mix of media which will be used to deliver the message. The range of media types which can be useful for tourism is as follows:

- campaign
- business-to business (B2B) sales missions/workshop/exhibitions
- print advertising
- direct mail/customer relationship management (CRM)/newsletters
- online advertising/e-CRM (including e-newsletters)
- brochure distribution
- agent training programmes
- familiarisation visits
- lead generation research
              (www.tourismtrade.org.uk/marketingopportunities)

Campaign

Refers to a specific communications drive directed towards potential customers through a communications campaign which includes the full range of above-and below-the-line advertising and media.

B2B Sales Missions

B2B sales missions, workshops and exhibitions refer to communications made to other businesses such as travel agents and tour operators. This is particularly useful for the travel trade where destinations promote themselves to tour operators, tour operators promote their activities alongside destinations and transport and visitor attractions also promote themselves to a travel trade audience. However, customer-oriented travel or holiday exhibitions or 'fairs' have emerged as a new form of promotional activity directly targeting customers.

Print Advertising

Print advertising generally refers to the printed media, advertisements in newspapers, magazines, advertorials and other printed forms.

Online Advertising

Online advertising, including e-CRM and e-newsletters, refers to advertising placed on websites or to e-mail database advertising. Online advertising is the subject of Chapter 10 and so will not be covered here.

Direct Mail/CRM/Newsletters

Increasingly, tourism and hospitality organisations alongside many other sectors are turning to database marketing, or 'direct marketing' and communication approaches as mentioned previously. The advantages of these types of communication are that they can be personalised and thus make appeals on the basis of familiarity, which in turn may lead to customer loyalty. Direct marketing techniques are discussed in Chapter 9 and so will not be covered here. Hotels are particularly good at exploiting their databases and their client preferences to direct personalised advertisements.

Brochure Distribution

In tourism and travel, there remains a heavy reliance on brochures and so the development and distribution of brochures forms an important part of the communications mix. Brochures have always been a vital communication tool in tourism (Wickes and Schuett, 1991) as a source of information and in aiding consumer decision-making (Molina and Esteban, 2006). Brochures traditionally helped overcome some of the problems of intangibility and also allowed the organisation to deliver some strong messages about the destination or organisation in an advertising format. Mostly, brochures are requested by potential consumers so there is a good chance to sell. However, they are often very generic, undifferentiated, and so they may not have enough appeal for niche market audiences. Brochures create representations of the resorts, destinations and brands featured by the organisation. They use a standard mix of images and narrative and the authenticity of these representations has been the subject of much debate in tourism social science (Dann, 1996).

Agent Training Programmes

Agent training programmes are largely designed to enable destinations, tour operators and visitor attractions to brief sales personnel so that they are more aware of the products and their benefits and features. In this way, agent training programmes can be equated with familiarisation visits. However, these can also be targeted at journalists to generate press coverage in the travel and lifestyle sections of the printed or broadcast media. This type of communications strategy is explained in more detail in Chapter 9.

Lead Generation Research

Lead generation research is concerned with the identification of the names and addresses of potential customers to target with personal selling through telephone or house visits.

Message Design

As argued throughout this book, marketing messages must reach the target audiences and make a strong enough impression to penetrate the mass of information and messages being sent and received. However, in Chapter 1 we argued that advertisers in tourism and hospitality have the challenges of intangibility which need to be tackled in terms of both objective and subjective claims.

The intangibility problems identified in Chapter 1 by Mittal and Baker are related to advertising strategies in Figure 8.1. Messages must be designed to provide a physical representation of the components of the service in situations where consumers might not know what to expect from the incorporeality of the experience. This is particularly necessary in the case of new service innovations or new products or destinations. Generality is overcome through the presentation of messages which demonstrate service performance episodes. Testimonials or independent auditor's reports/reviews (such as guide books and rating schemes) can be used to overcome issues of non-searchability. Presentations of people benefiting from the service are often used to overcome the abstractness of settings, as are narrative descriptions of experiences which can also be captured in images.

The messages must also connect with the values, desires and drivers of demand amongst significant numbers of the segments so that

Intangibility problem	Advertising strategy	Description
Incorporeal existence	Physical representation	Show physical components of service
Generality: • For objective claims • For subjective claims	System documentation performance documentation Service-performance episode	Objectively document physical-system capacity Document and cite past performance statistics Present an actual service-delivery incident
Non-searchability	Consumption documentation Reputation documentation	Obtain and present customer testimonials Cite independently audited performance
Abstractness	Service-consumption episode	Capture and display typical customers benefiting from the service
Impalpability	Service-process episode Case-history episode Service-consumption episode	Present a vivid documentary on the step-by-step service process Present an actual case history of what the firm did for a specific client An articulate narration or depiction of a customer's subjective experience

Figure 8.1 Strategies for overcoming intangibility in tourism and hospitality advertising messages.
Source: Mittal, B. (1999). The advertising of services: Meeting the challenge of intangibility. *Journal of Service Research*. 2(1): 105.

the communication objectives are met by people taking the desired actions. Thus the content of advertising must creatively engage people's thought processes, either in terms of rational responses or by provoking appeals for empathy and/or emotional responses. Even if the advertising content is truly great, unless it is seen by the right people, the target audiences, in times and places in which they will be receptive to the messages, the message may fail to provoke the appropriate response. Given these complex factors it is not surprising that much advertising fails to meet stated objectives.

The key for marketers is to ensure that the advertising messages are

- noticed (by the target segments)
- remembered
- actioned.

Following include the main reasons why advertising works:

- The target audience recognises the organisation and its products or services and the benefits they could derive from consuming them.
- They feel positive about the organisation, or they have some loyalty towards it.
- They are actively able to recognise a need for the products or services either at the time or at an unspecified time in the future.
- and, most importantly, they feel that what is offered actively meets their needs, values and/desires outcomes.

The message should specifically have

- appeal (defined in terms of benefits to the target audience)
- specificity (evidence of benefits to them in terms of copy or images used)
- appropriate tone (couched in the language of customers).

Common promotional themes contained within advertising messages are now discussed.

- *Sales promotion* – messages contain references to a specific price offer for the product for a specified time. The type of strategy used is often a rational response model, where the consumer is expected to make an immediate response to a direct stimulus. Sales promotions are discussed in further detail in Chapter 9.
- *Relationships* – messages stress the potential for relationships between the service provider and destination. Examples include associations made between place and identifications of 'home', or the membership or loyalty benefits associated with joining a specific scheme are outlined. These types of messages often employ an 'involvement' approach, developing a deeper emotional response, perhaps by concentrating on associations of 'family' and 'belonging'. Often, messages contain themes of 'home from home', which emphasise security and the ability to meet likeminded people and to feel included. These types of messages also include images of food and drink, to stress the inherently social nature of hospitality services and to provide reassurance that basic needs will be satisfied.
- *Adventure/escape* – travel and being (staying) 'away' from routine places and people create the ability for organisations to stress messages of adventure. These types of messages can encompass any tangible facet or destination attribute or experience, such as relaxing on a beach, relaxing in a hotel room, Jacuzzi or spa as well as adventurous activities. These could also refer to messages of 'escape' from routines which are familiar tropes in tourism and hospitality marketing communications. These types of messages apply a 'persuasion' approach, tapping into deeply held motivations and beliefs about the value of holiday experiences.
- *Convenience* – these types of messages relate to the value that consumers place on the need for advice, information and informed wisdom in helping them negotiate their decision-making. Messages often stress the value of informed experts, people whose opinion can be trusted. These types of messages recognise that consumers have limited amounts of time to spend on deciding on choices which are almost endless given the global scope of contemporary travel. These messages are largely conveyed by travel intermediaries or global

hotel, food and beverage chains. These types of messages employ a 'valence' approach, drawing on utility function of messages.

- *Desire/aspiration* – these types of messages appeal to the realisation that many products, services or destinations are luxury, discretionary items of consumption which are deeply connected with a sense of identity and self-actualisation. Many forms of tourism and hospitality remain beyond attainment for many members of even the wealthiest nations. These services and experiences are couched in messages of aspiration, emphasising 'once in a lifetime' experiences which require a high financial commitment. Honeymoon packages, long haul, extended stay travel experiences, and luxury, iconic or 'hip', boutique hotels often use imagery and text which speaks about 'ultimate desires'. These types of messages also employ an 'involvement' type approach, as the brand or destination experience will form part of the long-term memory.

Creative Development

There are generally five key stages in the development of the advertising process:

1. strategic development
2. creative brief development
3. creative development
4. communication assessment
5. campaign evaluation

The first two stages were covered in earlier chapters in terms of the strategic development of communications campaigns (Chapter 5) and the structure of the industry (Chapter 3), and we will now focus on the issues to be considered in creative development, communication assessment and campaign evaluation. Getting the creative content right is possibly the most crucial aspect of any marketing communications campaign. Creative content concerns not only the creation of the 'message': the words used to convey as aspect of the organisation's activity or products and services. It also concerns the look, feel, colours and tone, images used as contributing to the symbolic content of the communication. It is through the use of innovative, directed and creative content that marketing communications has the power to break through the 'clutter' of most advertising messages to deliver real competitive advantage and powerful impact.

However, this will only happen if the message presents either a new or different product or service or if the message is executed differently and in an interesting way, and importantly if the message concerns something of personal significance to the targeted audience at a particular point in time (Fill, 2005: p. 193). Advertising is most often used to develop positive associations between the individual and the brand, to ensure that a brand's values are communicated towards which the audience has empathy.

As identified in Chapter 3, the role of the advertising agency is to translate the communications brief from the client and to bring together the relevant specialists and professionals to create and coordinate a marketing communications campaign.

Fill (2005) identifies four key elements to the creation of a suitable message. It must contain balance, structure, be presented in a suitable manner and be credible.

Balance

The need for balance is necessary to make a message effective from the perspective of the receiver. Balance refers to the need for information and the need for the information to be presented in a suitable way. This might mean the use of humour or it can refer to a no-nonsense, pleasing or pleasant use of colour and imagery. In the following example, Thomsonfly, a division of Tui Travel, using the recognisable Tui smile logo, employs a balance in a non-humorous way. The use of corporate colours, (pale blue – symbolising the colour of the clear blue skies, red Tui Smile, white lettering), a gently rounded, plain font style, and simple images of Palm trees to denote Palma de Mallorca and distant planes crossing the sky to advertise its routes between the UK and Palma fares from Coventry airport to Pisa (Plate 8.1).

Plate 8.1 Thomsonfly uses Balance in a simple but effective manner.

Go
somewhere
you can't
spell this
weekend

4★ Tatiń, Tallinn
4 nights from £229
4★ Koala-Loompa, Kuala Lumpur
4 nights from £530
3★ Rokaviĉ, Reykjavik
3 nights from £239

lastminute.com

Prices correct at time of going to print, subject to availability & conditions. Offers are limited, once they've gone, they've gone.
Prices include flights, based on 2 sharing accommodation, departing in April 2006. Booking fees may apply. lastminute.com acts as an agent for ATOL protected operators.

Plate 8.2 Lastminute.com use of humour and colour in poster ads.

In contrast, Lastminute.com uses its characteristic company colours (bright pink) together with the image of a directional road sign in a humourous way to advertise short breaks in a variety of destinations, both short and long haul. By suggesting that readers should 'go somewhere you can't spell this weekend' lastminute evoke a sense of exoticism which highlights unusual, off-the-beatentrack short break product destinations and thus differentiates lastminute breaks from those offered by competitors and appeals to consumers sense of adventure (Plate 8.2).

Message Structure

Message structure refers to the content of the message. Key considerations are the level of knowledge of the receiver and the extent to which the message should lead the viewer/reader into drawing a set of conclusions about what they should do. Consideration needs to be given to the type of action required. The previous two examples which both use competitive pricing strategies in their promotional advertising do not explicitly call potential consumers to action, although the means of accessing the products are provided through the provision of the website address. Instead both organisations imply that consumers would and should find a decision to book either a trip to Pisa or a five-star break in Egypt easy and commonsense. These examples do not propose that the travel/tourism services are complex or require a high level of involvement in terms of the decision-making processes. Messages could also be structured to create awareness of an organisation, brand or event which helps to legitimise the organisation or its representatives to the audience.

Message Appeal

Issues of message appeal have already been discussed in an earlier section of this chapter. What needs to be reinforced here is the importance of having the *right* appeal. It is very difficult to quantify or qualify what makes good appeal. The main issue is whether there is a need to present functional product-oriented information about the product or service or whether there is a need to appeal to the emotional needs or states of the potential consumers. This is often boiled down to a basic choice between the levels of textual, factual information required against the amount of visual imagery. The choices are important, because in some cases it is better to let images speak for themselves and so the message must be conveyed only in a headline. The headline then must contain the organisation or brand name – or destination name. Good headlines are able to link a customer benefit or attribute to the name of the organisation/destination. If the organisation identifies a need for 'body copy' (supporting information flowing from the headline), it should be relevant to the target audience. In some cases, there is a need for detailed descriptive information as identified earlier in the chapter, especially for high-involvement decisions or special occasion purchases. Finally, the message should also contain the company contact information or 'call to action'. This allows the audience to communicate with the organisation and respond in the appropriate way.

Also, in terms of appeals to emotional response, the use of sexual imagery to promote tourism and hospitality services has been noted (as per the example of Club 18–30 in Chapter 2). In tourist resorts it is common to see semi-naked persons enjoying themselves on the beach, by the pool, spa or sauna, or in a nightclub having fun. But naked bodies can also be used to convey purity, nature, openness as well as the opportunity or possibility to meet potential sexual partners. Research has shown that physical attractiveness of models in advertisements does have an impact on consumers' evaluations (Baker and Churchill, 1977).

Music (particularly indigenous musical forms) and cultural activities, including language, can also be used to convey a sense of adventure, create mood states or link destinations to emotions.

Fill (2005) also distinguishes between factual, persuasive advertising, demonstration advertising and comparative advertising as forming the basis for an appeal. Fill describes these differences largely in terms of manufactured products/brands. In our context, however, the latter has been used effectively to create associations between current 'feeling states' and expected feeling states upon consumption of the place or the hotel. In positioning a hotel spa as being the ultimate place to relax and unwind, hotels often present images of (largely women in this example) executives under stress interposed with images of them receiving therapy treatments in the spa.

Credibility

In terms of the credibility of the source, the key here is the ability of the organisation to meet its stated values and promises in relation to service quality and other crucial factors. The power of brands to communicate high-quality products and services is a key determining factor in the ability of an organisation to be perceived as credible, since many people may not be active consumers of the products or services, but still may have a perception of the quality of the brand. For example, many people will never experience a stay at the Jumeirah Burj al Arab hotel in Dubai, the hotel has developed a reputation as one of the finest hotels in the world through its unique architectural design, suite-only accommodation and lavish attention to every aspect of service quality.

> Designed to resemble a billowing sail, the hotel soars to a height of 321 metres, dominating the Dubai coastline. At night, it offers an unforgettable sight, surrounded by choreographed colour sculptures of water and fire. This all-suite hotel reflects the finest that the world has to offer.
>
> With your chauffeur driven Rolls Royce, discreet in-suite check in, private reception desk on every floor and a brigade of highly trained butlers who provide around-the-clock attention, you can be assured of a highly personalised service throughout your stay.
>
> (Source: www.burj-al-arab.com/)

Fill identifies that source credibility is determined in relation to the degree of expertise, the degree of attractiveness of the source and the degree of power they hold (2005: p. 530). The credibility of source in relation to the Burj al Arab is given by the growing stature of Dubai as an attractive and very high-quality tourism destination. This is primarily linked to perceptions of Dubai as a wealthy nation built on oil whose citizens demand very high levels of service quality.

Credibility can also be established through association with famous patrons, referrals by relevant peer groups or third-party endorsements.

Case study 8 at the end of this chapter recalls Travelocity's successful campaign fronted by Alan Whicker as a further example; however, the use of celebrities is increasingly important as consumers identify themselves with famous personalities who in turn have become synonymous as brands in their own right.

> ### Illustration
>
> Celebrity chef and superbrand Gordon Ramsey has achieved iconic status through his television shows, books and restaurants which show his excellence in cooking, fiery character and legendry bad language, epitomised by his show 'The F word'. His name-brand restaurant empire is linked to some of the finest hotel properties in the world, with Gordon Ramsey Restaurants at Claridge's, Petrus at the Berkeley, the Savoy Grill, and Gordon Ramsey at The London Hotel, NYC. The Ritz-Carlton is hoping that the Gordon Ramsey restaurant will create competitive advantage, bring in additional business and add to the profile of the new hotel due to his status as a national and international iconic chef.
>
> *Source*: www.travelweekly.co.uk/Articles/2007/03/01/23890/

Of course, not all celebrities convey a sense of distinction and high quality. David Dickinson, a popular UK television personality and antiques expert, whose shows centre on the idea of being able to find a 'bargain' has been used to promote the bargain deals for low-cost airlines.

Advertising Value and Trends

In terms of the effectiveness of advertising, it may be useful to consider the value of spend for different types of media as an indicator of consumer impact. Looking at the changing nature of advertising spending enables an analysis of the shifting character and emphasis of advertising and the effects of new media platforms. Table 8.1 provides an analysis of the breakdown in advertising expenditure by type of media over a six-year period in the UK. It is important to note that over the whole period the value of expenditure on advertising in the UK has risen considerably, to £17.5 billion, and whilst the backdrop of increasing fragmentation of media channels across all forms of media (i.e. the proliferation of television channels across terrestrial, digital, satellite and interactive and mobile platforms, and the great increase in print media including free daily newspapers, consumer and professional magazines) and an increasingly segmented audience indicate a challenge to advertisers, what has resulted is an increasing overall expenditure recognising the need to target consumers across a number of media platforms.

Table 8.1 Trends in UK Advertising Spend by Media Type between 2001 and 2006

	2001		2002		2003		2004		2005		2006	
	Spend	% share	Spend	% share	Spend	% share	Spend	% share	Spend	% share	Spend	% share
Outdoor	677.4	4.50	701.5	4.59	786.4	4.96	847.8	5.02	896.8	5.17	932.5	5.35
TV	3,525.1	23.41	3,689.7	24.14	3,721.5	23.50	3,954.8	23.42	4,097.0	23.63	3,904.5	22.42
Radio	486.8	3.23	492.2	3.22	525.7	3.32	545.2	3.23	520.7	3.00	480.5	2.76
National newspapers	2,062.5	13.70	1,929.6	12.63	1,901.5	12.00	1,974.2	11.69	1,908.9	11.01	1,914.4	10.99
Regional newspapers	2,833.5	18.82	2,878.0	18.83	2,962.0	18.70	3,132.4	18.55	2,993.8	17.27	2,782.4	15.97
Consumer magazines	779.0	5.17	785.0	5.14	783.6	4.95	818.9	4.85	827.1	4.77	812.4	4.66
Business and professional magazines	1,201.5	7.98	1,088.0	7.12	1,048.4	6.62	1,082.1	6.41	1,064.5	6.14	1,015.8	5.83
Cinema	140.3	0.93	154.4	1.01	148.9	0.94	160.2	0.95	158.0	0.91	152.9	0.88
Internet	165.7	1.10	196.7	1.29	465.0	2.94	825.1	4.89	1,366.5	7.88	1,927.0	11.06
Direct mail	2,228.2	14.80	2,378.0	15.56	2,467.3	15.58	2,468.6	14.62	2,371.3	13.68	2,321.8	13.33
Directories	959.0	6.37	990.0	6.48	1,029.0	6.50	1,075.0	6.37	1,131.0	6.52	1,174.0	6.74
Total	15,059.0	100	15,283.1	100	15,839.3	100	16,884.3	100	17,335.6	100	17,418.2	100

Source: OAA/AA/WARC: The Outdoor Advertising Association market data on outdoor advertising as a percentage of all advertising spend, last accessed via http://www.oaa.org.uk/default_frame.asp June 2007).

Although television advertising expenditure is the largest by volume and share, the overall category of print media is by far the largest: grouping together, the expenditure across national and regional newsprint, and consumer, business and professional magazines gives a total share of over 45.5% for 2001. However, it is also interesting to note that the overall share of print media advertising spend fell to a total of just under 37.5%, with regional newspapers and business and professional magazines being the biggest losers.

Another major problem area is the share held by radio advertising, which has remained static over the same period in the face of increasing numbers of radio stations, despite their increased accessibility to the market via the Internet and mobile telephony. These types of media have struggled to remain competitive in the light of the rapid increase in terms of real spend and market share of revenue for the Internet as an advertising medium whose share has grown from 1% to over 11% in 5 years and the value of expenditure has grown over 1000% to a little under £2 billion (this will be discussed in more detail in Chapter 10).

The assault of the Internet on regional newspapers in particular but in the majority of traditional media in general will have a significant and profound impact on the types of media channels used by tourism and hospitality organisations in the future. However, one important factor to consider is the traditional importance placed on printed media as an information source for inspirations and ideas for travel. The weekend travel supplements have remained and will continue to remain a staple of the print media, whereas other sectors might incur more severe shifts towards interactive and Internet and mobile media forms for advertising, it is likely that a core sector of the industry's advertising spend will remain print based. Increasingly common is the trend towards complementary online platforms for the major print media players. Plate 10 shows the online pages of the *UK Times* with an advertisement for the *Sunday Times'* April 2008 issue of *Travel* magazine. This cross-fertilisation between different online and offline media, across different media platform types (newsprint and glossy consumer magazine) is designed to ensure reach and spread across the target market for *Times* newspapers.

Remaining fairly stable over the period in spite of the growth of the Internet are the directories and direct mail media, and outdoor has managed to retain and grow to just over 5% of the overall market. This may be explained by the rise in more ambient forms of outdoor media such as mobile billboards and hoardings, innovative forms of outdoor media campaigns and advertising on parking tickets, petrol pumps, public places, bathrooms, restrooms and washrooms and so on. Whilst as a society we are increasingly connected to each other through the Internet and mobile telephones, we are also a more mobile society, and being exposed to advertising messages in a range of public and open spaces or connected to our travelling behaviour in private cars or on public transport means that we spend more and more time being on the road or travelling between places and are often more receptive to advertising messages in these environments (plate 8.3 shows a travel advertisement in a related public transport environment, the London Underground network).

Plate 8.3 Example of travel poster in a related transport environment.

Illustration

A small guest house might traditionally derive a significant amount of business through advertising with a directory, for example. In the UK, directories such as 'Hoseasons' has been the leading self-catering holiday intermediary providing holidays for over 60 years and now has over 12,000 places to stay throughout the UK and mainland Europe, serving over a million customers each year and dealing with over 2 million telephone calls and hits to its website (www.hoseasons.co.uk/Information). Typically, holiday rental owners or bed-and-breakfast providers pay a subscription to the directory to advertise and may deal with more than one directory depending on the cost and the strength of the business derived from the directory. In addition, such properties or owners may send out direct mailings, place leaflets with the local tourist office, develop a website with online booking facility or subscribe to an online directory.

Similar types of directories exist for a full range of accommodation service providers, and the "Mr and Mrs Smith" directory of boutique hotels is an example of a top of market version.

Source: http://www.mrandmrssmith.com.

Thus the choice of media is crucial to make the most effective impact. And the shifting emphasis of advertising between different media has had the effect of increasing the diversity of communications mix available to organisations in tourism and hospitality. The technological processes are now advanced to the point that online booking or availability systems are cheaply available and so organisations can set up for a relatively low cost a website and place Internet advertising alongside more traditional forms of advertising.

Other forms of print media which have managed to survive the recent volatility in advertising markets for tourism and hospitality are the dedicated special interest travel magazines such as *Conde Nast Traveller*.

The use of creative outdoor media or the appropriation of forms and symbols in a unique and quirky way makes a lasting impression. Outdoor creative advertising is particularly useful in highly mobile societies. Tourism and hospitality environments themselves can be lent very usefully to marketing communications. Billboards in tourism destinations such as national parks might not be appropriate, but the use of ambient media within visitor attractions and tourist destinations is a good way to catch consumers when they might be expected to be more receptive to advertising stimuli. In the destination resort, often tourists are indeed actively looking for new possibilities or experiences and the use of in-destination advertising can have a particularly strong effect. The example (Plate 8.4) of the giant tee together with the distinctive round white dome of a radar detection facility provides a unique and interesting advertisement for the Gleneagles hotel in Scotland, combined with using a mobile billboard advertising hoarding.

Plate 8.4 Creative outdoor – Glenagles hotel.

Current Issues in Tourism and Hospitality Advertising

Often links to *motivations* are made implicit within the messages of tourism and hospitality organisations; after all, most people can empathise with a stated 'need for a holiday'. The DMO or hotel provider needs to remind people of the ability of the destination or hotel to meet the needs for relaxation, 'unwinding', shopping, adventure, culture or pampering – whatever the values being communicated. Services providers understand that the choices facing individuals for these types of purchase decisions are often not low involvement, fast-moving consumer goods, where habit, routine and convenience, familiarity and security dominate cognitive processes. Depending on the type of service, holiday decisions are often high involvement 'shopping' decisions, where family (or peers or significant others) collaboration is often required, significant information search and evaluation of alternatives is conceived as the norm.

However, in recent years, the most successful tourism and hospitality sectors have employed product and promotional strategies which appear to have drawn on similar approaches to marketing communications as those used for fast-moving consumer goods. The 'low-cost' airlines and budget hotels sectors have been successful in employing 'unbelievable' pricing strategies, based on an aggressive cost-control operations and product development model for air travel and overnights, which have firmly established brand values, positive associations and have driven consumer demand over the last 5 years.

Although new wisdom in integrated marketing communications has challenged the ability of advertising to change buying behaviour, it is clear that in the context of Europe and the advanced economies of the world considerable shifts in behaviour have been witnessed, driven by conventional marketing mix strategies that include aggressive mass media advertising, heavy discounting, focus on good value products and online distribution. When easyJet, Ryanair and Travelodge advertise and promote heavy price discounts for seats and bed-nights, there is a ready market which waits to snap up bargain short breaks and trips, which is something that might not easily equate in terms of consumer reaction to similar communications for toothpaste or car shampoo products, for example. Conventional habits around seasonality and timing, planning and response, anticipation and experience, cognitive and behaviour processing have all been affected recently by new travel and hospitality products.

An emotional connection between the brand and type of product does not need to be established in the same way largely because holidays and trips away from home are of significant value to many people in the advanced and emerging economies. It is in this sense that it is too simplistic to argue that tourism and hospitality marketing communications shares the same characteristics as trends in marketing communications for wider fast moving consumer goods.

Advertising must convey knowledge or associations between brands and often between people, places and experiences. It must build up a set of images, beliefs and positive perceptions, favourable attitudes or intentions towards the product, place or brand that also provide some ideas about the experiences that can be expected. The message can also be used to tie in some specific promotional mix information together with these fundamental underlying messages.

Summary

This chapter has outlined the role of advertising in marketing communications for tourism and hospitality products and services. The chapter defined advertising and discussed issues relating to the impact of advertising on consumers behaviour. It linked specific issues in message design to the intangible nature of the various services offered by the industry. Key differences were identified between current thinking in relation to messages for fast-moving consumer goods and tourism and hospitality services. Advertising types and media were discussed, compared and evaluated and key trends in the development of advertising platforms were identified. The reminder of the chapter compared and analysed how advertising messages are constructed for different purposes and audiences.

Discussion Questions

1. Discuss the main debates around the ways in which advertising affects consumers. Refer to consumer processes, theories of 'strong' and 'weak' advertising and other relevant frameworks.
2. Discuss the main issues surrounding the persuasiveness of advertising in the current environment for marketing communications.
3. Choose two advertisements for different organisations that highlight different approaches to marketing communication. Interpret and outline the main aims of each campaign, drawing on theories of communication.
4. Outline the main types of media for advertising, explaining how and why the balance of these is shifting.

Case Study 8: Making Travelocity the Number 1 Choice for Online Travel Bookings

Source: Travelocity.co.uk, *Hello World, hello sales: How Travelocity became an overnight success* by Dominic Hall and Andy Nairn, Miles Calcraft Briginshaw Duffy. IPA Effectiveness Awards 2006 as published in *Advertising Works 15* (www.warc.com).

One way in which an organisation can establish its credibility is through associations with famous patrons, referrals by relevant peer groups or third-party endorsements. Travelocity employed this approach very successfully in the UK with its 'Hello World' campaign featuring Alan Whicker. Although Whicker was seen not as the source of the message, as often happens in celebrity-style endorsements, in reality, his being in impossible situations (a contemporary office drawer of a working woman) doing highly improbable things (playing Flamenco-style guitar) lends a witty and postmodern edge to the way the message plays with the believability of his endorsement. In other words, whilst the core audience might seriously doubt or question the credibility of a mature gentleman of Whicker's high social class actually using the Internet to search for travel destinations and packages, they can put aside these doubts and focus on his credibility as a traveller of distinction and poise, being ever so slightly demeaned in this way (Plate 8.5).

The challenge

Back in 2004 Travelocity was a little known brand. Rivals spent more on marketing and there was no clear reason to visit the online travel agent, which had been launched in the UK in 1998.

At the time just 9% of UK households had Internet access but by 2003, 48% were online and 59% of these had purchased travel, accommodation or holidays over the Net. The market was growing fast but Travelocity remained a minor player. It had fewer visitors than lastminute, Expedia and Opodo and was also behind these three brands in consumer consideration.

Research highlighted the key issue; Travelocity simply was not famous enough. It needed fame to get people to its site but with a small share of voice thanks to a minimal marketing investment and a lack of differentiation it was not generating its own awareness or getting a strong boost from word of mouth.

The challenge for 2004 was to reverse this situation. The agency identified a core target audience of 1.3 million travel aficionados who flew three times a year for pleasure. This group not only spent heavily on travel but would also have significant word-of-mouth power.

To appeal to this group Travelocity was repositioned as 'the inspirational travel experts' and its new spokesman would be the original television traveller Alan Whicker.

The television solution

If fame was to be the key and the spokesman was a television veteran then television would be at the heart of the campaign. Whicker would appeal to 25–35-year-old travellers because of his track record and the fact that he had been off the radar for a few years gave him a cult status.

Plate 8.5 Travelocity and Alan Whicker.

To promote Travelocity he would be seen in unusual places around the world commentating on Travelocity's expertise. Creative executions have been rapidly switched and in the first 15 months of the campaign he was seen in eight different locations including Japan, Morocco and Peru.

The television advertisements, which ran as 40-, 30- and 10-second executions, ran in shows that over-indexed against the target audience of travel aficionados.

The campaign started as regional activity in London and Scotland backed up with national coverage on satellite channels in 2004 before going fully national in 2005. There were bursts of television activity in key periods for the travel business including January and February, Spring and Autumn.

Television was used to drive awareness and reach and be backed up by radio with additional messages about the benefits of using the Travelocity website.

Outdoor would provide a further boost in travel-specific locations such as tube or train stations and airports. Press would provide tactical advertising, and the idea would also be translated online.

Viral stunts such as Alan Whicker dolls and paying people to stand in airport arrivals lounges holding signs for the travel maestro added a sense of fun to the activity.

Results

Within days of the activity's launch the business noted immediate results. Visits to the website more than doubled, a significant year-on-year improvement despite the fact that January is a key time for travel.

The number of unique users nearly trebled in the first month and for 2004 as a whole as up 86% on 2003.

The campaign has also boosted the number of pages that people look at online. By January 2005, page views were increased eight times that the level of January 2003.

And all these visits have led to booming business with sales for 2004 up 135% on the previous year and the growth continued in 2005.

The additional fame provided by Alan Whicker has helped Travelocity boost its market share significantly, in 2004 it showed a 44% increase in its market share, while Opodo and lastminute declined and Expedia showed a 15% rise.

Advertising has played a key role in driving the Travelocity business. The brand's advertising awareness has shifted from last place in the market to first place as soon as the new creative was unveiled.

The differentiation scores have also risen with the number of people who believe the brand is different shifting from 6% in November 2003 to 28% by June 2004. The brand also scores highly on values such as 'inspiring', 'knowledgeable', 'modern' and 'Understands the needs of travellers such as me'.

All this has been achieved despite no other changes to the brand's pricing strategy. In fact, during 2004 rivals reduced their booking fee to £4 to undercut the £10 charged by Travelocity.

Extracting the contribution to the brand's 135% growth in 2003/04 from 39% growth in the online travel market, advertising can claim credit for 71% of that figure. That means £26.3m in new revenue and a return on investment of £5.60 for every £1 spent on advertising.

Travelocity is now well placed for the future. In a market where fame is important it now has buckets of the stuff, its new revenue enables it to increase its fame and it's all down to one man: Alan Whicker, the vehicle for a fantastic journey on television.

Databank

Campaign objectives: Produce a step change in awareness and use of Travelocity.
Target audience: Aficionados, people who fly for pleasure three or more times each year.
Budget: More than £5 million.
Campaign shape: The campaign launched in January 2004 with a primarily regional campaign targeting London and Scotland via macros on ITV, C4 and Five. The activity has used a mix of shorter and longer executions to drive frequency among the target audience of AB 25–54 Adults.
Advertisements have been scheduled in bursts, often running one week on one week off, particularly for the 10-second executions.
Media Mix: television, radio, press, outdoor and online.
Channels used: ITV, Channel 4, Five, Sky, Sky Sports, ITV2, ITV3 and Travel Channel.
Creative agency: Miles Calcraft Briginshaw Duffy.
Media agency: Klondike.

Learning Activity

Choose a tourism or hospitality organisation (this can include a DMO such as a national or regional tourism organisation). Collect as many samples of different types of marketing communications materials used by this organisation and undertake the following tasks:

- Classify the types of media used.
- Evaluate the objectives of the campaign.
- Classify the range of images and words used in the advertising and other materials.
- What messages are being conveyed?
- Discuss the appeal of the message (does the organisation expect consumers to take action, if so, what? Or does the organisation aim to create positive brand associations?)
- Referring to models and concepts used in this chapter, discuss the extent to which the organisation achieves its objectives, referring to evidence from the images and texts.

References and Further Reading

Baker, M.J. and Churchill, G.A. (1977). The impact of physically attractive models on advertising evaluations. *Journal of Marketing Research*. 14(4): 538–555.

Clements, C.J. and Josiam, B. (1995). Role of involvement in the travel decision. *Journal of Vacation Marketing*. 1(4): 3–16.

Dann, G.M.S. (1996). *The language of tourism: A sociolinguistic analysis*. Oxon, England: CAB International.

Fill, C. (2005). *Marketing communications: Engagement, strategies and practice* (Pearson Education). 4th edn. Harlow, Essex: FT Prentice Hall.

Hackley, C. (2005). *Advertising and Promotion: Communicating Brands*. London: Sage.

Hirschman, E.C. (1992). *Postmodern Consumer Research: The Study of Consumption as Text*. Newbury Park, CA: Sage, in association with The Association for Consumer Research.

Loda, M.D., Norman, W. and Backman, K.F. (2007). Advertising and publicity: Suggested new applications for tourism marketers. *Journal of Travel Research*. 45: 259–265.

Mittal, B. (1999). The advertising of services: Meeting the challenge of intangibility. *Journal of Service Research*. 2(1): 105.

Molina, A. and Esteban, A. (2006). Tourism brochures: Usefulness and image. *Annals of Tourism Research*. 33(4): 1036–1056.

Morgan, N. and Pritchard, A. (2001). *Advertising in Tourism and Leisure*. Oxford: Butterworth-Heinemann.

Wickes, B.E. and Schuett, M.A. (1991). Examining the role of tourism promotion through the use of brochures. *Tourism Management*. 301–312.

Key Resources and Links

http://www.tourismtrade.org.uk/marketing opportunities
http://www.marketingweek.co.uk/
http://www.oaa.org.uk/
http://www.asa.org.ukwww.asa.org.uk

Other Communications Strategies

At the end of this chapter, you will be able to

- Define and understand the roles of a range of marketing communications strategies as elements of the communications mix.

- Recognise the importance of alternative forms of communications to the promotion of tourism and hospitality organisations.

- Develop an appreciation of the application of the broader range of communications mix to an organisation's integrated marketing communications strategy.

Introduction

This chapter considers the application of a range of communications channels which support and complement integrated communications strategies for tourism and hospitality organisations alongside advertising. Integrated marketing communications are strategically led and seek to integrate all forms of communications created by organisations to achieve a wide set of organisational goals for delivery of messages to all stakeholders of the organisation. In this way, brand values and orientation to customers can be communicated in a coordinated way. In this chapter, a range of supporting communications techniques are considered. Some of these types of communications are integrated into an advertising promotional campaign to enhance the reach of an advertising campaign and to reinforce the messages through different media channels and platforms. At other times, other methods of communication can be used outside of promotional marketing campaigns to achieve different goals. The following types of approaches to the promotions mix will be considered:

- sales promotions
- personal selling
- sponsorship
- publicity and personal relations
- events and exhibitions
- direct marketing

Although these types of communications have a major role to play in promoting sales, broader, – non-selling – goals are also considered. It is also possible to conceive of these as media channels or communications platforms.

Sales Promotions

Sales promotion is generally considered to be a 'below the line' activity, the point of which is to stimulate sales or otherwise direct consumers to behave in a particular way. Although it may seem as though there is very little difference between sales promotion and advertising since many promotional messages are delivered through an advertising medium, the difference is that advertising, as noted in Chapter 8, is used to develop brand or organisational awareness. In fact, a great deal of advertising is used to drive sales through a specific promotion available for a limited period of time and increase brand awareness at the same time. Often, sales promotions are used alongside a more general communications strategy to raise awareness of the brand or product, to launch a new service or relaunch a brand or product. In these cases, awareness is raised, interest created and sales stimulated through a single communications campaign. Sometimes, different communications mix tools are used at different points in a single campaign if it is lengthy, for example, or to move consumers through the different stages of reaction (cognitive, affective, conative – see Chapter 2) very rapidly.

How Sales Promotions Work

Sales promotions take the form of enticements or inducements. They are delivered in a communications message. The sales promotion must provide an incentive often in the form of a price deal, reward or upgrade, which is time limited. The consequence being that consumer must act within a short time period in order to take advantage of the offer. Most often, it is a price-related incentive which adds value to the service, whether that be price discounting or offering extra nights for free (as in the Thomson case study in Chapter 7). However, it is important to note the distinction between sales promotions that are value increasing and those that are value-adding. Value-adding entails the offer of additional services or service upgrades which augment the basic service for the price paid. This can be in the form of upgrade of room type (from standard to deluxe or from garden view to sea view) or free gifts. The upgrades can be accumulated over time through loyalty programmes, for example. However, sales promotions can also be targeted towards members of staff or agents in the distribution network.

Sales Promotions Techniques

Sales promotions stimulate demand, but it would be wrong to think of sales promotion as being concerned solely with the clearance of unwanted or unsold stock in a reactive, crisis management way. Indeed, the contemporary and competitive tourism and hospitality sector using yield management software and aggressive sales or occupancy targets that sales promotions are now built into strategic planning, which are connected to various points in the seasonal cycle of the trade.

It is also wrong to confuse sales promotions as a marketing communications mix technique with cost leadership as a generic marketing strategy as discussed in Chapter 5. Cost leadership as a strategic choice may also include some sales promotions on a regular or ad-hoc basis throughout the business cycle. However, cost leadership represents an enduring commitment to provide the lowest possible cost for a service and is often accompanied by a guarantee as such. In the UK, First Choice holidays, for example, carries a guarantee of the lowest UK prices, its website claiming that 'If you find your holiday at a lower price elsewhere after booking online, we'll refund you 110% of

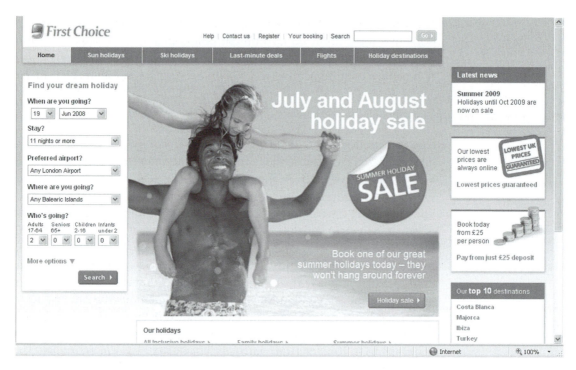

Plate 9.1 First Choice UK summer sale 2008.

the difference (Plate 9.1). Our best deals are always online!' (http://www.firstchoice.co.uk/). The commitment to long-term low costs for services relies on an aggressive cost saving strategy across all levels and activities of the organisation. This is entirely different to the service offered by www.laterooms.com which acts as a clearing house for unsold, last-minute hotel room stock. This is similarly not a sales-promotion exercise but represents a commitment to bring price reductions on a wide range of accommodation properties.

Reasons to employ sales promotion as part of a communications strategy include the following:

- to stimulate sales over the short term
- as an ongoing way to meet longer-term marketing objectives for market share
- to react to competitors' actions

A typical example of a travel company that has excelled at the cost leadership generic strategy but which also, due to the competitive nature of the low-cost air-travel sector, regularly engages in sales-promotions activities to stimulate short-term tactical sales is www. Ryanair.com. Ryanair's strategies are sometimes induced by competitor actions which is another feature of sales promotions.

In very cyclical types of businesses such as the tourism and hospitality sector, the role of sales promotions can be seen as a positive and regular aspect of the business or can be seen as a necessary evil. Many service providers in this sector rely on the general peaks and troughs of demand to enable their businesses to maximise the returns within a limited cycle. High yield during the high season mitigates against the costs of trying to achieve more evenly distributed demand cycles for some organisations. The impact of labour availability in the low season compared to the relative level of demand, coupled with other fixed and variable costs of discounting, advertising and remaining open, often means that businesses in this sector can find sales promotion in low season counterproductive. This is particularly the case where high yields at peak times can be achieved, and again sales promotion in these circumstances is neither a necessary or desirable technique. A good example is in the case of ski resorts which rely on the availability of snow in the peak season. Perdue (2002) provides a useful example of the need to think about sales promotions, yield management and pricing strategies together with promotional communications strategies in a coordinated way in trying to combat issues of perishability in ski resorts.

Illustration

In the food and beverage sector, the UK has seen a shift in patterns of usage and consumption, particularly in the pub sector. J D Wetherspoon is one of the UK's leading pub brands, and it has undertaken extensive sales-promotion work in relation to its themed nights, such as 'curry night' or 'steak night'. It now claims to sell in excess of 60,000 curries a week on the offer of a curry and a pint for £4.95, becoming one of the UK's largest retailers of curry. Wetherspoon argues that the pub business has changed dramatically in the recent years. In the past, pubs were the preserve of men who stopped for a few drinks in an evening. However, more recently, the business has developed into an all-day food and beverage market, with coffee sales, all-day meals and drinking. Whereas sales promotions in the pub trade were often previously focused on offers relating to driving sales of alcoholic drinks (two-for-one deals, double measures for the price of singles on spirits, etc.), promotions now focus on combinations of food and drinks.

Types of Sales Promotions in Tourism and Hospitality

Business-to-Customer Promotions

Point-of-sale material, the full range of advertising techniques, can be directed towards sales-promotion messages, such as competitions;

piggybacking (joint promotions with third-party businesses or organisations, such as travel supplement reader offers, discounted hotel rooms with vouchers collected on purchases of other goods, money-off vouchers through the accumulation of purchase points on credit cards etc.); free samples, giveaways or discounted 'degustation' menus; and direct-mail promotions. Sales promotions can also include loyalty schemes, such as preferred guest membership or frequent-flyer programmes. These programmes work through an accumulation basis, whereby points are awarded for repeated purchases to develop brand loyalty. These schemes have been widely implemented across the sector but the nature of the relationship, as well as the benefits, have been questioned. Sales promotions are often targeted towards particular channel purchases, such as Internet purchase, to try and drive sales through specific channels to alter behaviour.

Business-to-Customer Promotions

Giveaways such as pens, calendars, brochures, local food, souvenirs and incentives are often offered to company staffs in competitions for driving sales and achieving targets. These can include free travel or accommodation in the organisations property in the form of bonuses, which can act as familiarisation trips (see the following section) so that sales teams are better able to deliver sales growth or meet customer satisfaction targets.

Personal Selling

Personal selling is that part of the marketing communications mix concerned with direct interaction between the seller and buyer. This is a highly effective form of communication because the seller can respond to the individual needs of the consumer and provide a tailored and flexible solution. The seller can answer questions, gain feedback instantly, and adapt the message accordingly. This effectiveness is driven by the expertise, motivation and personal qualities of the sales force. Personal-selling techniques and sales management as a management function are an integral part of marketing and have been the subject of much theorising and debate. Personal-selling techniques are often most effective in high-involvement decisions, where there is a high degree of risk and/or complex decision-making. These characteristics do match up with some forms of tourism and hospitality services as discussed elsewhere in this book. Wedding planning, conference and event coordination, honeymoon travel, long-haul travel, gap-year trips, volunteer tourism are all examples of complex and high-involvement decision-making aspects of these services.

There are many tasks and functions of the sales team:

- finding new customers
- selling services
- communicating
- representing the organisation
- establishing and maintaining relationships with customers or other stakeholders

In the tourism and hospitality sector, there are many contexts in which staff responsibilities include a sales function. The service orientation of the sector means that there are many opportunities in which the staff has the opportunity to make a sale, even if the primary role is not part of the sales team. Tour operator resort representatives, for example, have dual roles, a main function of which is a sales function, but also they have a customer care role, communicating with customers during the trip. Flight attendants have a primary service role but a secondary sales role. Many hospitality workers in a range of different departments can 'sell up' or 'cross-sell' services once a customer is in the service encounter. This aspect of personal selling is very important to this sector and yet has received little attention in the academic literature. As more and more organisations find that they have to compete on the basis of low base prices for the core service (flight, ferry trip, accommodation, visitor attraction, etc.), they find that higher profit margins can be attained once the customer is enduring/enjoying the service by selling additional products and services (tours within the destination, souvenirs, gifts and consumer items such as duty free on flights, and even scratch cards). This represents a different form of personal selling than in the conventional sense, since sales professionals focus on sales as a communications channel.

One important example of personal selling as a communication approach is the use of familiarisation 'fam' trips by tour operators and the hospitality trade to agents. Fam trips are also used widely in terms of generation of tourism destination, hotel or restaurant reviews in the media in the context of publicity and public relations (PR), and is discussed in the following section. The focus here is on the role of fam trips within the tourism industry through travel agents.

Familiarisation Trips

Familiarisation trips for intermediaries and the travel press have long been associated with the tourism and hospitality industry. The relationship between the media and the travel and food and drink supplements has relied on these types of promotions, which in return often result in greater positive exposure for the establishment or destination. Fam trips are critical to overcome intangibles in tourism. If word

Illustration

Sometimes publicity about a destination or a tourism organisation can create extraordinary circumstances. Fam trips can help overcome huge communications challenges in some circumstances. In May 2007, the world's media spotlight was drawn to the disappearance of a 3-year-old British girl, Madeleine McCann, from her holiday complex, the Ocean Club at Praia de Luz on the Portuguese Algarve coast, which was allocated through UK tour operator Mark Warner. It seems clear that 'Maddie' was abducted in her sleep from the holiday apartment where the family was staying. Mark Warner resort staff assisted the Portuguese authorities and the family who remained in the resort and led a high-profile media campaign from there to find the missing daughter. There was no question that Mark Warner was in any way responsible for Madeleine's disappearance, but the company has reviewed its security despite being committed to more open-plan holiday complexes. The Warner staff was devastated by Madeleine's disappearance, and the company sent counsellors in the resort to help the staff. The company not only had to deal with other customers who were staying at the resort at the time, but also offered alternatives to customers who had booked for later in the season. It also cancelled a trade advertising campaign.

However, by the end of September 2007, when Madeleine had still not been found (and sadly remains missing), the company had to begin the process of starting to sell the resort once more. It organised a fam trip for 30 agents to show them how it had coped with the extraordinary and difficult circumstances and to try and ensure that the Ocean Club did not receive long-term negative reputation as a family-friendly resort. Even though the company reported that sales were only marginally down for the area, there was potential that the resort could have been eschewed by customers, and it was offering sales promotions. The fam trip for agents was designed to reassure them that Ocean Club was open for business and agents gave the company their blessing and praised Warner for its sensitive handling of the situation. After a period of intense media scrutiny and the overwhelming sadness of the story, for which a happy resolution looks increasingly unlikely, Mark Warner had to show the best of the property and to allow agents the chance to experience Praia de Luz resort outside of the spin of the broadcast media's focus on the Madeleine story. The fam trip was the best way in which Warner could have approached the situation, given the impersonal nature of advertising and the strong possibility for negative reaction to straightforward sales promotions.

(Sources and further references:

http://www.travelweekly.co.uk/Articles/2007/09/27/25313/agents-praise-mark-warners-madeleine-resort-fam-trip.html

http://www.travelweekly.co.uk/Articles/2007/05/10/24303/mark-warner-prays-for-abducted-girls-safe-return-10-may.html

http://www.ttglive.com/NArticleDetails.asp?aid=8573)

of mouth is one of the most important and effective forms of marketing communication, it is because the stories of people's experiences in a destination or of a hotel or restaurant can create evocative and emotional associations for others. Fam trips are important because travel agents can be conceived as opinion leaders (see Chapter 2) for tourism services, and so the need for agents to have first-hand knowledge of the destination, resort or hotel can make a huge contribution to the sales function. Agents are more likely to sell a destination or an operator which has provided fam trips, and so the use of fam trips by operators and destination marketing organisations (DMOs) can be considered a form of encouraging loyalty amongst the sales force.

Personal selling is useful if the organisation opts for a push strategy, but it requires significant investment in personnel and training, knowledge of where sales are most likely to be achieved so that sales territories can be identified – such as through the segmentation, targeting and positioning (STP) process discussed in Chapter 6. Personal selling can complement other forms of communication in the mix, especially advertising, so that the brand is already positioned in the mind of the consumer, and the sales personnel become representative of the brand.

Sponsorship

Sponsorship has been defined as 'a business relationship between a provider of funds, resources or services and an individual, event or organisation which offers in return some rights and association that may be used for commercial advantage' (Sleight, 1989: p. 4, cited in Jobber, 1995: p. 452).

Sponsorship generally takes the form of broadcast (such as television or radio programmes) or events (such as sports, music, cultural events). There are four main forms of sponsorship which can be used as part of the communications mix strategy:

1. sports sponsorship
2. programme sponsorship
3. arts sponsorship
4. events sponsorship

Each of these types of activity has the benefit of having the power to bring the brand to the attention of a very large market, largely through the potential of televised or other broadcast media coverage.

There are five main reasons for an organisation's choice of sponsorship as part of its communications strategy (Jobber, 1995):

1. creation of favourable brand associations
2. creation of promotional opportunities

3. creation of additional publicity

4. creation of corporate hospitality opportunities

5. creation of corporate social responsibility (CSR) profile

Creation of Favourable Brand Associations

The right choice of sponsorship arrangement can create favourable associations between the target audience and the brand. This can help position the organisation or its brands in the minds of consumers.

Creation of Promotional Opportunities

A further benefit derives from the opportunity to promote the brand through the event or sponsorship activity. Additional merchandising containing the brands logo can be sold at events, for example.

Creation of Additional Publicity

Sponsorship of televised sports, such as football teams (as described in case study 9, at the end of this chapter), creates additional publicity and exposure to the brand through wider media. Sponsorship of a Premier League football club in the UK means that the name of the organisation appears on the players' shirts, which is seen by the spectators and potentially by millions in the global audience on television.

Creation of Corporate Hospitality Opportunities

Sponsorship of events creates opportunities for organisations to provide incentives for staff sales teams as part of a rewards scheme; undertake selling opportunities with key customers (particularly in relation to corporate clients) or to provide incentives for intermediaries.

Creation of Corporate Social Responsibility Profile

Increasingly, sponsorship is used in an alternative charitable way to create associations between the organisation and its image, reputation or aims in respect of CSR. This is particularly important where the services are offered in underdeveloped areas of the world, where the impact of the tourism activity is great or where natural or physical resources are shared between local communities and visitors. Charitable sponsorship of local community initiatives can help an organisation to improve its reputation as a caring organisation and contribute to promotional initiatives of wider strategic aims. This was discussed in Chapter 3 in the context of organisational ethics.

Sponsoring the weather reports in the regional UK Central television by East Midlands-based low-cost airline 'Bmi baby' builds positive brand image for the airline within the region. Sponsoring weather reports is important as it is a key driver of UK outbound tourism.

Considerations on which type of sponsorship arrangement to enter into centre on the following:

- What are the objectives for choosing this approach?
- In what ways does the image of the event or programme match up to the 'personality' of the brand or organisation?
- Do the target audiences of the organisation match those of the event/programme?
- What are the opportunities for sales promotion and publicity?
- What are the risks for unfavourable publicity?
- Does the activity represent value for money for the organisation as a part of its communications strategy?

These questions are critical for sponsors as there are many issues which remain outside the control of the sponsor organisation. Unfavourable publicity may be generated if there is a poor reaction to an artist's exhibition or violence erupts at a football match or a sports personality's reputation becomes tarnished by reports of drug misuse (doping) or other forms of misconduct. There is often no tangible evidence between the use of sponsorship and an increase in sales. The purpose of sponsorship as a function of advertising or sales promotion or public relations is quite unclear, and so it is not possible to conclusively identify the benefits of sponsorship to the sponsoring organisation other than through awareness research and evaluation.

Publicity and Public Relations

Publicity and PR can be described as a management activity and one aspect of the communications strategy that is focused on the management of attitudes and opinions held by publics of the organisation. According to the Institute of Public Relations *public relations* is defined as 'the discipline which builds and maintains reputation, with the aim of earning understanding and support and influencing opinion and behaviour. It is the planned and sustained effort to establish and maintain goodwill and mutual understanding between an organisation and its publics.'

In previous chapters, the distinction between the creation of messages which are directed at selling products and services and of messages directed towards impression management has been highlighted. Thus the focus of PR activity can be divided into two aspects:

1. the delivery of information at the level of corporate communications
2. the marketing- or promotion-related PR activity in the communications mix

The difference between the two can be delicate and inter-related because favourable impressions made in the media through corporate communications can lead to general brand awareness through exposure and ultimately the generation of sales. However, the PR activity is different in that the communications messages are generally very different from advertising messages. A further aspect is the importance of internal communications, especially in the context of large-scale or multinational, global organisations. Lack of or deficiencies in internal communications is a major factor behind inefficiency in these organisations, and in labour-intensive organisations with high staff turnover such as the tourism and hospitality sector, effective internal communications strategies can also impact upon the quality of service delivery and hence the short- and long-term profitability of the organisation.

The organisations publics can be broken down into external and internal.

External

Media – television, radio and press

Public – local communities, pressure groups and the general public

Government – local, region, national authorities, non-governmental organisations

Internal

Internal stakeholders – shareholders, banks, board of trustees

Internal representatives – staff, trades union representative

Internal commercial – suppliers, agents and intermediaries, customers

Therefore, the role of PR and publicity is wider than advertising. There are generally two types of reasons to engage in PR, reactive and proactive, which are driven by external or internal events. Reactive messages are required as responses to requests from media and press as the following illustration will prove. Proactive messages are created in response to a range of information stimuli, the production of the annual report, for example, can (especially in very large organisations) provide detail on the financial performance of the organisation over the previous year which in itself can become a newsworthy item. Similarly, new research, new product development (such as an unusual new package tour theme), alliances and mergers and acquisitions, price changes and conferences and seminars are all examples of activities which could be deemed newsworthy and require input from the PR team. The use of PR and publicity is growing rapidly, and organisations, particularly DMOs are pumping a great deal of investment into publicity media strategies. Happily, Lubbers (2005) found that travel journalists and tourism professionals often share the same point of view and agree about the main issues in the representation of the industry/destinations in the press. In the case of tourism destinations, the use of 'press kits' (Gladwell and Wolff, 1989) has been widely used by DMOs to pull travel writers to the destination so that a review can be facilitated. A press kit informs travel writers about the features of the destination with the aim of enticing writers to feature them, and thus the press kit becomes a promotional tool to generate publicity. In terms of internal stakeholders, newsletters are often created to alert audiences to changes in personnel or organisational structure, sales figures, awards and prizes, new products and mergers, new developments in respect of a re-positioning or re-branding exercise.

Illustration

Most companies, especially those involved in travel, face the risk of a serious incident occurring at any time. One such situation occurred in January 2008 when during the final approach to London Heathrow, a British Airways' plane lost all control of its engines and the flight crew were forced to make an emergency landing. The plane was 'glided' into the airport, just managing to skim over the perimeter fence, and upon touching down in the rough grass, the plane lost its entire undercarriage and very nearly one of its wings.

This was a potential PR disaster for British Airways (BA), yet only 24 hours later the press was not condemning or criticising the airline. Partially this was because there were no serious injuries luckily. However, mainly, it was the way that the situation was handled by BA that made all the difference. BA's chief executive, Willie Walsh, was quick to step in front of the cameras to make a statement in which he praised the flight crew for their professionalism and courage in landing the aircraft safely and for evacuating the 136 passengers. He stated, 'they are heroes and everyone at British Airways is very proud of them.'

The speed and timing of the statement gave the media a different focus than the stricken plane, and it portrayed the company as one in control. Moreover, the refocus of attention on to the positive actions of the crew set the tone for the media attention that followed. Thus, the following day *The Daily Mail* reported how the pilot had 'saved the lives' of 151 passengers, and the headlines of *The Mirror* called for the pilot to be 'given a medal the size of a frying pan', whilst the headlines of *The Telegraph* stated simply, 'crash pilot averts disaster'. The prime minister said, 'I think it's right to pay tribute to the calmness and professionalism of the British Airways staff and the captain and what he achieved in landing the aircraft.' All this demonstrated how professional crisis management can avert a PR disaster.

Source: http://www.media-mentor.co.uk/newsdesk_two.html

In the context of messages directed at an external audience through publicity, Jobber (1995) identifies that there are five key characteristics:

1. message credibility
2. no direct media costs
3. loss of control over publication
4. loss of control of content
5. loss of control of timing

Although the first two characteristics are very positive, they are tempered by the loss of control the organisation has once the message has been created. Messages delivered through publicity are reported by the broadcast media and so to the general public and carry a high degree of trust because they are delivered through a trusted third-party source. Similarly, there are no direct media costs, and so publicity is a relatively cheap way to gain exposure for the brand. However, once the message has been created and sent out through the press channels, there is no direct control of the organisation over its publication. PR specialists often have many contacts in the media which they rely on to ensure that a story gets taken up (and strength of contacts is one of the ways in which PR companies differentiate between themselves), but there is no guarantee that a story will get published. Also part of the role of the PR firm is to ensure that the story is written in a way that it is seen as newsworthy by the media. In this process, however, the key message might be altered, and similarly, the organisation looses control of the message content if the media picks up on a different angle to the story. A final point is that the organisation looses control of the timing which is critical for tourism and hospitality services which are perishable.

Public relations is increasingly being seen as a very persuasive and powerful aspect of the marketing communications mix, and organisations now place a great deal of effort into this tool. The role of PR has traditionally been exploited best by the not-for-profit sector as a cheap and reliable way to publicise fund-raising activity, or to raise goodwill, awareness and interest in the cause. However, in recent years, the private and public sectors have sought to explore the benefits that PR can bring to enhance the visibility of messages or brand values and to integrate the external and internal communications between an organisation and its publics.

Events and Exhibitions

Events, exhibitions and trade shows are becoming an increasingly important additional element of the communications mix. Big trade events in tourism, such as the ITB in Berlin and the World Travel Market (WTM) in London, become a central part of the B2B marketing process in tourism. Of course, these are not solely the preserve of tour operators or DMOs but hotel chains and resorts are widely represented since it is through these trade events that allocation deals and package-tour arrangements can be made between the principals and the destinations.

The main purposes of trade exhibitions are to

- launch new products
- meet new contacts with a view to product development
- gather competitor intelligence
- learn about new trends and market developments.

Illustration

The World Travel Market proclaims to be *the* global event for the travel trade. According to its website, the 2007 event was attended by over 48,000 travel professionals representing the whole of the tourism and hospitality sector. Over 20,000 exhibiting staff from 197 countries and regions represented the event. There were 618 exhibition stands, and almost 10,000 exhibiting companies and partners with specialist programmes for travel agents on product-knowledge training. WTM is held each year on the second week of November. The UK delegates make up just under 50% of all representatives (www.wtmlondon.com).

The ITB is held each year in early March in Berlin. It too claims to be the world's leading travel show. In 2008, it had over 177,000 visitors of which 110,000 are trade professionals, according to its website. It has representation from 180 different countries and is the leading B2B platform for travel professions with one-third of all stands taken by German organisations to two-thirds international (*source*: www.itb-berlin).

It is no coincidence that these two huge travel events dominate the international travel trade exhibition market. The German and UK outbound travel markets dominate, and they are geographically well located to draw in a global trade audience.

However, it is not just for the B2B market that events and exhibitions are important. Trade shows can present a focal point of contact with customers, particularly in relation to travel and tourism, or holiday shows and events. These exhibitions have a number of benefits for organisations:

- They are often organised by a third party which minimises the financial commitment, has the potential to reach a large audience through advertising can create opportunities for sales.

- They provide an opportunity for the organisation to meet with prospective customers in an environment in which the customers voluntarily choose to participate.
- They allow the organisation to gather competitor intelligence and informal market research, especially in the form of feedback on its products and, potentially, its communications materials.

This allows organisations to communicate with customers in a non-sales-oriented environment, so there is the potential to develop deeper relationships. This may include generation of sales leads or information to feed into customer databases. However, the organisation must see exhibitions as part of a wider marketing communications strategy. They can take up a lot of valuable time and resources and divert sales staff away from selling environments.

Events can also take the form of one-off special events which are totally designed to drive a communications strategy. The drinks company Innocent Smoothies in the UK organised an event called Fruitstock during 4–5th August 2007, a weekend event which essentially took the form of a free rock music festival. In 2008, the company is looking to repeat the event with a young twist on the traditional English village fete (http://www.innocentvillagefete.co.uk/). Not only do events such as this have the potential to play a major role in an organisation's efforts to build brand awareness through association with other activities which might be of interest to the target audience (in this case through music acts, a sense of English country life in the heart of London, free fun and lots of activities for families and so on), they are also good for providing a focus for marketing campaigns. This is because PR, advertising, sales promotions and all other forms of marketing mix activities can be driven around the theme of the event.

Direct Marketing

Direct marketing is a broad term, but can be defined as all the media activities, communications and responses which are directed at individual customers or potential customers. In other words, direct marketing is targeted at individual users instead of through intermediaries. Traditionally, we tend to think of direct marketing as direct mail, which is only one form of direct communication. However, the direct marketing industry is now a much more complex proposition.

The purpose of direct marketing is to capture information about customers and potential customers from the responses they make to direct 'calls to action'. A call to action can be delivered through a range of media platforms, and so it is not uncommon to include posters and press (sometimes in the form of inserts as per the Visit Wales case study in Chapter 5), the Internet and e-mail, as well as direct mail.

The purpose of the call to action may be to

- make a purchase
- request a brochure
- visit a website
- send in your details.

The ultimate marketing purpose of direct marketing techniques is to establish and manage direct relationships with customers, through the capture of personal information in a database. This is growing because organisations want to maximise the effectiveness of their marketing communications strategies and target-specific groups/segments of users directly, and this represents a much more cost-effective method than above the line-media activity. Direct marketing techniques do this by driving sales growth and are mainly tied to sales promotions effects alongside advertising campaigns and a broad marketing communications strategy for larger organisations.

However, direct marketing can also be a very useful means of communication for very small organisations. Guest books and visitors lists provide a ready source of in-house database of personal mailing information about customers. Lists of enquirers can also be generated if the organisation identifies that direct marketing is to be a key part of its communications strategy. In many small tourism firms, relying on repeat business and with high levels of retention, direct marketing communications are a vital part of the relationship they have with customers.

The main types of direct marketing for tourism and hospitality organisations include

- direct response advertising
- direct mail
- e-mail
- inserts.

Direct response advertising are those that include a call to action (visit the website and enter details, send off for a brochure, fill in a response coupon). Inserts in catalogues and newspapers is a prolific form of direct marketing. E-mail will be discussed in Chapter 10 in the context of broader advertising and communications strategies based on technology platforms.

Direct mail is generally a tool which is used based on databases. An organisation either sends material through the post to customers from its own database list of addresses or it can buy addresses from a third-party organisation. The latter is becoming increasingly common as specialist companies use software which can be used to segment the market by postal code (zip code). This point is critical for direct marketing decisions as a tool in the communications mix:

- Who are the target market?
- What is the response we want (sale or further communication)?
- Why should we contact them now (what is the news/sales promotion)?
- What will direct methods contribute to the achievement of communications objectives?

The main benefits of direct marketing are that it allows organisations to personalise the message and direct it towards specific targeted individuals. Because direct marketing is often tied to a sales-promotion strategy, the outcomes can be easily measured and the return on investment evaluated. It allows organisations to stimulate new sales to existing customers which minimises marketing effort and is a more efficient use of the marketing budget. It actively seeks to bypass channel intermediaries which can also reduce costs by removing commission charges; however, there are negatives. Costs can be higher than advertising, direct mail can produce a negative response in customers, and indeed the message might not even reach many in the list if people immediately suspect that they are the target of junk mail. This means that customers might react unfavourably to further communications in the future.

Direct marketing techniques can be effective at building and maintaining relationships with customers, but the relationship needs should be based on a real connection between the values of the organisation and the customers. This puts the emphasis on the credibility and value of the database list.

Summary

This chapter has discussed and evaluated a range of alternative tools in the communications mix. In the present context, it was shown that all these forms of communication can be used very effectively to achieve particular communications goals. The applications to personal selling, sponsorship, PR, direct marketing and events and exhibitions were discussed. However, this range of communications channels was also shown to work most effectively in conjunction with a broader communications strategy following the principles of an integrated marketing communications approach. Organisations can make an effective impact with consumers using a variety of channels and communications platforms. However, similarly with advertising and other strategic decisions discussed in previous chapters, a note of caution was given in that marketing communications of any sort need to be targeted effectively towards the organisation's identified segments and that measures of effectiveness also need to be implemented to ensure that the methods do add tangible value or returns to the organisation.

Discussion Questions

1. Define the role of alternatives to advertising in the communications mix for tourism and hospitality.
2. Discuss the effectiveness of public relations as a communications tool for tourism and hospitality organizations.
3. Explain how could these tools complement advertising strategies as part of a broad communications strategy.
4. Assess the value of direct marketing techniques for contemporary hospitality organisations, explaining how such techniques could be used more effectively.

Case study 9: XL.com Sponsor West Ham United to Grow Awareness

'XL Leisure Group is hoping to tempt West Ham footballers to holiday with its luxury Aspire brand, after sealing a sponsorship deal with the Premiership club. The partnership will include shirt sponsorship, pitch-side advertising and a bespoke XL design that will cover the roof of one stand. The multimillion-pound deal also gives XL access to West Ham's database of fans, while the club's website receives 500,000 unique users each month. Bosses claim that the 3-year tie-up will seal its position as the third-biggest player in the UK market once the big four have consolidated. Phil Wyatt, XL Leisure Group chief executive, said, 'After these mergers, we are the third-biggest travel firm in terms of Atol numbers, but we still need to get more awareness.'

'We must build the brand, as it is still young, and this gives us a chance to establish ourselves as a major player.'

He added 'There are some great opportunities for cross-fertilisation, not just for the XL Airways brand, which already has good recognition, but also for the operating brands.'

In addition to the airline, the XL group also operates in the UK as Kosmar, Aspire Holidays, Freedom Flights, trade-only Excel Holidays and Travel City Direct. Scott Duxbury, West Ham deputy chief executive, said, 'We are thrilled XL.com will be an integral part of the club's future as we look to grow on and off the pitch. We have been seeking the right partner for West Ham United and, in XL.com, we have the perfect match." Wyatt confirmed that the deal was for a "multimillion-pound" figure but would not disclose the amount.'

(*Source*: XL Aims to Score with West Ham, 8 June 2007; http://www.ttglive.com/NArticleDetails.asp?aid=7734)

In this case the XL Leisure Group realises that the brand means very little to its potential customers. The use of a sponsorship deal with an English Premier League football club based in London is significant because of the high degree of media exposure the brand will achieve through its brand being on the players' shirts and on pitch-side, and other advertising and promotional materials at the club, as well as the exposure gained through the West Ham United website. The other major benefit for the XL group is the additional access to the database of West Ham supporters.

The major reason for this type of major sponsorship deal is to position the XL brand. Currently, the brand suffers from a lack of positive associations, or recognition, as the company 'accepts that, for most consumers, the name XL means nothing.' The vehicle through which XL can achieve this step change in public awareness is through the sponsorship deal with West Ham. This is appropriate given that the organisation has a large range of subbrands which has the potential to appeal to a wide audience. The aim of the activity is, according to Peter Owen, CEO, 'We want to make XL.com famous. Initially bulk it up, in terms of our own product, and then next year introduce third-party product.' The sponsorship deal needs to be supported by other marketing activities and communications mix tools, because fans might see the brand and not realise that it is a travel company (http://www.ttglive.com/NArticleDetails.asp?aid=9414)

Learning Activity

- Discuss the rationale behind the XL.com's strategy for sponsoring West Ham United.
- Explain why tourism organisations choose to sponsor sports teams.
- In small groups, propose a range of additional marketing communications mix tools which you would choose to complement the sponsorship activity.
- Evaluate the potential benefits and problems which might arise for XL.com through their deal with West Ham United.
- Outline any segmentation or market-related challenges you foresee, if any, arising from this form of activity.

References

Gladwell, N.J. and Wolff, R.M. (1989). An assessment of the effectiveness of press kits as a tourism promotion tool. *Journal of Travel Research*. 27: 49–51.

Jobber, D. (1995). *Principles and Practice of Marketing*. London: McGraw-Hill.

Lubbers, C.A. (2005). Media relations in the travel and tourism industry: A coorientation analysis. *Journal of Hospitality and Leisure Marketing*. 12(1/2): 41–55.

Perdue, R. (2002). Perishability, yield management, and cross-product elasticity: A case study of deep discount season passes in the Colorado ski industry. *Journal of Travel Research*. 41: 15–22.

Sleight, S. (1989). *Sponsorship: What Is It and How to Use It*. Maidenhead: McGraw Hill.

Key Resources and Links

http://www.ttglive.com/NArticleDetails.asp?aid=9414

http://www.ttglive.com/NArticleDetails.asp?aid=7734

http://www1.messe-berlin.de/vip8_1/website/Internet/Internet/
www.itb-berlin/englisch/index.html

www.wtmlondon.com

www.cipr.co.uk/

Interactive and E-communications Issues and Strategies

At the end of this chapter, you will be able to

- Understand the value and importance of online marketing communications and advertising strategies in tourism and hospitality.

- Recognise the changing nature of Internet interactivity, the changing behaviour of users and the impacts of these changes on marketing communications in tourism and hospitality.

- Understand and define a range of online forms of marketing communications and their value for the tourism and hospitality industry.

- Understand how online advertising and other communications form part of organisational marketing communications strategies.

Introduction

At various points in this book, the importance of technology has been stressed as a driver of change in the tourism and hospitality sector. This chapter looks at the growing influence that the Internet is having on the marketing and distribution of this sector. It outlines the main forms of interactive and e-communications available to organisations. It begins by quantifying the growing importance of the Internet as a media channel for advertising. This is reflected in the value of online advertising which is outlined. Issues of online behaviour are discussed. The discussion then moves onto define and describe various forms of online marketing open to organisations. Finally the chapter concludes with a discussion of the importance and characteristics of user-generated content for the organisations in this sector. User-generated peer-to-peer communications forms an exciting and challenging medium, providing them not only with potential opportunities to capitalise on the trusted and objective content but also serious challenges in terms of marketing control and reliability.

Growth of the Internet

For many people in the advanced and technologically developing world, it is difficult to imagine life without or before the advent of the Internet. Yet Internet technology is a relatively recent phenomenon. In 1995, the fledgling Internet was largely confined to academic users and regionally within the USA and Europe. In the early days of the growth of the technology, the business community concentrated on getting their businesses online, developing organisational content. However, the rapid rise and uptake of e-commerce activity and the use of information communications technology (ICT) has received ample attention in the literature and is discussed elsewhere (Buhalis, 2000; Buhalis and Laws, 2001). Instead, this chapter outlines the dramatic changes that Internet access and computing technology and use are having on the marketing communications of tourism and hospitality organisations.

The surge in the growth of penetration of personal computing and Internet access has rapidly changed the patterns of work, leisure, access to information and media exposure across large parts of the world. The proportion of the population with Internet access in the UK, for example, stands at over 60% in 2006, double the 30% in 2000 (according to *The Communications Market 2006*, Office of Communications [Ofcom], cited in Keynote, 2007: p. 7). A revolution in Internet connection speeds has been enabled by broadband connectivity and its uptake. By 2008, 65% of UK households had Internet access, of which over 56% had a broadband connection, some 8.9 million households. This was an increase of 5% on the previous year (Source: Office of National Statistics, 2008). Broadband reduces download times and so allows users to view more pages than ever before. In recent years, there has been an explosion of content of different types and forms, largely driven by the capabilities of broadband technology. The Internet Advertising Bureau (IAB) identifies that broadband penetration is predicted to continue growing and will be 63.5% of all homes by 2010 (PriceWaterhouseCoopers [PwC], Global Entertainment and Media Outlook 2006–2010, cited from www.iabuk.net). This dramatic growth in the uptake of broadband Internet technology, coupled with the increased speed and memory capacity of personal computers, has enabled a technological leap in the types of applications made possible. Music and film clip downloads are cheap, simple and quick to undertake, for example. Multimedia content is rapidly becoming the norm for organisations wishing to present themselves over the World Wide Web in a dynamic and interesting way.

This has had an enormous impact upon the range of media and types of marketing communications which are now possible through the Internet. This chapter assesses these changes and highlights the possible effects of this explosion of Internet use for tourism and hospitality sector. First, however, the chapter defines online advertising and some key terms. It goes on to analyse various types of online advertising strategies before it considers the broader implications of advertising and communicating information through this exciting and rapidly growing medium.

Growth of Online Advertising

The advertising content of the World Wide Web has grown extremely rapidly, to become one of the major new forces in marketing communications spanning all sectors, but particularly within the tourism and hospitality sector. After the dot-com bubble burst in 2000, there was a slowdown in Internet advertising, but there has been a huge surge in advertising expenditure since 2003. Keynote reports that, in the UK, there was a 136.4% increase for that year, partly attributed to the development of new forms of Internet advertising, such as paid listings and sponsored advertisements on search engines (ibid, 2007: p. 5). This was followed by 77% growth in 2004, 65% in 2005 and 40% for the first half of 2006 compared with the same period in 2005. Despite this deceleration in growth, Keynote argues that these figures represent a consolidated position as the fastest growing advertising medium (ibid, 2007: p. 5). The IAB notes that online advertising took an 11.4% share of the UK advertising industry for 2006 (IAB/PwC, April 2007, cited from www.iabuk.net); this growth has continued despite the limited research on the effects of online advertising on consumers responses. In one of only a handful of studies, Wu *et al.* (2008) found that only when consumers had a higher involvement in the product content of the online travel agencies advertising did they notice some effects on consumers' attitudes and responses.

The Value of Online Advertising Spend to the UK Market

The value of online advertising is enormous and currently growing continuously as new developments drive users' – customers' – engagement with the technology and the capacity of the Internet to connect with their lifestyles, user (purchase)-cycles, needs and values. This is also particularly the case in the context of the travel industry in Europe. The rapid and intense growth of online travel retail, for example, is forecast to continue, with the market forecast to increase by 20% to $69 billion in the European Union between 2006 and 2011, according to Euromonitor International.

The case of the UK provides a good example of the growing importance of the Internet to the advertising industry. In 2006, Internet advertising expenditure in the UK was over £2 billion. Whereas all other types of media expenditure weakened, the share of Internet advertising grew over 7% and pushed the entire industry to a 1% overall growth for 2006 (WARC/IAB/PwC, 2007). All other forms of advertising spend ('adspend') fell in relative percentage terms over the same period. Indeed, adspend on the Internet overtook national newspapers, which recorded a market share of just over 10%. The UK market is important since (according to the IAB) the global average for Internet advertising is currently 5.8% of all adspend, whereas in the UK this climbed to a total of over 12% for the latter half of 2006.

In terms of the share by format of adspend, the IAB found that display advertising, including banners and online sponsorships, also rose 35% in 2006. However, the real leader in terms of growth was the paid-for-search (discussed later) category, which rose by over 50% in 2006, which amounted to £1.2 billion of total online adspend, almost 58% market share.

However, whilst it is important to note the great increases in market share and performance of Internet advertising, it is also pertinent to note that the IAB identifies that the major growth sectors were automotive, technology, property and retail sectors. It may be, however, that the tourism and hospitality industry was at the forefront of the Internet advertising revolution, and so the proportionate increase in its market share of advertising activity may not be so great.

The IAB does, however, identify that the key drivers for growth are the increasing capabilities derived from the uptake of broadband Internet technology, which in turn allows for greater application of 'rich media' in advertising over the Internet, particularly in terms of film (video) and sound files, which is in turn connected to the growth in user-generated content over sites such as YouTube and MySpace and the related types of format sites for travel and tourism in particular (www.iabuk.net).

Illustration

While the impact of this technology adoption may be seen as only tangentially relevant to the broader food service and hospitality services, the hotel industry can certainly benefit from the adoption of such technological changes. Some hotel chains are making the most of the available technology in creating dynamic websites, incorporating full audio-visual means to make the desired impression with the target audience. This adds interactive and tangible elements to the experience of using the sites and, through virtual tours of the hotel itself over the web, making the ambience of the hotel more tangible. The development of hotel intermediary sites which focus on niche products such as boutique hotels or mass-market-oriented portals selling rooms at discounted rates to appeal to the last-minute purchaser (such as www.laterooms.com) reflects a growing recognition of the importance of recent trends to book the individual elements of the trip separately. The ability to create unique and individual package trips using online services is driving the growth of e-intermediaries, new product development and new travel and hospitality services, which is creating a new direction to advertising both online and offline.

Online Behaviour

Not only is the spread of Internet access changing the type and nature of advertising online, a further consideration is changes in the types of user activity which also impacts upon the ways in which messages should be directed towards appropriate actions.

Sites where people can buy products or services are still proving to be the most popular online destinations with 19.4 million people doing so in January 2007. The importance of the leisure and travel market to the Internet presence cannot be understated. According to the British Market Research Bureau, the most popular online activities undertaken in January 2007 in the UK (BMRB, February 2007; in millions) were

- using email, 26.1
- sourcing information on activity/interest, 22.8
- making travel plans, 16.7
- cinema/theatre/concert listings, 14.1
- to look at job opportunities, 12.2

According to Keynote's 2007 report on Internet advertising in the UK, searching for information about travel and accommodation was the third most popular activity, with 71% of UK adults who had used the Internet in the 3 months prior to the interview having undertaken this activity. In terms of buying behaviour, 51% of UK adults who had made a purchase over the Internet in the last year had bought travel and accommodation products, which was the second highest type of product after films and music.

It is clear that the leisure and travel information market is a huge market and is ripe for brands to target their marketing communications strategies. The online market for sourcing information and making purchases is expected to grow steadily over the next 5 years. Consequently there is also an expected strong growth in the market for online advertising, with Keynote identifying that online advertising is the fastest growing medium in advertising history, forecasting that for the UK market:

> The Internet advertising market will continue to expand at a strong pace in the immediate future (with a predicted 48% increase in expenditure in 2007). Growth is expected to steady at around 25% by 2010 and 2011, with the market reaching a value in the region of £7.97 billion by 2011.' (Keynote, 2007: p. 22)

However, the travel and accommodation sector is only fifth in the rankings of advertising spend by sector, behind recruitment, finance, automotive and entertainment, and, according to Keynote's assessment in 2007, was actually dipping in volume of campaigns and banner advertising between 2004 and 2005. It is apparent that in the UK case for online tourism and hospitality services, there is a possible gap between the volume of online activity in the marketplace and the volume of advertising spend by the industry.

Online Behaviour and Marketing Communications Strategy

The purposes of an online communications strategy can be largely similar to those of a traditional campaign. It is now expected practice that any organisation has a website that potential customers can explore to search for relevant information about the products, services or offerings of the organisation. The website can form part of the wider integrated communications strategy of an organisation in terms of the provision and distribution of directed information. Similarly, websites are increasingly becoming the focus for transactions and so the functionality of the website must allow for potentially large volumes of traffic through its purchase procedures. Online advertising can therefore be directed towards: the provision of information, raising awareness of the brand, shaping or changing attitudes, or; a call to action, such as making a purchase or requesting further information, or; developing customer retention and loyalty, reminding customers.

Types of Online Advertising

Advertising on the Internet comprises essentially three different types of format:

1. search marketing
2. classified advertising
3. display advertising

Figure 10.1 (IAB, ibid.) shows the proportions of all online UK advertising expenditure in the three main areas. Not only is 'search' the largest proportional recipient by type of advertising expenditure, but it is also the fastest growing of the three formats.

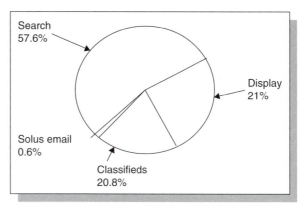

Figure 10.1 Proportions of online advertising spend, UK.
(*Source*: IAB/PwC Online Adspend Study full year 2007.)

Classifieds

Online classified advertising is similar to print forms in that they generally take the form of listings services such as directories such as those proved by Hip Hotels (www.hiphotels.com), or theatre tickets direct (www.TheatreTicketsDirect.co.uk).

Display Advertising

Online advertising has developed rapidly over recent years from the early forms. The main forms of online display advertising are similar to print advertisements or short moving image clips, sometimes called 'banners' or 'skyscrapers' depending on where they are positioned on the screen. These can take the form of 'interruptive advertisements', or 'pop-ups'. These are advertisements which automatically open a new window of the advertiser's site when a link is clicked on from a host site. Pop-ups have a range of types, including pop-overs, which sit on top of the website being viewed, or pop-unders, which stay behind the website being viewed until the window is closed. This form of advertising has been heavily criticised by consumers, who feel that it is overly intrusive. Many consumers have exercised control of this type of content and now own software that blocks interruptive advertisements. Organisations need to think carefully about the strategy they employ to communicate to potential consumers online. New forms of advertising have recently been developed which appear to be less contentious with consumers.

The Internet and its marketing communications applications have created a new lexicon of advertising terms. The IAB (see www.iabuk.net) has developed a helpful glossary of terms on Internet advertising which have been edited and adapted to include the following main concepts and terms.

Search Marketing

'Search marketing' is the generic term for advertising which is placed with Internet search engines and is given a number of synonymous terms which are explained below. Search advertising works when a user logs onto an Internet search engine, such as Yahoo, Google, Ask, etc., and performs a keyword search. The results of any search provide the user with a list of sponsored and unsponsored links. The sponsored links are those that have been paid for by organisations who pay the search engines a commission if they can tempt users into clicking on their websites.

This is sometimes also called 'keyword marketing', where organisations effectively 'buy' keywords so that their website links appear in the search results boxes when the keywords are entered by the user.

Another key term is – 'pay per click' (PPC) whereby advertisers pay a biddable rate for each time a user clicks through from the search engine to their website.

This is a competitive arena whereby lots of competing companies or organisations might sponsor similar keywords through the same search engine. Therefore advertisers bid for placement in the paid listing search results on terms that are the most relevant for their business sector. This is sometimes referred to as search engine marketing or SEO (search engine optimization). This is the process which aims to ensure that the organisation's website is most prominently listed in search engine results and in certain cases the organisation can pay – called 'paid inclusion' – to ensure that the link to their website is guaranteed to appear in search results, although it is not possible to guarantee the rank order in which websites appear in the results, which still relies on the search engine's software governing the statistical measures of relevancy for the terms.

Illustration

Travelocity.co.uk found twice the projected bookings with Google AdWords.

A pioneer in the online travel market, Travelocity continues to be among the most popular travel services on the web. The company operates sites in four continents giving 40 million registered members access to hundreds of airlines, thousands of hotels and cruises, vacation packages and car rentals. The UK Travelocity site (www.travelocity.co.uk) engages media agency Klondike to manage its offline media strategy as well as its online marketing, media planning and buying, including keyword advertising.

Approach

With the immense growth of the online travel business, Klondike's Account Director Joshua Krichefski says travel planning has moved from being predictably seasonal to being constant. 'Today, people book their holidays whenever they want,' he says, adding, 'as people rely increasingly upon Internet search engines to navigate the overwhelming choice of information, the use of paid for keyword advertising has become an extremely important final communication with Travelocity customers.'

Krichefski says that Google has recently become a major player in the UK market, adding, 'With some of the highest volume of relevant travel searches in the UK, and users who are a good match to our target audience, our account team felt we had to approach Google for help with Travelocity's keyword advertising,' he says.

Klondike arranged a test campaign for Travelocity using Google AdWords™. 'We briefed Google to help identify all the relevant search terms for the Travelocity service, bearing in mind our need to drive flight, car hire, hotel, holiday and city break bookings,' says Krichefski. 'We set up spotlight tags on the Travelocity site and click commands directed to these tags on all the keywords that we bought. This way, we were able to constantly track how many bookings were coming from each of the keywords. With our target cost per acquisition in mind, we constantly changed our bids, and hence, cost-per-click, so as to ensure that our bookings were delivered at the right cost.'

Results

Krichefski says that part of Klondike's job is 'to deliver bookings using keyword marketing at a lower cost per booking than can be achieved through offline advertising, including TV, radio, print.' In this regard, the test was very successful. 'We have continued to utilise AdWords ever since,' he says. 'The campaign has been extremely effective at both driving users to the Travelocity site and converting them to booking reservations.'

Source: http://www.google.co.uk/ads

Email Marketing

Email marketing is a form of direct marketing. It applies the same principles and relies on similar types of processes. A user or potential customer logs onto an organisation's website and the site asks him or her to provide certain contact details, either at the point of purchase or in order to register to gain access to the website's content. The information demanded generally includes demographic details and email contact address. The organisation builds up a database of email addresses, which it then uses to send direct marketing emails.

Organisations can also buy lists of email addresses. In some sectors there is a move to email for direct mailing which is not advertising. Email is more and more used to confirm a hotel booking or to send details of an itinerary or to provide a customer reference number in the case of airline e-tickets. In terms of integrated marketing communications (IMC), it is important that email communications with customers as well as email advertising reflect the brand value and is integrated with other forms of communication.

Viral Marketing

The concept of 'viral advertising' is literally a type of word of mouth that uses an online platform as opposed to the spoken word. Viral marketing works on the assumption of peer-to-peer communication and recognises that people will pass on and share relevant and striking content which reflect their personal values most often by email or in social-networking spaces. These types of marketing content often take the form of funny video clips or interactive Flash games, images and even text. Viral campaigns can be sponsored by a brand looking to build awareness of a product or service.

Many organisations are now using viral methods alongside their main marketing communications campaigns. UK tour operator, Thomson sponsored an online 'holiday questionnaire' in 2005 which categorised holiday makers by their answers and compared them to a celebrity. In this campaign, Thomson was emulating rival First Choice, who created an online game in association with its sponsorship of the television series 'I'm a Celebrity – Get Me Out of Here'. The key to successful viral campaigns is to offer value by being fun or shocking or by offering a sales promotion alongside. The problem is that many of the most successful viral's feature sexual innuendo and the use of controversial material may conflict with organisation's core values or the audience's image of the brand (http://www.ttglive.com).

Affiliate Marketing

This type of online marketing is different to display or other types of advertising in that it relies on links between a 'host' website or online publisher, the affiliate and the organisation placing the advertisement. An affiliate can be an organisation or an individual which promotes similar values or content, or complements the activities and so the display of an advertisement (such as a banner or link) on a site for a merchant (the brand or advertiser). If an individual visits the affiliate's site and then clicks on the advertisement or link and goes on to perform a specified action (usually a purchase) on the advertiser's site, then the affiliate receives a commission.

Sponsorship

Similarly to sponsorship approaches using other media, advertisers can promote their products through sponsoring online content areas (e.g. entire website, site area or an event).

Tenancies

This refers to the 'renting' out of a part of a website by an advertiser or brand who then pays commission to the media owner on any revenue generated from sales which have been derived from this space.

Podcasting

Podcasting involves the production of audio content mainly in the style of a radio programme that is stored as an MP3 compatible file format and made available to download from a website. Online audio communications are at an early stage of adoption as a form of marketing communications but have been used effectively in non-advertising messages for the voluntary sector. In the UK the Family Holiday Association (http://www.fhaonline.org.uk/default.asp) has made very effective use of online audio and video content in order to make its case for fund-raising for holidays for families in need. In association with a specialist third sector audio communications enterprise (http://www.sounddelivery.org.uk/index.php) 'Sound Delivery'. This form of media is particularly useful in cases where a strong emotional content needs to be delivered cheaply and effectively. This is now moving rapidly into the mainstream of online communications. Leger Holidays, for example, has added video podcasts of its battlefield tours to its online brochure which were co-produced by the History Channel. The videos are also being posted on YouTube to maximise the potential exposure. This type of approach adds value to the research consumers undertake in planning their holidays online, but also importantly is a novel and entertaining method of communication which has the potential to reach and connect with audiences more effectively (www.travelweekly.co.uk).

More recent developments in the technology of video streaming mean that in the near future online audio and video marketing communications will be more prevalent. These recent developments have been powered by advances in microprocessor technology and high-speed Internet connections which can support such applications.

Online Advertising Applications

Online advertising is suitable for most conventional types of promotional strategy. Direct marketing via email is very cost effective, can be easily tailored for different segments and can be personalised. Email can be used frequently and effectively to communicate with a market and can support a number of functions. Common approaches used include newsletters, PR style announcements and sales promotions.

Email lists are often created by the organisation and are based on permission being given. Online travel organisations use this type of strategy to great effect (such as www.lastminute.com), whose use of newsletters to its email database are centred around a fun, youthful and vibrant creative content with strong use of colour and images of young people. The appeal of this type of strategy is based on an ability to engender empathy on an emotional level about the importance of 'experiences' to the lives of its customers. Unsolicited email communications using bought databases of email addresses can also be used for particular types of strategy, such as awareness building. Sales promotions can also be communicated either via direct email or through banner advertising.

User-generated Content

An important development in tourism and hospitality online activity is in relation to user-generated content. Specifically web-logs or 'blogs' containing accounts of people's travel experiences and, online review sites, where people post their opinions about destinations and accommodation in ratings system, have become very important informal means of communication between users. These have been equated with virtual communities of like-minded people. Wang *et al.* (2002) discuss the implications of online communities for tourism marketing. They argued that for tourism organisations, virtual communities have widened the marketing scope and can impact on sales, product and service development, supplier networks, information quality and distribution channels. They conclude that these impacts are in the areas of brand building and relationship management as well as in cost reduction. Although not specifically online advertising, these represent peer-to-peer communications which appear to have a lot of credibility and are equally trusted as word-of-mouth communications.

Blogging

A 'blog' is an online space which is created by a single user whose content presents the opinions or activities in a diary-style format, often applying a chronological order to describe events, activities or situations of the individuals. Travel blogs are an extremely important and growing activity and are in the general area of user-generated content (Pan *et al.*, 2007). These types of sites can be useful affiliates for tour operators, travel agencies, accommodation providers or destination marketing organisations (DMOs) online advertising (examples follow).

Online Community

Online communities also provide an outlet for user-generated web-content often through the use of traveller forums or special interest groups. These types of sites are becoming increasingly popular with users and the business community, and in turn will lead to the attention of marketers, although these new developments are not without challenges (Dellarocas, 2003). This type of content is often very useful for consumers and advertisers alike, since they emphasise descriptions and explanations about places, include photographs, video or audio clips providing reviews of places. Sites that encourage user-generated content include MySpace, YouTube, Wikipedia and Flickr. The sites become the focus of advertising.

A key example is Virtualtourist.com (www.virtualtourist.com) which claims to be the largest source of 'unbiased' user-generated content for travellers in the world. It applies peer-to-peer word-of-mouth communications through worldwide social networking. People register to become members and can share experiences, photos and tips about places they have visited and/or lived in, which creates powerful and trusted message content about brands, destinations and services. According to the company's website it has

- 800,000 registered members from more than 220 countries and territories
- 1.4 million travel tips on more than 25,000 locations worldwide
- 2.6 million photos
- 2 million mapped destinations
- 85% of forum questions are answered
- dozens of VirtualTourist meetings happen every week around the globe
- 25 VirtualTourist marriages (that we know of!)
- 5 million unique users per month*
- 30 million page views per month*

*comScore Media Metrix, May 2006
(*Source*: http://members.virtualtourist.com)

Recently there has been an explosion in the use of this type of user-generated content on the Internet in the form of social networking sites such as www.youtube.com; www.facebook.com; where are you now – www.wayn.com; www.travelblog.org; and www.virtualtourist.com. These sites represent one of the fastest growth areas of content on the Internet. Travel blogs, for example, are often about the personal events in the lives of the writers and are directed towards a narrow and very specific readership of family and friends – they do have a direct impact on the ways in which messages about tourism and places are communicated via the Internet. However, many of the 'shared content spaces' such as www.travelblog.org generate revenue through the sale of sponsored advertising links, and these will usually be relevant to the places mentioned in the diaries.

The example cited from 'TravelBlog' given in Plate 10.1 is typical of the ways in which tourism information of the type usually generated by authorised and legitimate marketing agencies on behalf of tourism DMOs, private sector tourism organisations or governments, is increasingly being created and delivered by users. Travellers post their descriptions of places and experiences on the site which are linked up to relevant advertisers to match the destinations featured.

Plate 10.1 Travelblog: user-generated tourism communications on the web.

Issues with User-Generated Content

Images and personalised testimonies can be a powerful form of communication and there is no doubt that they could be seen as more authoritative or trusted than official communications. These types of blogs are becoming increasingly used as networking tools and also as a means to showcase literary or photographic skills, and tourism and travel experiences are one of the most popular mechanisms through which people aim to develop a professional writing or artistic career.

The problem with user-generated content is the obvious lack of control and often the lack of informed, insider or detailed knowledge about the issues in different countries which hamper the trustworthiness of some information. Also, some users can create a superficial and often false impression of political, cultural or other issues within a destination.

The point of this discussion is to highlight that the Internet allows for the presentation of information from a very wide range of sources to be posted and thus messages are communicated that can come from a very wide diversity of perspectives which is unfiltered, or varying degrees of authority. There are competing viewpoints about the quality of information available on the Internet. One view is that it is extremely useful and positive, since many people can very quickly gain access to information from a range of perspectives anywhere in the world which is well informed, cheap to access and can enhance individual's informed choices. However, there is also the risk that people could be overwhelmed by the choice, assume that all information is of equal value in terms of objectivity or accuracy, or simply discover only one perspective out of the competing, multiple viewpoints available. The mass of information created for open access over the Internet makes regulation and control almost impossible (many would argue for the benefits of this), and yet in the context of places (destinations), organisations and individuals, there is an overwhelming need from a marketing communications perspective that misrepresentation does not occur, and to ensure accurate, objective (if possible) and a fair interpretation is provided. This creates further issues relating to ethical behaviour and regulation outlined in Chapter 3.

Virtual Worlds

Another interesting development is the growth in uptake of subscribers to virtual worlds such as 'Second Life'. These are Internet sites where individuals subscribe as a member and create a computer-generated version of themselves an avatar to populate or live in a virtual community or 'world' where real activities can take place: business transactions; meetings and virtual tours. 'Second Life' (http://secondlife.com/) currently has a total of 7.8 m 'residents' and is rapidly growing. The amount spent in Second Life is over $2 m per day (according to their website, last accessed on 4 July 2007). Businesses are already trying to work out marketing communications strategies through a presence on Second Life and other virtual worlds.

This type of web space is becoming targeted by the travel and hospitality industry. Starwood Hotels, for example, has attempted to incorporate user-generated content and marketing communications in virtual worlds. It has created virtual versions of its Hot Hotels in Second Life, so that customers can go to view and feedback on a yet to be completed hotel. It has also incorporated peer-related, user-generated, customer-to-customer (C2C) marketing content by posting a link to an unofficial website www.starwoodlobby.com, on Starwood's official website www.lobby.com. Starwood lobby was created by two Starwood customers (who are unadulterated fans of the group's brands and provide exclusively positive endorsements about the group's service orientation, properties as well as the brands) that has unofficial reviews of Starwood's properties via a link to their website on Starwood's official website lobby.com (according to Travelmole.com).

The main aim is that, through virtual communities such as Second Life, companies are able to attract different consumer segments that do not go to travel fairs or travel agencies. For example, Gratistours, a German travel agency allows its virtual potential clients to view travel offers and interact with other virtual customers who are on the same site.

One of the main problems is that organisations do not know who the 'real' consumer is behind the avatar identity. This creates problems for brands, since all the principles discussed throughout this book about the need for an IMC approach being based on a deep understanding of customers is lost in the virtual reality of virtualscapes such as Second Life. At the moment, the key growth in business activity on Second Life and other virtual reality worlds is in business-to-business marketing, and this largely in the domain of technology, software and systems support. However, as growth rates continue to surge in virtual communities (worlds) their reach into political, public and social and economic spheres of activity is spreading. The Maldives has recently opened an embassy in Second Life to encourage investment opportunities and the US Government Internal Revenue Service is currently investigating ways in which to raise tax on spending on 'Lindens' the Second Life currency.

It is undoubtedly the case that online communities and virtual worlds will continue to develop and dominate efforts to develop and sustain brand images and generate new business opportunities.

Issues of Online Developments on Marketing Communications

The impact of this in terms of marketing communications on the Internet is the following:

- Many organisations advertise their products and services on user-generated content sites such as travelblog.com and there is the possibility that communication messages can be confused, mis-interpreted or mixed up, if the information content presents a differ-ent type of message from that with which the organisation wishes to be associated.

- Advertising messages may be considered less or more impor-tant than other types of content on the Internet and thus attitudes towards the value or validity of information presented via the Internet may be subject to increased or decreased levels of trust or confidence. Fill (2005: pp. 582–583), for example, argues that web-based information is poor at managing attitudes but good at gen-erating awareness and attention. Internet-based information about products, services but especially places is difficult to manage, con-trol or regulate, and 'official' communications might be contradicted from different perspectives and/or users.

- Because of this difficulty for organisations to manage and control information which is presented on the Internet, information may have to be monitored, countered and managed that responds to rep-resentations or other types of information that might impact upon the ability of the organisation to achieve its aims and goals. This can lead to higher communication costs.

- Advertisers have little knowledge about the 'real' lives of virtual or online users and so it may be increasingly difficult to ensure that brand images and marketing messages effectively reach out to the right target groups.

Uncertainty in regulation and the effect of marketing and other communication via user-generated content is masked, however, by the huge growth in advertising spend and the enormous and sustained growth in spending over the Internet. Misrepresentation is always a risk from a wide range of media sources. In the current climate, tour-ism and hospitality businesses and organisations are content to con-tinue to pour marketing budgets into the development of online media content, paid advertising spend and in communications activities which drive traffic towards and sales through their online presence. By understanding the importance of C2C networking and building this into their online strategies, travel companies will build brand loyalty through repeat visits and consumer interaction.

Summary

The range of activity on the Internet is growing and developing at a rapid pace. This is being fuelled by the dramatic growth of uptake in broadband network connections, which in turn allows the development of more sophisticated, interactive and rich media applications. The travel and accommodation sector is one of the most important sectors of Internet activity currently on the Internet. The types of products and services made available over the Internet have many synergies with users needs and activity cycles for information, comparing prices and products and making purchases. The traditional role of the travel agency, for example, is being replicated online. New e-mediaries allow tourists to book the different elements of their travel arrangements separately, enabling them to compare and assess the individual component prices, create unique tailored travel experiences and choose the quality rating of their products independently. In this way, a traveller might use a low-cost airline ticket brought at a very cheap rate but stay in an up-scale boutique hotel in the destination. Thus, customers can create travel experiences which connect with their needs and values for the different component parts.

The Internet enables customers to form communities according to preferences, attitudes or peer-group affiliation. All this activity is ideally suited to the development of new online services, which is fuelling the marketing communications strategies of many tourism and hospitality organisations. Much offline (conventional) advertising and communication is now being directed towards driving traffic to or sales from organisation's websites. Online advertising itself is growing at the highest rate of any form of media in history. Search for information about leisure, travel and hospitality activities is one of the most important sectors of Internet activity. Purchase of travel and accommodation is the third largest sector of activity in the UK. The potential for growth in business activity, the provision of information and thus the potential for online marketing in the future is huge. However, there are potential issues. The unregulated and open access information, the vast rise in user-generated content giving rise to potential problems of misrepresentation and the falling off of spending on online advertising across the sector were all highlighted as challenges for the future for the sector.

Discussion Questions

1. Assess the current value and future potential for online marketing communications strategies in the tourism and hospitality sector.
2. Discuss and evaluate the potential applications to tourism and hospitality marketing communications of virtual world Internet sites such as 'Second Life'.
3. Identify three major challenges posed by the Internet to destination's ability to control and determine their destination image.
4. Discuss the role of user-generated content to the promotion of tourism and hospitality organisations.

Case Study 10 How Far should We Trust Website Reviews?

Article written by Fred Mawer

Published in *The Mail* on Sunday, 11 June 2006

'Try this for a hotel review – 'Superlative in every way. Fantastic breakfast, magical dinner. Our room was truly luxurious and, as for service, they pulled out all the stops. I can't recommend it strongly enough.'

That's how one contributor to www.tripadvisor.co.uk, the hugely influential website that promises 'unbiased travel reviews' that give you 'the real story about hotels from people just like you', describes the Ritz in Paris.

But be aware. I was that contributor – and I made up that glowing description. I've never set foot in the hotel in my life. I also submitted a fake review of a hotel in Lanzarote to other websites that concentrate on reviews of accommodation used on package holidays.

Again, I'd never been anywhere near the place yet my opinions were soon posted up on www.holiday-truth.com and www.holidays-uncovered.co.uk.

Such review websites, on which people share their opinions on all manner of things, are all the rage. The leading one in the travel world, American-based TripAdvisor, claims to hold reviews on more than 160,000 hotels and have an astonishing 20 million visitors each month, including 3 million from the UK. British-based www.holidaywatchdog.com, which focuses on package holidays, says it is getting 1 million visitors a month.

To give you an idea of the influence of these sites, I was dining recently in a hotel in St Lucia in the Caribbean. 'Look around', said the manager. 'I reckon 90% of the guests in this dining room have read reviews about us on TripAdvisor. It has more effect on our bookings than anything else.'

There must be, therefore, a temptation for unscrupulous hoteliers to submit fabricated reviews extolling the virtues of their own establishments or even to rubbish their competitors, I've heard of hotels offering perks to guests, such as free room upgrades, in return for positive reviews.

TripAdvisor is cagey about fake reviews. It admits 'a small handful' of people try to manipulate the system but insists the majority are identified before reviews appear on the website.

Other sites are more open about the issue. Andrew Burton, head of Holidays Uncovered, estimates that around 2% of reviews submitted to his site are bogus. This would suggest that review websites as a whole must be receiving hundreds every day.

Burton says some are easy to spot. 'They are often written by bar owners, who mention, in capital letters, how fantastic their bar is and how cheap the drinks are'. Another tell-tale sign is where the review is 100% positive. 'Most honest reviews include some criticism,' he says.

Chris Brown, managing director of Holiday Watchdog, says some unprincipled British Travel agents are to blame. 'When they want to push a deal with a particular hotel, they'll submit a clutch of enthusiastic reviews of that hotel. The agent will then refer clients to the reviews of the hotel on our website to persuade them to book.'

Brown says Holiday Watchdog uses software than can detect clusters of reviews coming from similar Internet provider addresses and will delete them where discovered.

But he admits that if Holiday Watchdog suspects a hotel has submitted its own fake review, normally it will still put it on the website because the presence of one review encourages more contributions.

Worryingly, Holiday-Truth.com doesn't appear to vet reviews before they're posted. I know this because the fake review I submitted to it appeared immediately (the ones I wrote for the other sites took several days to appear).

Holiday-Truth.com does, however, say that reviews submitted from resorts will be deleted, presumably to try to deal with the problem of foreign hotels making them up.

TripAdvisor reviews are usually anonymous – you don't need to provide your name or email address. Several hoteliers I've spoken to think this is unfair and encourages abuse. The owner of a well regarded hotel in Cornwall told me he believes a reviewer who claimed he'd got food poisoning at the hotel was in fact a chef who had worked there and left on bad terms. 'The timing of the review was mighty coincidental and we had no other reports of food poisoning,' he says.

Hotels, incidentally, are allowed to post responses to reviews on TripAdvisor, but that doesn't properly address the issue. Despite these concerns, I still believe review websites are incredibly helpful resources. The vast majority of reviews are from honest punters, and their comments, whether positive or critical, are usually far more revealing than any puff in a hotel or tour operator's brochure or website.

And, dare I say it, they are often more useful than travel writer's hotel reviews in guidebooks or newspapers – not least because you'll often get a range of opinions and an enormous amount of detailed feedback.

TripAdvisor's 'hotel popularity index', which uses a mathematical formula to rank establishments based on reviews on the website plus those in guidebooks and newspaper articles, is an especially useful tool. Nonetheless, I'd exercise some scepticism about a review that lavishes unremitting praise, or vitriolic abuse, of a hotel, particularly when the review seems at odds with other write-ups.

And I'd be wary of judging a hotel based on a single review – TripAdvisor and Co are at their most trustworthy when they have lots of reviews of a hotel, and the comments repeatedly make similar assertions about, say, the food or service. Also, bear in mind that the more detailed the review, the more reliable it is likely to be because it will have been harder to fabricate.

Finally, remember reviews are just subjective opinions from people whose expectations may be different from yours. You should also be aware that most reviews on TripAdvisor are written by Americans, they are used to vast bedrooms and beds when travelling in their own country, and often carp about how small bedrooms and beds are in European hotels.

Learning Activity

- Perform an online search for a travel destination of your choice. Try to ensure that you have found a range of examples including the following: the official DMO; an unofficial destination information site ('what's on' guide for example); a tour operator, travel provider or (e-)travel agency featuring products for this destination; a weblog about the destination; a travel guide.
- Find reviews about the destination which have been posted on sites such as Tripadvisor and virtualtourist.
- Discuss and compare the range of information and evaluate the quality of the information you have found.
- Discuss to what extent the reviews from the different sites match those created by the DMO.
- Discuss the ethical and regulatory issues arising from user-generated review content. Whose views should be trusted most?

References and Further Reading

Buhalis, D. (2000). Marketing the competitive destination of the future. *Tourism Management*. 21(1): 97–116.

Buhalis, D. and Laws, E. (eds) (2001). *Tourism Disbribution Channels*. London and New York: Continuum.

Dellarocas, C. (2003). The digitization of word of mouth: Promise and challenges of online feedback mechanisms. *Management Science*. 49(10): 1407–1424.

Fill, C. (2005). *Marketing Communications: Engagement, Strategies and Practice*. 4th edn. Harrow, England: Prentice Hall.

Hackley, C. (2005). *Advertising and Promotion: Communicating Brands*. London: Sage.

Keynote (2007). *Internet Advertising: Market Assessment*. 4th edn. Jane Griffiths (ed). (ISBN 978-1-84729-102-8). Mintel.

Morgan, N. and Pritchard, A. (2001). *Advertising in Tourism and Leisure*. Oxford: Butterworth-Heinemann.

Morgan, N., Pritchard, A. and Pride, R. (2004). *Destination Branding: Creating the Unique Destination Proposition*. 2nd edn.. Oxford: Butterworth-Heinemann.

ONS (2008). *Internet Access 2008: Households and Individuals*. Newport: Office of National Statistics.

Pan, B., MacLaurin, T. and Crotts, J.C. (2007). Travel blogs and the implications for destination marketing. *Journal of Travel Research*. 46: 35–45.

Shimp, T.A. (2007). *Advertising, promotion and other aspects of integrated marketing communications*. 7th edn. Mason, Ohio: Thomson South-Western.

Wang, Y., Yu, Q. and Fesenmaier, D.R. (2002). Defining the virtual tourist community: Implications for tourism marketing. *Tourism Management.*. 23: 407–417.

Wu, S.I., Wei, P.L. and Chen, J.H. (2008). Influential factors and relational structure of Internet banner advertising in the tourism industry. *Tourism Management*. 29: 221–236.

Key Resources and Links

http://www.iabuk.net
http://www.ipa.co.uk/
http://www.ukaop.org.uk/
(Glossary of internet marketing terms)
http://www.iabuk.net/en/1/glossaryatod.html
http://www.tripadvisor.co.uk
http://www.holiday-truth.com
http://www.holidays-uncovered.co.uk
http://www.holidaywatchdog.com
http://www.secondlife.com/
http://www.laterooms.com
http://www.youtube.com
http://www.facebook.com
http://www.wayn.com
http://www.travelblog.org
http://www.virtualtourist.com

Conclusions and Future Issues in Marketing Communications

At the end of this chapter, you will be able to

- Identify and describe a range of critical issues affecting the future direction of marketing communications in tourism and hospitality.

- Assess a range of factors which will influence the nature of marketing communications in the tourism and hospitality sector.

- Evaluate the possible future changes in marketing promotions.

- Analyse industry implications of changes in the marketing communications environment.

Introduction

This chapter synthesises the issues discussed in this book and proposes a series of critical developments which will impact upon the marketing of tourism and hospitality products, services and destinations over the next decade or so. The book has highlighted the fact that these products and services are unique contexts for marketing communications in that the challenges they pose for marketers are inevitably linked to their characteristics as lifestyle services, part of discretionary leisure spending and intangible experiences. This impacts on how communications should seek to connect up with consumers' values, beliefs and attitudes towards these services. Other issues were also highlighted as changes in the dynamic external environment, whereas yet others are more specifically located in the changing environment of marketing, distribution and promotion of these services. Some issues relate to the changes in the consumption of such services across the globe. Changing patterns of consumption affect the ways in which customers view and respond to certain types of marketing messages. Other challenges and changes involve the marketing industry itself as it becomes more fragmented and compartmentalised, targeting highly segmented audiences, requiring sophisticated research methods, and these issues similarly affect the marketing communications strategies that organisations select.

The book has outlined these contextual concepts. It has then sought to describe and evaluate a range of strategies for marketing communications in the sector, which are primarily associated within the broader context of marketing strategy. And so, Part 2 outlined competitive and organisational strategies, and how they shaped and are shaped by marketing functions. This was linked to segmentation, targeting and positioning decision-making processes and segmentation strategies, which in turn provided the context for marketing mix strategies. As with all such exercises, there is an element of gloss, yet the book has tried to relate issues and concepts to current trends and developments. Finally in Part 3, the range of communications strategies and concepts were discussed and applied to communications issues in tourism and hospitality sector. In many ways, marketing of various services in this sector has changed very little in the past 30 years, and yet consumers have changed in their use, responses to and attitudes towards marketing. Tourism brochures and word-of-mouth communication are still resonant to consumers; however, the ways in which they are created and distributed have changed. Chapters 8 and 9 tried to capture some of these developments whilst covering core concepts in advertising and other communications approaches. Chapter 10 assessed the growing importance of e-communications strategies, which are of such importance to the organisations in this sector.

The Importance of Marketing Communications to Tourism and Hospitality Organisations

This book has argued for the fundamental role of marketing communications to the tourism and hospitality business sector. Although there are differences in the promotion and provision of information – which may be about tourism destinations, attractions, transport providers, intermediaries, tour operators, hotel and accommodation services providers and food and beverage, conference, banqueting and events services – there are also many similarities. This is particularly true in relation to the function of communications – the creation of messages about places, services and products and brands for consumption. To reiterate, these services and products often

- are experientially consumed
- involve a highly emotional orientation in terms of decision-making
- are perceived as discretionary consumer items
- play a significant symbolic role in contributing to consumers' identities.

The importance of designing and implementing an integrated marketing communication (IMC) strategy development and the importance of an orientation to marketing planning with a consumer focus have been stressed to highlight how marketing communications can contribute to the success of organisation's goals in a competitive and dynamic global business environment.

Marketing communication was defined as the provision of information to a defined audience, including an understanding of how the information is received. The messages contained therein are purposefully created with specific intentions, goals or aims in mind. These are generally concerned with sales promotion or building up of awareness about and a favourable attitude towards an organisation's offering to a market. However, the range of marketing communications is extended in the context of tourism destinations to include a consideration of the impact of adverse media coverage about events or activities within a destination, which might lead to some misinterpretation or other incorrect image being portrayed to potential markets. The need for marketing communications to account for the production of information to counteract negative media coverage is vital in understanding the wider role of marketing communications to the creation and management of 'impressions' or images about places, products and services. And so marketing communications is concerned with *the methods through which information is delivered to a defined audience about some aspect of an organisation's activity.*

The various approaches to communication theory were outlined and their application to tourism and hospitality marketing communications strategies were discussed in this book. The key concepts underpinning marketing communications are that an organisation or an individual identifies that there is a need to communicate something to a group of people, most often a target market, but this can also include all other stakeholders such as suppliers and internal marketing communications to employees. Most communications models now assume a reciprocal communication exchange approach, whereby the dialogue between sender and receiver is geared towards the achievement of at least partially mutual interests. Consumers are becoming more sceptical of marketing messages; the 'suspension of disbelief', which has fuelled marketing communications in the tourism sector for the past 40 years, although still potent and relevant, is waning. There is an increasing tendency amongst tourism and travel marketing communications strategies featuring more peer group or celebrity advocacy rather than the conventional images of isolated, sun-kissed beaches or wilderness environments or, indeed, the 'natives' of the destination. This is no coincidence. Consumers respond better to messages about the potential for 'experiences' in the destination based on their affiliation to or association with the images of their peers or affiliate celebrities. The importance of relational and network communication approaches underpins the use of people in advertising especially in the case of consumption, which is oriented towards the emotional needs and values of consumers.

The role of consumers – who are becoming increasingly sophisticated in their tastes – was also considered. The more experience they develop, the more power they exercise to choose and actively produce their own experiences. However, there is a tendency to make broad generalisations about the distribution of this powerful across all social sectors in all societies. Even in advanced societies, the middle classes with high levels of disposable income are driving demand for new and independently organised travel, a diverse and vibrant short-break market, they are fuelling the growth in the long-haul market, and they are driving tastes in hospitality services. However, there are newly emerging markets in the advanced economies for long-haul packaged tourism experiences, for more experiential short-break trips and for themed visitor attractions and hotel experiences.

In short, it is clear that new market economies for packaged, standard or themed tourism and hospitality products exist in significant numbers alongside strong demand for a very wide range of niche products particularly in the short-break market and for independently booked travel. Demand in emerging economies is likely to grow significantly in the next 10 years in South and East Asia, the Middle East, South America and Africa, so there is still significant growth yet to be made in the packaged holiday market with chained hotels continuing to drive the hospitality sector. However, consumer demand is becoming more and more fragmented in the advanced economies in particular. The clear winners in recent years have been those companies that truly understand their consumers and their values and can connect up with them through their marketing communications. Consumers communicate with each other and the most successful companies create value, which generates a buzz, positive word-of-mouth and media coverage. Consumers are more influenced in their choices of services by their peers than by advertising appeals. Chapter 4 discussed how consumers interacted with and responded to marketing communications and identified the relationship between consumer behaviour analysis and the marketing strategy.

The marketing strategy that an organisation devises ought then to underpin the marketing communications it selects to use. It should be rooted in an orientation towards and a deep knowledge of consumers and their value orientations. For many organisations in the current market it is unthinkable that they should aim to attract broad cross sections of society as their main customers. Customer tastes becoming more diverse, greater competition within some core market groups and an increasing reluctance amongst customers to 'settle' for service which does not meet their expectations mean that businesses and organisations are increasingly adopting a more focused strategy on specific target markets. The process of selecting and then targeting strategic groups of consumers was discussed as a competitive strategy. Not all potential consumers will share the same attitudes or orientations to the same product. The STP processes help organisations to focus on those groups for whom their services will have the greatest relevance. This strategic approach makes marketing communications more effective and also allows the organisation to communicate in a very meaningful way.

The role of branding was also identified as being significant to tourism and hospitality organisations. Branding is important in its role in communicating the symbolic qualities of the product, organisation or place. It is now more and more common for destinations to draw on branding concepts and practices to create effective images and associations for potential tourist consumers. Consumers' experiences of brands and their emotional attachment to brands are foregrounded by and interrelated to their attachment to people and places. Therefore, the ability of organisations to construct meaningful and enduring brand associations may be directly attributed to their ability to understand and really know their target customers, their values and concerns.

In an increasingly competitive and fragmented business and audience environment, the challenge for these organisations is to create meaningful messages, which connect with the values and beliefs of specific groups in society. The sheer volumes of information and advertising across a broadening range of media formats are changing the way in which consumers react to and interpret marketing stimuli. Thus the need to create marketing messages that really stand out from the competition and find new ways of engaging the interest of consumers is becoming a real challenge. This book has argued that it is not possible to look at the creative marketing communications function in isolation from a broader analysis of the function of marketing to the achievement of wider corporate objectives and, in particular, the competitive strategy.

This process creates an environment in which organisations can recognise and articulate – and thus communicate – the special qualities, differences or subtle attributes that make its products and/or services different from those of the competition. In a very crowded and diverse competitive marketplace, it is vital that companies can, through their marketing communications strategy, differentiate their offers from those of the competition in a way that is meaningful to consumers' values. For example, in the crowded budget hotel market, a brand needs to be able to distinguish what makes it more attractive to consumers than its competitors: maybe it boasts about the cheapest room rates, the best city centre locations, friendliest staff, loyalty scheme, most comfortable rooms in its class, service delivery and customer satisfaction ratings and so on. Some of these differentiating characteristics are based on product attributes, but others are based more on experiential aspects of the consumers' stay in the hotel. The more an organisation can specify the position (the image) it holds in the minds of its customers or potential customers, the more it is able to differentiate itself from the competition and develop new and/or more sophisticated channels of communication flow between itself and its customers.

Customers are only one of an organisation's publics, however. A range of stakeholders were identified in earlier chapters including shareholders, employees, suppliers, competitors and governments. Each requires particular forms of communications at different points in their contact or activity cycles with the organisation. It is wrong to assume that all marketing communications are concerned with advertising. Communication is concerned with the creation and delivery of appropriate and directed information to specific groups at specified times. An IMC approach was identified as a tool to ensure that brand values are communicated in a consistent and coherent way across this broad range of information to diverse publics. IMC can be interpreted to mean the integration of messages across a range of media within the context of one advertising campaign. This book argues for a broader interpretation and application of IMC philosophy.

The range of media and the diverse types of communications were discussed in this book. Advertising was defined and a range of strategies were highlighted. A rush to Internet-based marketing communications was identified which held challenges for organisations in the sector. The value of Internet advertising was outlined and I considered the impact of a change in buying behaviour on the use of the Internet for information search and purchase behaviour and how this affected the scope, potential and challenges for the Internet, and interactive forms of marketing communications in the future. The Internet is the fastest growing advertising medium in history and the adoption of the Internet and broadband technology has created a whole new potential for rich-media advertising including radio and video streaming online.

In considering all these themes, the aim was to critically assess the challenges and opportunities facing the tourism and hospitality business sector in terms of the impacts on future marketing communications issues. This last section of the book goes on to highlight those challenges, issues and trends for the future.

Future Challenges

An analysis of the current trends and developments in the advertising and promotion of tourism and hospitality services in the context of the strategic environment of the sector suggests that brands and organisations face a series of key challenges in the short to medium term:

- the changing structure of the advertising industry
- the changing structure of the tourism and hospitality industry
- the emergence of new markets and the conflicts that might arise in mature markets
- climate change and how marketing communications will be affected
- the changing media environment

The Changing Structure and Nature of the Advertising Industry

Characterised by increasing fragmentation of media and diversity of platforms and channels of communication, the structure of the advertising industry will be driven by changes in consumer demand and their reactions to marketing messages.

The rise of Internet-based advertising messages is not only affecting the traditional forms of media for advertising, but also impacting upon the types of messages being generated. A great deal of conventional advertising in tourism and hospitality is currently focused on driving traffic to the websites of organisations.

Destination marketing organisations (DMOs), on the other hand, tend to use conventional TV, radio and print media as the means to create emotional attachment to places, which is more difficult to achieve through Internet marketing communications, which tend to focus on more rational messages. Future challenges are that the impact factor of different media platforms will change through audience fragmentation. This will have an effect on the price of advertising through different channels.

Some forms of advertising may become more expensive; however, all organisations may need to invest ever-growing budgets to marketing communications to maximise the reach and spread of their messages across a range of platforms.

Ever more innovative forms of media use, from viral marketing, sponsorships, events as marketing and ambient outdoor coupled with continuing innovation in message creation will make the difference in an increasingly competitive business environment sector. The impact of this diverse and dynamic advertising environment will lead to the increasing specialisation in marketing communications agencies.

The challenges posed by the Internet as a valued and valid, reliable and trusted medium of information provider were highlighted in Chapter 10. Organisations in the future will have to work very hard to make sure that their messages cut through the clutter of information on the Web, to ensure that their information is trusted more than rival, or unofficial, information content. Websites which presently work to provide more rationally oriented, functional content will in the future need to develop more content-oriented to emotional values of consumers to try to increase the length of time people use the websites, the rates at which they click through to other organisations and the level of attachment consumers have with web brands.

The Changing Structure of the Tourism and Hospitality Industry

The industry itself is characterised by increasing concentration of large multinational corporations, including the emergence of the growth in powerful web-based intermediary organisations such as Sabre Holdings. This is contrasted by the increasing fragmentation of types and forms of tourism and hospitality organisations at the small and medium-sized scale whose focus is largely on niche market segments. Not only does this reflect the awkward trading conditions facing the major holiday providers in the UK, but it also reveals the difficulties faced by large multinationals in the face of competition, the low-cost airlines and the rise in independent booking.

Recognising the shifts in customer demands towards more personalised and intimate, unique accommodation experiences, Marriott have announced partnership with Schrager to develop a new brand of up to 100 boutique lifestyle hotels. This will be the first attempt to apply the ethos of boutique hotel products on a globalised level (www.travelmole.com).

Increasing globalisation will ensure that the large multinationals continue to exploit emerging markets in the South and East Asian region, South America, Middle East and Africa. They will be able to achieve increasing economies of scale and rely less on promotional advertising spend, but will be able to enhance direct communications with customers through loyalty programmes and an enhanced knowledge of their needs. The global multinational organisations will also continue to acquire smaller brands whose offer complements their core customers' demands for increasingly personalised, tailored and unique services yet with the guarantees and security of a trusted brand. The ways in which the large global organisations communicate with their consumers will be consolidated through database and direct marketing.

On the contrary, the micro and small organisations will continue to develop niche markets through a diverse range of communications strategies including the following:

- maintaining a web presence in terms of advertising on directories, display advertising and search listings
- direct communication
- affiliate marketing strategies
- small-scale, tightly focused advertising

The Emergence of New Markets

New markets for tourism and hospitality services are emerging in Eastern Europe, South and East Asia, Africa, the Middle East, North Africa and South and Central America as their economies are expanding and increasing numbers of their people have a disposable income, for the first time. Reaching these markets requires specific packages and promotions. As a first step in devising their marketing communications strategy, organisations will have to collect a great deal of information about these diverse markets.

The United Nations World Tourism Organisation prediction that international arrivals will continue to grow until 2020 to a forecast 1.5 billion, from a current 800 million suggests a huge growth in the outbound markets in some regions (Asia – America/Europe), inter-regional (Middle East and North Africa) and inbound (Europe).

The differences in experiences and expectations of these groups require different products and forms of marketing messages.

Packaged tourism products as well as 'separates', individualised and customer-created packages will all achieve growth and so there is an opportunity to see a whole diverse range of marketing communications strategies in evidence targeting different markets with different messages about a wide range of products.

Messages based on the emotional experience of tourism places and hospitality services will become the norm. However, in the short term, messages which concentrate on the rational aspects of decision-making will continue to dominate the message content of some media channels and for some sectors of the industry. A great deal of emphasis will be placed on the communications of brand values throughout all media channels.

The attitude of consumers in diverse markets towards the information they are exposed to and the impact of the proliferation of advertising messages in non-traditional environments may affect the impact of advertising on consumer behaviour. Attitudes towards information will be a constant challenge in the future for brands and organisations that will work hard to try and develop meaningful relationships with key customers and to build and maintain loyalty. To these ends, organisations will go to increasingly deep depths to ensure that customers are involved in the production of holiday experiences, are used to enable the development of new products and services and are also used as ambassadors through peer-to-peer marketing communications. The use of endorsements by peers and celebrities for products and services will continue to grow.

The Challenge of Climate Change

In the more advanced economies at least, the debate about climate change in relation to tourism and hospitality has been coupled with the general move to a more responsible thinking as regards travel and holidays. This debate is centred very much on the emotional level.

The impact of climate change has been discussed in passing in various short illustrations in this book, particularly in relation to competition in the travel and transport sector in Chapter 3. It has been noted that organisations, especially in the travel sector, but also increasingly in the hospitality sector, are being forced to, or actively feel that it is important to, communicate to their core audiences about their stance on the environment or regarding climate change.

Because of the debates about global warming and the changes which are perceived to be a result of this, there is a continual debate about what constitutes good, moral behaviour. Air travel appears to be bearing the brunt of the accusations about pollution and carbon dioxide emissions, and this is leading to intense debate around the world about the impacts of the growth in air travel on emissions and climate change. Already there have been competitive and aggressive marketing strategies which have seen train companies aiming to steal back market share from the low-cost, short-haul airline routes based on the impact on the environment posed by cheap and accessible air travel. As noted in Chapter 3, this leads to aggressive counter-marketing communications. The effects of these types of negative activities are unlikely to impact very greatly on consumer demand. In fact, the most likely outcome is that consumers become less interested in the messages which are irrelevant to their values and not directed towards their needs.

In contrast, the climate change debate also opens up new opportunity for new product developments in niche markets. The arguments for or against air travel do have implications for the industry and the debates engender a strong emotional pull in very important sectors of the market, particularly middle class families who are opinion leaders or shapers. If public opinion were to force action by governments to increase the tax on aircraft fuel or levies on air travel duty, then the international travel market suddenly becomes quite precarious. The rise in demand for domestic and short-haul overland travel would then grow.

The Challenge of the External Media Environment

This was the focus of discussion in Chapter 3 and also in relation to the role of public relations in Chapter 9. The external media environment brings challenges linked to globalised media coverage of events, activities or extreme conditions in a highly fragmented media market. The potential impact of this type of globalised, instantly accessible, snapshot media coverage is a lack of balance in reporting and a 'sound-bite' approach to coverage of issues in regions or countries of the world. This has the potential to impact on the destination image of countries and the ability of organisations to reach their target audience and make the messages meaningful.

The impact of this media coverage can be positive as well as negative, however, and the challenges arise out of the preparedness of the DMO or individual businesses to counteract negative communications or capitalise on opportunities brought about by such media coverage.

Summary

This chapter has highlighted a range of future challenges for the tourism and hospitality sector arising from current trends and developments both within the industry itself and in the wider competitive external environment. All these factors, potentially, have a direct influence on the marketing communications of the organisations in this sector seeking to compete effectively in the contemporary world. The chapter concludes that although it is a challenging environment, there remains a great many opportunities. Many of the case studies used in this book have shown how organisations can create distinctive marketing messages to make an impact. These have shown that through the use of integrated and strategic marketing communications approaches, which seek to connect with specific consumers' needs for the service, tourism and hospitality organisations can overcome a range of challenges and achieve success.

Index

4/09